Educating for Civic-Mindedness

Imagined at their best, how might professions contribute most effectively to their local and global communities, and how could higher education support graduates/ future professionals in making this contribution? The answer proposed in this book is to educate students for 'civic-mindedness', an overarching professional capability grounded in certain dispositions and qualities, ideals, types of knowledge and political emotions. 'Civic-mindedness', and its internal counterpart, the practitioner's self-cultivation, give rise to an engagement with professional practice that is authentic, civic and democratic. The tension between responsiveness or regard for others and regard for self is overcome by recognising that authentic professional identities are constructed through practices around shared purposes and ideals.

Drawing on a wide range of theorists including Dewey, Arendt, and Nussbaum, professions are envisaged to play a vital role. Primarily, professions support society's well-being by ensuring a connection to public goods, such as local and global justice, access to information, health, education, safety, housing, the beauty and sustaining power of the ecological environment, among others. Yet professions also protect the fundamental good of citizen participation in free deliberation and decision-making on issues affecting their lives. The book concludes with a vision of higher education that is transformative of graduates/professionals, pedagogies, professional practices and communities.

Issues of increasing social awareness are a key concern for anyone involved in teaching professionals, and this book, which builds best practice around a sound theoretical and philosophical framework, will prove both thought-provoking and practical in application.

Carolin Kreber is Professor of Higher Education at the University of Edinburgh, UK, and Dean of the School of Professional Studies at Cape Breton University, Canada.

Educating for Civic-Mindedness

Nurturing authentic professional identities through transformative higher education

Carolin Kreber

Routledge
Taylor & Francis Group

LONDON AND NEW YORK

First published 2016
by Routledge
2 Park Square, Milton Park, Abingdon, Oxon OX14 4RN

and by Routledge
711 Third Avenue, New York, NY 10017

Routledge is an imprint of the Taylor & Francis Group, an informa business

British Library Cataloguing in Publication Data
A catalogue record for this book is available from the British Library

Library of Congress Cataloging in Publication Data
Names: Kreber, Carolin, author.
Title: Educating for civic-mindedness: nurturing authentic professional
identities through transformative higher education/Carolin Kreber.
Description: New York, NY: Routledge, 2016.
Identifiers: LCCN 2015049691 (print) | LCCN 2016011820 (ebook) |
ISBN 9780415735490 (hbk: alk. paper) | ISBN 9780415735506 (pbk: alk.
paper) | ISBN 9781315559872 (ebk)
Subjects: LCSH: Citizenship—Study and teaching (Higher) | Transformative
learning. | Service learning. | Professional ethics. | Higher education—Aims
and objectives.
Classification: LCC LC1091 .K74 2016 (print) | LCC LC1091 (ebook) |
DDC 370.11/5—dc23
LC record available at http://lccn.loc.gov/2015049691

ISBN: 978-0-415-73549-0 (hbk)
ISBN: 978-0-415-73550-6 (pbk)
ISBN: 978-1-315-55987-2 (ebk)

Typeset in Galliard
by Keystroke, Station Road, Codsall, Wolverhampton

Contents

Acknowledgements

In writing this book I benefited enormously from the thought-provoking conversations with many students and colleagues. Given our shared interest in social philosophy and professional practices I profited in particular from supervision meetings with Charles Busani Silvane and Sue Chapman, both soon to graduate with a PhD in Education from the University of Edinburgh, and their outstanding co-supervisors, Pete Allison, Andrea English, and Morwenna Griffiths. While the ideas and arguments expressed in this book (with all their limitations) are my own, there is no doubt that they have been greatly enriched by our monthly meetings. Discussions with colleagues at Cape Breton University in Nova Scotia made me realise and admire the genuine commitment to the scholarship of engagement and civic-mindedness that can develop especially in small universities that feel a strong connection to their place and a passion to make a difference in their local and wider communities.

I would like to thank Sage Publishers for allowing me to make use of the manuscript 'Transforming employment-oriented adult education to foster Arendtian action: Rebuilding bridges between community and vocational education', previously published online in *Adult Education Quarterly* in 2014 (DOI: 10.1177/0741713614566674). Likewise, I would like to thank Taylor and Francis for allowing me to make use of two manuscripts: 'The "civic-minded" professional? An exploration through Hannah Arendt's "vita activa"', previously published online in *Educational Philosophy and Theory* in 2014 (DOI: 10.1080/00131857.2014.963492), and 'Rationalising the nature of "graduateness" through philosophical accounts of authenticity', previously published in *Teaching in Higher Education* in 2013, 19(1), pp. 90–100. None of these articles appear as full chapters in the book. However, I took the liberty of borrowing selected pages, at times with adaptations, and integrated them into some of the chapters. Specifically, several pages from 'Transforming employment-oriented adult education to foster Arendtian action: Rebuilding bridges between community and vocational education' (*Adult Education Quarterly*) were incorporated into Chapters 8 and 9; some material from 'The "civic-minded" professional? An exploration through Hannah Arendt's "vita activa"' (*Educational Philosophy and Theory*) was incorporated into Chapters 2 and 9; and large parts of

'Rationalising the nature of "graduateness" through philosophical accounts of authenticity' (*Teaching in Higher Education*) appear in Chapter 3.

Carolin Kreber
Edinburgh, UK and Sydney, Nova Scotia, Canada
November 2015

Chapter 1

Introducing key issues and concepts

Life in modern society seems inconceivable without professions. On an individual level we have come to rely on professionals to correct our teeth, prescribe drugs, give us a by-pass, care for us when we are old or sick, teach us essential knowledge, values and skills that prepare us for life, provide us with safe food, water, housing and transport, respond effectively to emergencies, keep us informed about what is happening in our community and, increasingly, do our accounting for us, handle our legal matters, fix our computerised automobiles and heating systems, and so much more. On a larger scale we rely on professionals to secure our economy, protect our planet (with all its magnificent species), work towards peace and social stability and ensure there is enough food, water and energy around to nourish us and keep us warm, and at least try to distribute these fundamental public goods more equitably in society.

This book is about the role of professions in society and how higher education programmes might best help prepare future professionals for practice. It asks questions about the motivations behind, and the consequences of, professional actions, including difficult ones such as whether it is the principal role of professionals to provide a useful service to individuals and society or to facilitate community engagement in matters of public concern. It also explores two contrasting desires of professionals, self-cultivation and responsiveness to the needs of others, and asks whether these are necessarily in conflict with one another. A key theme is the contribution professionals can make to civic life, civil society and greater social justice.

Although the focus of this book is the professions, specifically the role professions could or should ideally play in modern society, and the implications of this ideal for university-based professional education, part of the argument advanced here applies not only to students enrolled in programmes that prepare for a *particular* profession but students on any degree programme. The point is that higher education needs to change to better serve the fundamental purpose of educating people for the *world*, which implies preparation for both work *and* life in our local and global communities. The humanities tend to fall short in this endeavour for two reasons: first, the extent to which they are recognised as being foundational to professional programmes has been diminishing (e.g., Brint et al.,

2005; Sandeen, 2013); second, humanities programmes tend to be too one-sidedly concerned with the critical and abstract and often neglect making explicit how the critical, analytical and interpretive skills they help develop are of relevance to the world, let alone the varied work contexts many of our graduates will enter into.

Yet, where the humanities are not practical enough and not sufficiently concerned with relevance to work and life in modern society, the professions, by contrast, prepare for practice only in a narrow domain, and increasingly through training in a set of technical skills and instrumental knowledge. What our society needs instead, however, is critical, social and civic engagement with practice and our local and global communities, acknowledging that professional environments are complex, problems ill-defined and what constitutes the 'best solution' often uncertain. Ultimately, neither traditional professional programmes nor programmes in the humanities develop in students the capabilities needed by an increasingly complex social, civic and professional environment; yet, they can do so together. In the following chapters I shall argue that professional education is enriched by stronger and more critical engagement with our communities. This implies, as I shall suggest in Chapter 11, a capacity to understand complex issues from a variety of perspectives, which, in turn, presupposes not only the acquisition of instrumental knowledge and technical skill, but importantly communicative and emancipatory knowledge, the latter two, by definition, the natural playing field of the humanities.

Before I enter into a more comprehensive argument around these issues it is helpful to contextualise the discussion of professions within a broader context. Such is my intent in this and the following chapter.

Context

The professionalisation of the university

With the technological, political, social, cultural, environmental, health and economic issues confronting modern society becoming more and more complex, the need for professional expertise and services has likewise increased. It is not surprising then that the university curriculum has experienced some fundamental changes over the past fifty years.

Ron Barnett observed already a quarter-century ago that 'The professionalization of the higher education curriculum probably represents the biggest – and largely unrecognized – shift in UK higher education over the past 30 years' (Barnett, 1990, p. 75). The university's central mission has shifted from preparing people for life and careers in academia to preparing people for work. This change toward employability – sometimes captured in the notion of 'the professionalisation of the university' – is not only observable in the expansion of professional fields taught within the academy, but is pervasive across the curriculum (e.g., Barnett, 1990; Boys et al., 1988; Taylor, Barr & Steele, 2002; Collini, 2012).

These developments have not remained free of debate, principally spurred by two contrasting positions. One group of critics warns of the risks of knowledge becoming increasingly instrumental and of the university gradually succumbing under the pressure of the market or the state. The other sees in the push toward professionalisation an opportunity for the university to reorient its theoretical and fragmented disciplines towards the resolution of the many complex problems confronted by modern society (Serrano del Pozo & Kreber, 2014).

The orientation of higher education towards the preparation for work over the past fifty years is perhaps not unexpected given the strong appeal of human capital theory underlying government policy (e.g., Keeley, 2007; Wolf, 2011) in many countries. Education, or rather an educated population, is seen as an instrument to economic growth, an idea strongly reflected, for instance, in the Leitch Report in the UK, which emphasised the importance of skills for a thriving competitive economy:

> In the 21st Century, our natural resource is our people – and their potential is both untapped and vast. Skills will unlock that potential. The prize for our country will be enormous – higher productivity, the creation of wealth and social justice. The alternative? Without increased skills, we would condemn ourselves to a lingering decline in competitiveness, diminishing economic growth and a bleaker future for all.
>
> (Leitch Report, 2006, p. 1)

One assumption underlying human capital theory is that highly educated workers will naturally find employment in areas that require their specialised knowledge and skills, thereby offering them good returns for their investments plus strengthening the economy. A further and related assumption is that if the resources invested in education are to result in the most profitable returns, then it makes sense to focus investment principally on those areas that promise to be of greatest economic value. It is of interest that Brint (1994) observed two decades ago that because of their recognised economic value, professional schools within the universities over time received superior status compared to liberal and social studies, which historically had served as a foundation for professional formation. As already noted, several observers in the US since then have remarked that the liberal arts increasingly have moved into the background of professional programmes (e.g., Breneman, 1990; Brint et al., 2005; Sandeen, 2013).

The above developments have also had some bearing on the nature of knowledge taught in academic institutions (e.g., Young, 2008; Young & Muller, 2014). The occupations we recognise as *professions* today achieved their legitimisation within the academy, and wider society, on the grounds of being rooted in a distinct body of specialised formal knowledge and skills grounded in abstract theories. Think of the specialised knowledge of medicine, law, or theology, but also accounting, engineering, or architecture and newer professions such as nursing, teaching, city planning, social work, and so forth. The German term for professionals, 'Fachleute' (referring to people who are experts in their subject ('Fach') or domain and ought to be consulted on issues related to their domain of expertise), conveys this understanding well. It is of particular interest, however, that within the discourses of 'employability' (or the 'professionalisation of the university'), the kind of knowledge increasingly celebrated as vital to success in work contexts is not necessarily that which is specialised and principally discipline-based but that which is transferable and principally skills-based. Does this shift matter, or more to the point, is it a problem as suggested by those who express worry about the pervasiveness of transferable skills (and perceived resultant decline of specialised content knowledge) in the higher education curriculum? Do these commentators blow the issue out of proportion? Do we not need transferable knowledge and skills to address the problems of our times?

I think there are at least two responses needed, one exploring critically the value of 'disciplinarity' and the other that of 'transferability'. As for 'disciplinarity', or alternatively 'specialisation', we might argue that while content knowledge clearly is important, disciplines, given that they are chiefly concerned with the advancement of knowledge through their distinct ways of inquiry, are perhaps too narrow and inward-looking and not sufficiently connected with the world that is made up not of individual disciplinary silos but of multifaceted phenomena and challenges (e.g., Gibbons et al., 1994). Professions, by definition connected to the field of practice, need to be open to exploring interdisciplinary solutions (within and importantly across professions) to the many complex problems our society faces. However, it is equally important to recognise that there can be no *inter*disciplinarity without at least some *disciplinarity*. Being capable of interdisciplinary thinking presupposes having acquired disciplinary knowledge. Disciplines offer theoretical frames of reference from which to inquire and critique (that is, they offer a lens to look *through*), but they themselves also can be looked *at* and critiqued from the vantage point of other disciplines. This critique of one discipline from the point of view of another, ideally, brings about a more sophisticated and integrated and, thereby, interdisciplinary perspective (Rowland, 2006). The notion of transferable skills that is so dominant in the discourse on employability, and often associated with a rather superficial notion of interdisciplinarity, runs the risk of becoming a concept void of meaning unless it remains strongly connected to disciplinary knowledge (Young, 2008).

Yet, we might also ask whether there is something to be rescued about the notion of transferability and whether and how it may be of value to professional knowledge and practice. It is helpful to keep in mind that while professional knowledge is grounded in a body of abstract knowledge and advanced skills, this abstract knowledge cannot altogether *determine* professional decisions but instead provides *guidance* for practitioners when making judgements regarding what actions to take in particular and often highly complex situations (e.g., Carr, 2000; Eraut, 1994; Schön, 1983). What is at stake is the capacity of the practitioner to make sound judgements in changing and often uncertain contexts. The question, of course, is whether this capacity is properly conceived of as a 'transferable skill'.

If we see the knowledge base of the professional largely as a matter of technical know-how or expertise, we may conclude that it is a *skill*, but might nonetheless conclude that it is *not transferable*, at least not outside the given domain of expertise (although within the same domain it might be). The '*techne*' of a heart surgeon may transfer from one intricate heart problem to another, but not to hip surgery. If, on the other hand, we conceive of the professional's knowledge base more broadly, and as connected to the 'professional as person' (I will have more to say about this in Chapters 5 to 7), then we might be less inclined to refer to it as a *skill*, but at the same time be more inclined to consider it '*transferable*' across domains. The '*practical wisdom*' of the school counsellor is less a matter of knowing what broad rules to apply in order to achieve a particular outcome than it is of being prepared to act and do the wise thing in a given situation (although just what the wise thing to do is will always remain, strictly speaking, uncertain). This readiness to act and push oneself forward in the face of uncertainty, not with the goal of achieving a predetermined outcome but for the sake of acting well, is less a matter of skill than it is a matter of character; and the character of the school counsellor, we might then say, is likely to extend from the school environment to his or her relations with colleagues, friends, partner, children . . . and the wider community. Of course, the heart surgeon should not be excluded from this discussion of practical wisdom; yet, her 'techne' is clearly a different matter from the practical wisdom she also might be exhibiting.

A counter-discourse

Despite the emphasis on economic value and employability featuring strongly in public policy, there is a parallel or counter-discourse that educationalists, philosophers and political scientists have been contributing to for many years. This discourse highlights not the economic but social and, importantly, public purposes of higher education (e.g., Boyte, 2004, 2008; Bowen, 2010; Colby et al., 2003; Giroux, 2006; Gutmann, 1987; Jacoby, 2009; Lagemann & Lewis, 2012; McIlrath, Lyons & Munck, 2012; Nussbaum 2010; Watson et al., 2011). The argument underlying this counter-discourse is that higher education plays a key role in the formation of citizens (often conceptualised as global citizens) and, by extension, is a vehicle for creating a more democratic and fairer society.

In view of these developments – the growing 'professionalisation' of the university and the contrasting discourses on the purposes of higher education – it is timely to ask what our aspirations are concerning professional formation. Does the academy have a shared vision of what it considers a 'decent profession', or 'good professional practice' and, by extension, a 'good graduate', to be? Does it ask, '*Imagined at their best, how might professions contribute most effectively to their broader communities, and how might higher education support future professionals in making this contribution?*' Can there be some shared ideals given that new professional programmes, with their distinct bodies of expertise, continue to be added to the university curriculum while traditional ones become further divided into an ever growing pool of sub-specialisations?

Twenty years ago Damrosch (1995) observed that disciplines had become so specialised that scholars in the same department or discipline had lost the ability to communicate about their work to one another. 'One person', he wrote, 'cannot master more than a small handful of fields even in a single discipline, still less do really meaningful work across more than two or three' (Damrosch, 1995, p. 15). In parallel with this growing specialisation a series of studies carried out by higher education teaching and learning specialists over the past two decades concluded that different disciplines and professional fields have very distinctive ways of thinking and practising, and that, for this reason, decisions regarding *how* to teach (let alone *what* to teach, the latter closely linked to the implied aims and purposes of one's teaching) should be made according to the particular learning objectives and challenges characteristic of these special-isations (e.g., Hativa & Marincovich, 1995; Neumann, 2001; Pace & Middendorf, 2004). While there is certainly some value to recognising the distinctiveness of individual disciplines and professional subjects, overemphasising particularity of subject knowledge might carry a risk of losing sight of the shared purposes of higher education.

Although celebrated precisely for having recognised the importance of the teachers' discipline-specific knowledge when making pedagogical decisions (Shulman, 1987), Lee Shulman also made quite a different point in an article published a few years later. There he observed that:

> Each of us in higher education is a member of at least two professions: that of our discipline, interdiscipline or professional field (e.g., history, women's studies, accounting) *as well as our profession as educator.*
> (Shulman, 2000, p. 49, emphasis added)

According to Shulman there is more to being an educator than the teaching of exclusively discipline-specific knowledge. Stephen Brookfield, too, criticised a narrow sense of academic identity rooted in one's particular discipline, underlining instead the need for an overarching or cross-disciplinary vision for higher education practice:

> If college teachers define themselves only as content or skill experts within some narrowly restricted domain, they effectively cut themselves off from the broader identity as change agents involved in helping students shape the world they inhabit. What is needed to counter this tendency towards isolated separatism is an underlying rationale for college teaching. This rationale, although it would acknowledge the importance of specialist curricula and expertise, would go beyond these to *unite college teachers who work in very divergent contexts in the pursuit of shared purposes.*
> (Brookfield, 1990, pp. 17–18, emphasis added)

Shared purposes, I suggest, have to be identified in response to the question of what we consider 'the ideal graduate', and by extension 'ideal professional practice' in society, to be. We need to ask what kind of engagement with the world, and with professional practices, we hope to promote in future professionals, and what the implications of such desirable forms of engagement are for our university curricula and pedagogies.

Civic-mindedness

Recently the notion of *civic-mindedness* and the related question of how to bring about *civic-minded* graduates have engaged the imagination of those responsible for academic programmes (e.g., McMillan, 2015). Bringle and Steinberg (2010) describe civic-mindedness as 'a person's inclination or disposition to be know-ledgeable of and involved in the community, and to have a commitment to act upon a sense of responsibility as a member of that community' (p. 429), and understand a *civic-minded graduate* as 'a person who has completed a course of study (e.g., bachelor's degree), and has the capacity and desire to work with others to achieve the common good' (p. 429). Bowes, Chalmers and Flanagan (1996) defined civic-mindedness as the willingness of an individual to actively take on the role of being a citizen, while Smart, Sanson, Da Silva and Toumbourou (2000) referred to it as 'attitudes and behaviours that are beneficial to society' (p. 5) and 'the selfless regard for the well-being of others' (p. 4). Whether civic-mindedness is indeed *selfless* or rather *self-full*, and achieved through a process of self-cultivation (Erikson, 1965; Maslow, 1972), will concern us later. Of central importance in Bringle and Steinberg's (2010) definition are the words 'with others', and more will be said about this in later chapters as well.

The focus of this book is civic-mindedness in the professions (e.g., Boyte & Fretz, 2012; Dzur, 2008; Sullivan, 1995) and how to promote it through university-based professional education. It thereby aims to integrate the discourses of employability, citizenship, social justice and pedagogy in higher education. This integration seems especially timely given evidence from a range of studies across a number of different professions showing that doing a good job is increasingly conceptualised by practitioners as performing technical services effectively rather than as making a contribution that is fundamentally of public value (e.g., Brint & Levy, 1999; Brint, 1994; Sennett, 1998; Wilson et al., 2013). Although recently some contrary evidence emerged from a small number of studies suggesting a less dire picture (see for instance a recent study by Pederson, Durrant and Bentley (2014) demonstrating that teachers view themselves as civic educators), a diminishing sense among practitioners that the work they do is of public value is a recognised and unfortunate trend. This trend demands confronting the question of how universities might better support future practitioners in constructing professional identities that are formed not just around personal and/or economic gain and technical expertise but a civic mission (and it furthermore requires, as I shall argue in Chapter 8, critical engagement with the question of what precisely we mean by 'civic' mission). Janice McMillan recently summed up the general challenge when she wrote in the global magazine *University World News*:

> We need teaching and learning that engages the student not only as an emergent professional but also as a committed, thoughtful and civic-minded young citizen. This means rethinking pedagogy and the complex relationship between knowledge, skills and values.
>
> (McMillan, 2015, electronic source)

Expanding on Bringle and Steinberg's (2010) definition of civic-mindedness, I intend to tease out connections between civic-mindedness and the notion of an 'authentic professional identity'. I operationalise civic-mindedness as an over-arching professional capability that is grounded in an identity that is authentic. Universities, I shall argue in the chapters that follow, have a responsibility to nurture authentic professional identities through curricula and pedagogies that have the potential to be transformative. Higher education becomes transforma-tive when it brings about transformation in *students*, our *learning communities* and the *world* we share with others. Transformation is not just change; it implies a profound reorientation and has an emancipatory dimension. *Students* experi-ence transformation, I shall argue, as they become increasingly aware of the many blatant injustices in the world and decide to act upon this awareness, especially by giving voice to those who otherwise are silenced; as they develop greater toler-ance and openness towards others who are different from themselves; and as they recognise a sense of personal and public purpose in their work. They experi-ence transformation as they develop the overarching professional capability of civic-mindedness, which is grounded in 'authenticity'. Our *learning communities* become transformative as they encourage the development of civic-mindedness and thus professional identities that are authentic. Finally, the *world* we share with others becomes transformed as it becomes a better, and fairer, place to live.

While multifaceted, the notion of authenticity in relation to professional identity, at a minimum, relates to:

• constructing an identity around purposes of personal value;
• constructing an identity around purposes of public value, common good and social justice;
• being afforded the opportunity to enact this identity in practice (the latter clearly not to be taken for granted in public sector work); and therefore,
• having a disposition to cope with the state of affairs in which we find our-selves, which is one of '*uncertainty*', '*unpredictability*', '*challengeability*' and '*contestability*' (see Barnett, 2000, p. 159).

On a more general level we can add that authenticity in relation to professional identity involves a process of becoming aware of socially constructed (and often hegemonic) assumptions, beliefs and values that have led us to hold a limiting perspective on the possibilities of our professional practice.

In the remainder of this introductory chapter I will sketch out the core argument and introduce some central concepts that feature throughout the book. I will conclude with a brief overview of the chapters that follow.

Authentic professional identity

The notion of an 'authentic professional identity' here refers to the identity of people who practise a profession. 'Professions' are typically assumed to be characterised by an ideology of serving some transcendent value including that professionals are more motivated by doing good work than by economic reward (Freidson, 2001). The previous discussion, however, has shown that people's conceptions of 'good work' vary. Studies across a range of professions revealed that many professionals tend to equate good work with the efficient provision of technical services (often linked to a sense of economic security or advantages in return for the services rendered), thereby calling into question a sense of 'transcendent value' served by this work.

It is refreshing, therefore, that William Sullivan (1995, 2005) conceives of professions as special occupations that individuals can build a life around and that allow them to do something of value. Professions, he suggests, make it possible for individuals to make something of themselves. He further argues that being able to make something of oneself is intrinsically valuable and even *ethical*. Aristotle already recognised the importance of 'making something of yourself'. A happy life, or *eudaimonia*, he understood as one that is good for a human being (Nussbaum, 1986, p. 6). The ancient notion of eudaimonia, typically translated as human flourishing, has also been associated with 'authenticity' (e.g., Henderson & Knight, 2012; Thames, 2011). For instance, Wright (2008) submits that 'Eudaimonia refers to a state of well-being and full functioning that derives from a sense of living in accordance with one's deeply held values – in other words, from a sense of authenticity' (electronic source). Whether eudaimonia (or authenticity) derives primarily from living in accordance with one's deeply held values or also from a sense of 'the free flourishing of one's powers and capacities' (Eagleton, 2007, p. 96) should not concern us just now, although I will have more to say about this momentarily and again in Chapter 5. At this stage I would like to bring out the central point of a connection between having a professional identity that is *authentic*, and the opportunity to make something of oneself (*eudaimonia*), as doing so is good for a human being (Nussbaum, 1986).

Importantly, for both Sullivan (1995) and Higgins (2011), the flourishing of the practitioner, or the practitioner's self-cultivation, is a genuine *ethical* concern. This is in contrast to much of the literature on professional ethics where 'acting ethically' is understood principally as serving the interests of others. Leaning on Bernard Williams's (1985) distinction between ethics and morality, Higgins calls the perspective of professional ethics that is grounded in the duty of serving others 'moral professionalism'. From the perspective of 'moral professionalism', which is widespread, pursuing one's own interests is seen as violating one's duty to act in the interests of others, and, for this reason, must be rejected. However, Higgins (2011) and others would argue that it is not at all obvious that the self-regard or self-interest of the practitioner (that is the practitioner's pursuit of his or her own flourishing, self-cultivation or *eudaimonia*) and his or her regard for others are necessarily incompatible or two extremes to choose from (see also Chapman, forthcoming). Indeed for Higgins (2011), and I suggest also for Sullivan (1995), professional ethics is not just about doing good *to* and *for others* but also about doing good for oneself; in other words it is also about pursuing one's own *eudaimonia*, authenticity or flourishing.

The key to realising that the choice between self-interest and self-sacrifice (or we might say responsiveness to others) is avoidable lies in recognising the fundamental link between our personal flourishing and the flourishing of others, a relationship rooted in the significance of our social interrelatedness (e.g., Eagleton, 2007; MacIntyre, 2009; Nussbaum, 1998, 2004b). In a key section of his popular text *The meaning of life*, Terry Eagleton argues this point in the following way:

> If happiness is seen in Aristotelian terms as the free flourishing of our faculties, and if love is the kind of reciprocity which allows this best to happen, there is no final conflict between them. Nor is there a conflict between happiness and morality, given that a just, compassionate treatment of other people is on the grand scale of things one of the conditions for one's own thriving.
>
> (Eagleton, 2007, p. 98)

For Eagleton (2007) the fulfilment of each person is the foundation for the flourishing of the other, and thus is what enables personal well-being. He observes that this perspective is at odds with the predominant liberal worldview 'for which it is enough if my uniquely individual flourishing is protected from interference by another's' (p. 97) and where the other is recognised not as 'what brings me into being, but (as) a potential threat to my being' (p. 97). In a similar vein, Martha Nussbaum (2004b) highlights that our capacity to experience the emotion of compassion lies, at least in part, in us being able to recognise the plight of others as a real possibility for ourselves, suggesting that compassion is linked to us valuing others as our fellow human beings who are important to our own flourishing.

Communitarians, of either more liberal or conservative persuasions, also encourage us to recognise the 'essentially social nature of individuals . . .' (Gray, 1996, cited in Arthur, 2000, p. 18) and that 'autonomy . . . will only have value if it is exercised in a community providing worthwhile options and supporting individual well-being' (Arthur, 2000, p. 19).

So far I argued with Higgins (2011) and Sullivan (1995) that the flourishing of the individual professional is a genuine ethical concern, and that this ethical concern is entirely compatible with the same professional *also* acting in the interests of others. Indeed, for Sullivan (1995), 'Professionalism itself embodies the contradiction . . . between the enhancement of individual satisfaction and the demands of social well-being' (p. 23). His notion of 'civic professionalism' is based on the understanding that the concerns of the community are recognised as also one's own. Conceiving of a profession as something to 'build a life around' (p. 6), or, as we said earlier, an opportunity to make something of oneself, Sullivan argues that professional types of work 'by their nature . . . create goods that at some time are essential for everyone, and important for society as a whole' (p. 6). 'Civic-minded professionals', he suggests, integrate their personal goals with those of their communities, the latter comprising not just the professional group but the broader community of citizens. It is in this sense that for these professionals civic purpose is integrated with personal meaning. 'At its best', Sullivan (1995) writes, 'professional life enables individual freedom to find fulfilment as it advances the well-being of the larger society' (p. 221). The core of my argument has been (and will be) that practitioners who strive towards an authentic professional identity are motivated not just by self-fulfilment (or self-interest) but also by enabling the flourishing, or authenticity, of others. It is in this sense that professional practice can be a site of self-cultivation grounded in both pursuit of self-regard and responsiveness to others.

According to Martha Nussbaum (1986, 2000, 2011), a flourishing human life is one that is capable of functioning in a truly human way and, hence, is a life that is good for a human being. It is a life an individual has reason to value, and as such one of 'human dignity'. For a life to fulfil the conditions of human dignity, it would need to offer opportunities to realise essentially human capabilities, such as being educated, being healthy, having one's physical and psychological integrity protected, developing a vision of the good life, practising one's imagination, establishing friendships and affiliations with others (including other species), to mention just a few examples. Capabilities are 'freedoms of opportunity'; they are not simply abilities resting exclusively with the individual but are 'created by a combination of abilities and the political, social and economic environment' (Nussbaum, 2011, p. 20) in which people live. Nussbaum's concern with the basic right to a good life is not limited to humans, however. In 'Beyond compassion and humanity', Nussbaum (2005) develops the capabilities approach for non-human animals, making important observations about the importance of protecting our ecological environment.

Practitioners, across a wide range of professions, are in a unique position to support other members of society in being afforded capabilities needed to live a life that is supportive of their well-being. In this way professionals can contribute to greater social justice. This is the point made by Melanie Walker and Monica Maclean who applied Nussbaum's capability approach to professional learning and practice (e.g., Walker & McLean, 2013). In a two-layered argument (which we will revisit in Chapters 4 and 8) the authors suggest that if professional education is to make a difference to the many social injustices we find in the world, it needs to equip future practitioners with certain forms of knowledge, skills, values and dispositions that will enable them to support others in choosing a life of human dignity. Specifically they conceive of the kinds of knowledge, skills, values and dispositions (and we might add emotions) to be developed by practitioners through higher education as *professional capabilities*, critical for enabling practitioners to contribute to *capability expansion* in wider society (Nussbaum, 2011; Nussbaum & Sen, 1993; Sen, 2009). Translated into my own language, and reconnecting with the previous discussion, we might say that nurturing of authentic professional identities through transformative higher education encourages amongst future professionals a sense of civic-mindedness. Civic-minded professionals support the flourishing, or *authenticity*, of other members of society, by helping others achieve important human capabilities. These capabilities include also those of practical and public reasoning, which, as we shall see in Chapters 8 and 9, are especially important in the context of democratic professionalism.

In an article highlighting the many complex social and environmental issues our society is in dire need of resolving, Cortese (2003) asserted that 'It is the people coming out of the world's best colleges and universities that are leading us down the current unhealthy, inequitable, and unsustainable path' (p. 17), urging universities to teach students 'the awareness, knowledge, skills and values needed to create a just and sustainable future' (p. 17). In this book I argue that educating students for civic-mindedness by nurturing authentic professional identities through transformative higher education is one step towards addressing this need. The *main thesis* of the book is that university-based professional education should foster in future professionals not only domain-specific expertise, and facility in solving technical problems that arise in professional practice; nor is its task complete if it, additionally, succeeds in fostering among students a sense of personal meaning and commitment with regards to their chosen subject area and professional group. What is needed in addition is that professional education fosters in students a disposition to seek greater social justice. Importantly, students on professional programmes ought to recognise their social inter-relatedness with other members of their broader communities and thus develop a desire to invest what they have been learning in the interests of, and importantly *with*, individual clients and wider society. The emphasis on working *with* others is crucial in a society where we increasingly seem dependent on professionals making decisions for us (see the introductory paragraph to this chapter). An authentic professional identity, therefore, is underpinned by a civic and demo-cratic (and thus political) interest and desire to change the world to make it a better, that is, fairer, place to live.

Outline of subsequent chapters

In Chapter 2 I suggest that professions have become besieged by the 'culture of inauthenticity'. Four aspects of this culture can be distinguished. These include:

(1) strict accountability regimes leading to 'performativity'; (2) the effects of these regimes, and the overarching ideologies and new governance models giving rise to them, on professional work and identity; (3) the changing relationship between institutions and practices; and, lastly, (4) the continuing unequal access to the professions despite widening participation policies, and as such the ongoing inequality in terms of access to wealth, status and prestige associated with professional knowledge and power. As we continue to 'tolerate' this fourth point, I shall suggest that an authentic and inauthentic motivation can be distinguished.

While Chapters 1 and 2 provide the more general context of professions in contemporary times, it is in Chapter 3 that I begin to delve deeper into the key argument of this book. This chapter offers a philosophical investigation into the nature of 'graduateness', drawing on the work of British philosopher of higher education Ron Barnett, and North American philosophers William Sullivan and Mathew Rosin. Specifically, I argue that 'graduateness' is distinguished by three overarching core attributes: a fundamental disposition of *openness to experience* (and by extension an openness to risk and uncertainty), and the two human qualities or values of *moral commitment* and *responsible community engagement*. I suggest that these three attributes are significant learning outcomes irrespective of the discipline or programme students are enrolled in. I furthermore show how these attributes map onto three distinct but interrelated dimensions of authenticity: the existential, the critical and the communitarian (Kreber, 2013b).

Building directly on the model of graduateness introduced in Chapter 3, I propose in Chapter 4 that the disposition of *openness to experience* is imperative for students to develop as it constitutes the very basis, or fundamental resource, from which to deal with the many challenges characterising contemporary professional practice, the latter comprising uncertainty, unpredictability, challengeability, contestability as well as other work-related adversity. I then proceed to demonstrate that the three dimensions of 'graduateness' that were outlined in the previous chapter, together, provide a sound theoretical foundation for the concept of 'civic-mindedness'. Specifically, drawing on the capabilities approach of Sen and Nussbaum, as well as the work of Walker and McLean (2013), I suggest that in order to work towards the central mission of seeking greater social justice for others by helping expand basic capabilities among all members of society, future practitioners need to be afforded certain *professional capabilities* that culminate in their *overarching capability of civic-mindedness*.

While Chapter 4 makes a case for civic-mindedness as an essential overarching professional capability, Chapter 5 reacts to it arguing that in order to be civic-minded, and act in civic-minded ways, professionals also need to pay attention to their own self-cultivation. Work that is especially helpful to me in this discussion includes that of Jean Hampton, Chris Higgins, Charles Taylor and Alasdair MacIntyre and to a lesser extent Harry Frankfurt. The chapter distinguishes activities that are self-refreshing or self-maintaining from those that are self-cultivating, the latter associated with personal growth and development. Professional practices are revealed as potential sites of practitioners' self-cultivation.

However, once professional practices become corrupted by institutions this corruption can lead, on the one hand, to the neglect of the internal goods associated with the practice, and, on the other, to an unhealthy sense of duty or distorted civic-mindedness, that is not self-cultivating but self-negating, and in this sense is *in*authentic. The chapter identifies the tensions between civic-mindedness (responsiveness to others) and self-cultivation (pursuit of self-regard), drawing on the argument that true self-cultivation occurs in dialogue with others, or in community (e.g., Eagleton, 2007; MacIntyre, 2007; Sullivan, 1995; Taylor, 1989, 1991). While civic-mindedness presents the external side of 'civic-professionalism', focused on giving and being responsive to the needs of others, self-cultivation presents the internal side, focused on developing oneself and/or the professional practice as a whole. Importantly, though, the argument is that true self-cultivation of the professional, unlike the pursuit of pure self-regard, depends on recognising our social relatedness. Self-cultivation and civic-mindedness hence are interdependent.

Chapter 6 explores the knowledge necessary for responsible professional practice, distinguishing between instrumental, communicative and emancipatory knowledge. While all three types are relevant, civic–minded professional practice, it is argued, calls especially for communicative and emancipatory knowledge. These types of knowledge are intimately bound up with dispositions necessary for achieving understanding with others and identifying distorted assumptions. Distorted or invalid assumptions can be identified in relation to oneself as well as the practice one is part of. Professional education then is not simply a matter of fitting students into predefined social roles by teaching important scientific knowledge and skills; professional education is also about helping students think for themselves and about how to develop and improve the world of work, as well as the *world*. This broader purpose of professional education can be achieved by promoting the acquisition of all three types of knowledge.

Chapter 7 considers several emotions that are deemed necessary to stabilise the principles, ideals or aspirations of a decent profession, the latter understood as one oriented towards contributing to greater social justice in the world. Here I shall mainly, though not exclusively, draw on the insights of Martha Nussbaum, including her most recent work on political emotions. Chapter 8 moves the discussion of civic-mindedness to a different level and introduces the idea of professionals as enablers of democracy. Implied in this notion is that professionals and lay-people engage in task sharing, public deliberation and joint decision-making. I discuss the advantages 'democratic professionalism' (Dzur, 2008) holds over the social trustee model, which conceives of citizens as dependent on professionals and needy of their expertise and services. I argue that democratic professionalism (which is a particular version of civic professionalism) qualifies as informal democratic community education aimed at empowering citizens to make informed choices on important matters of public concern. I also draw linkages to capabilities (see Chapter 4), suggesting that democratic professionals, by facilitating spaces for public deliberation, allow especially for the capabilities of 'practical' and 'public reasoning' to be enacted by members of the public and offer opportunity for their ongoing cultivation.

Chapter 9 argues that democratic professionalism's aim to strengthen the public sphere has strong resonance with Hannah Arendt's call for freedom through 'action'. I explore some of the core concepts behind Arendtian *action* in the context of professionalism, especially her notions of representative thinking, 'freedom' and 'deliberation', 'plurality' and 'natality', 'unpredictability' and 'irreversibility', and 'forgiving' and 'promising'. A brief discussion addressing the question of whether Arendt is easily placed within any one particular political let alone educational tradition concludes the chapter. Chapter 10 builds directly on this discussion and considers what university-based professional education guided by Arendt's theory of action might look like. The chapter also addresses some of the challenges that make the enactment of a civic and especially democratic professionalism difficult for teachers and students on professional programmes. While some of these challenges come from within the academy, others are associated with the wider policy context in which universities operate. In the final chapter I reflect on how higher education might be transformed to promote authentic professional identities and practitioners' capacity to act as civic agents.

Chapter 2

Exposing the culture of inauthenticity

Introduction

In this chapter I am concerned with what I shall call the 'culture of inauthenticity' that has besieged the professions. Speaking of the 'culture of *in*authenticity' is perhaps unusual given that our modern era has been referred to as the 'age of authenticity' (e.g., Taylor, 1991, 2007). The age of authenticity, so goes the argument typically, is an age obsessed with the search for individual self-fulfilment, self-realisation and self-advancement (e.g., Potter, 2010). This culture, it is further suggested by some, is ultimately to blame for the weakening of the public sphere (Putnam, 2000; Taylor, 1991), the latter itself the consequence of the pervasive ethos of an extreme liberalism, emphasising individual choice and advancement as core values, rather than social responsibility and the common good (e.g., Arthur, 2000). I shall argue that this is a misconception, or at the very least a too narrow conception, of authenticity in that it fails to recognise that authenticity has two dimensions, one emphasising individual choice and desire and the other emphasising commitment to shared values and traditions within a community (Taylor, 1991). While these two dimensions can be in tension, they are not ultimately irreconcilable and both are vital for authenticity. Taylor (1991) articulated these two dimensions in the following way:

> Briefly we can say that authenticity (A) involves (i) creation and construction as well as discovery, (ii) originality, and frequently (iii) opposition to the rules of society and even potentially to what we recognize as morality. But it is also true . . . that it (B) requires (i) openness to horizons of significance (for otherwise the creation loses the background that can save it from insignificance) and (ii) self-definition in dialogue.
>
> (Taylor, 1991, p. 66)

Speaking of *in*authenticity would imply emphasising one dimension at the expense of the other; an extreme desire of self-fulfilment at the expense of community, or an extreme sense of duty to community (or the organisation) at the expense of self-fulfilment. I argue in this chapter, and throughout this book, that authenticity is imperative for professional life, but that it is made ever more difficult in the prevailing 'culture of *in*authenticity'.

The 'culture of *in*authenticity' that has besieged the professions has at least four different aspects. The first pertains to the stringent and often unhealthy audit and accountability regimes implemented across the public sector which lead to fabricated versions of professional effectiveness intended to demonstrate to others the worth of one's performance in relation to externally set targets or indicators. A second aspect lies in the consequences of these new accountability regimes, and the overarching philosophy of 'new managerialism' that gives rise to them (e.g., Exworthy & Halford, 1999; Kirkpatrick, Ackroyd & Walker, 2005), on professional work and professional identities. A third, and related, aspect of the culture of inauthenticity can be seen in the changing relationship between professional practices and the larger institutions that sustain (or perhaps rather constrain) them. Finally, the fourth aspect of the culture of inauthenticity pertains to the question of who has access to the professions, and, by implication, to the wealth, status and prestige associated with professional knowledge and power. This last aspect requires some further explication.

While allegedly widening participation policies have contributed greatly to increases in social mobility, this assumption is challenged by evidence suggesting that entry into high-paying professions is still more likely for a certain already privileged sub-section of society. This then raises the question of how one might justify this unequal access to education and professional careers. Of interest here is the motivation behind our tolerating this state of affairs. To the extent that the rest of society (including our most marginalised members) can be seen to benefit from locating privileges in the hands of a few, the underlying motivation for tolerating it may be judged as authentic as the decision takes account of everyone and recognises our social interrelatedness or common humanity. However, to the extent that the people graduating from our professional programmes understand their roles primarily as providing efficient technical services in return for monetary reward, rather than as contributing something of public value, the underpinning motivation suffers from a lack of authenticity. The argument is twofold.

First, we might simply observe that there is a problem with authenticity given the lack of correspondence between the professional's actual role identification (providing technical services in return for economic reward) and that assumed by the 'ideal type' or social trustee model of the professions, the latter viewing the professional's civic orientation as fundamental to professional identity (Durkheim, 1957; Freidson, 2001; Parsons, 1954). 'Inauthenticity' here would simply mean (as is common in the popular usage of the term) lack of correspondence to the real (or here we might say the 'ideal'). Second, we might suggest that the one-sided economic motivation of the professional is inauthentic to the extent that it is little concerned with seeking to ensure that all other members of society will be better off. Now, to be clear, economic reward is an entirely legitimate motivation of professionals; but it must not be the *only* motivation if we are serious about wishing to create a better and fairer society for all. Grimmet and Neufeld's (1994) argument from two decades ago is relevant here: an authentic motivation is not limited to doing what is externally rewarded; nor is it limited to also doing what is personally rewarding. An authentic motivation includes, *in addition*, doing what is in the important interests of those served by the profession, which is individual clients and society as a whole.

I shall elaborate on each of these four aspects of the 'culture of inauthenticity' in the four sections of this chapter that follow, tackling them in reverse order. Beginning with the question of access to status, wealth and privilege in section one, I shall, in sections two and three, address the new accountability regimes under new public management and new managerialism and how these affect professional work and identity. Here I employ as an analytical tool Hannah Arendt's important distinction between two modes of human activity – *labour* and *work* (her third mode of human activity, *action*, will concern us in Chapters 9 and 10). In the fourth and final section of the chapter I make brief reference to Alasdair MacIntyre's analysis of the relationship between practices and institutions, highlighting the potential of inauthenticity that arises when institutions lose their critical role as supporters of good practice.

Access to status, wealth and privilege

'Professions' fulfil important roles in society. Indeed, as the opening paragraph of Chapter 1 highlighted, the quality of life in modern societies depends, in crucial ways, on the quality of professionals' work (Sugrue & Solbrekke, 2011). It is because professional services are highly valued that society bestows on professions relative wealth, status and prestige. Although it has been suggested that with the rise of the internet and ease of access to expert knowledge, professional status has become more vulnerable (see, for example, Barnett, 2008 or Fournier, 2000), at present the attainment of specialised and formal knowledge typically obtained through a university degree, combined with the licence to practice, is the decisive factor in determining who is entitled in society to provide a particular service. The university degree, and accreditation by a professional body, keeps professional knowledge a rare and precious commodity and protects professional status. This then raises two questions: First, might some types of knowledge become delegitimised through this process of academic and professional credentialing and, second, who has access to the knowledge that is legitimate and thus 'precious'.

As for the first question, it is crucial to highlight at this stage that the process of credentialing by the academy and accrediting bodies serves to discredit the knowledge of all those who do not hold these credentials; a process that has been criticised as posing a fundamental threat to democracy. This point is made most strongly by Harry Boyte (2008) who argues that the power and politics associated with expert academic knowledge is the 'largest obstacle to higher education to authentic engagement with communities and the public world but also a significant contributor to the general crisis of democracy' (p. 108). This important issue will concern us again in Chapter 8 where we look more closely at the role of professions in enabling democracy. For the purposes of the present argument, however, it is the second question (i.e., who has access to 'legitimate' and thus precious knowledge) that warrants greater exploration.

Over the past thirty years access to higher education has been recognised as a social justice issue, and a range of different approaches have been taken towards widening participation. These policies have led to drastic increases in the number of people now participating in higher education. In Canada and the United States, participation of the eligible age group has exceeded 50 per cent for many years now, and the United Kingdom has been moving in this direction as well. These increases in participation, however, are unequally distributed across different sub-groups of society, as well as types of higher education institutions and programmes. There is evidence from across a number of studies (e.g., Croxford & Raffe, 2012; The Sutton Trust, 2012; UK Government, 2014) showing that access to (many) high-profile professions is still more likely for people from higher socio-economic backgrounds. Essentially this means that people from wealthier backgrounds are typically more likely to attend better-achieving schools, and, by implication, choose and obtain access to more high-status post-secondary institutions, and thus graduate from programmes leading to higher-status professional occupations (e.g., medicine, law, dentistry, etc.).

It would be wrong to assume though that success in access, academic attainment and economic reward through the occupation entered into could be explained exclusively in terms of social class. Women, for example, used to be vastly underrepresented in higher education, overall; yet, by 2010, in most wealthy developed countries, they outnumbered men in many programmes, at both undergraduate and master's level, but, notably, not at doctoral level which is still dominated by men (UNESCO Institute for Statistics, 2010). Research in the UK also noted modest improvements in access of people with disabilities, but cautioned that this could be a function of changing attitudes which might have made students more likely to disclose their disability, rather than more students with disabilities actually entering higher education (Riddell, Tinklin & Wilson, 2004).

Again in the context of the UK, a number of studies (e.g., Tackey, Barnes & Khambhaita, 2011; Richardson, 2010) showed that while ethnic minority groups, especially Blacks and Asians, were now overrepresented in UK higher education generally, compared to White people, they were more likely to study at lower-status universities, had lower entry qualifications due to attending schools that are ill equipped to help ethnic minority students succeed, were less likely to attain a higher degree class (equivalent of a high GPA in North America) and tended to achieve lower economic returns upon graduation. The latter is due to a variety of reasons including choice of professional subject, demand, and employer bias, among others. What these studies suggest is that widening access policies that are focused exclusively on providing access to any type of higher education institution are not sufficient for promoting social mobility. Moreover, appropriate supports and inclusive pedagogical practices need to be put in place so as to ensure that each and every student has an equal chance to succeed in higher education, and such supports ought to be put in place at all types of higher education institutions. Good academic attainment and a successful career in a professional occupation should be a fair chance for all students, not only those who arrive on our campuses already well equipped with the forms of capital (cultural, social, and symbolic) strongly valued in higher education, especially in the high-status institutions, giving these students from the start an unfair advantage over others to succeed in this field (Bourdieu & Passeron, 1977).

I suggested that the formal knowledge acquired through university education, certified by a good degree and professional licensing, is the pathway to relative wealth, status and prestige. Notions of wealth, status and prestige, of course, are relative. Looking only at the public sector, professions vary considerably in the status, prestige and wealth they are actually endowed with. Teachers, nurses, social workers and city planners have never enjoyed the same monetary reward, let alone social recognition, that have been extended to doctors, architects, or lawyers (and I add senior university professors). Nonetheless, while it certainly is the case that (even) within the public sector there is considerable disparity across the professions in terms of the wealth, status and prestige they are associated with, it *still* needs acknowledging that a good undergraduate university degree makes a substantial difference to lifetime earnings (e.g., Walker & Zhu, 2013). Assuming a labour market offering possibilities for employment in a relevant area, we can then argue that those lucky enough to graduate from a professional programme and enter into a professional occupation, including the 'lower-status' ones, still have secured certain advantages or privileges over those members of society who have not had this same opportunity open to them. This then raises the following question: is it justifiable locating these privileges in the hands of only a small sub-section of society? 'I worked hard for my degree' may not strike us as a satisfactory justification in light of the above discussion. A more convincing justification might be found in reference to John Rawls's concept of (distributive) justice as fairness. In a frequently cited section from *A theory of justice*, Rawls (1971) made this particular point as follows:

> All social goods – liberty and opportunity, income and wealth, and the (social) basis of self-respect – are to be distributed equally *unless an unequal distribution of any or all of these primary goods is to the advantage of the least favoured.*
>
> (p. 303, emphasis added)

Access to higher education, and by extension to the professions, is a primary social good, which continues to be distributed unequally in society. To be clear, by bringing in Rawls at this stage my intent is not to defend unequal access to the professions. Rather I want to argue that the concentration of privileges associated with being part of a professional group in the hands of a select few may be tolerated (at least temporarily) only if this concentration ultimately results in the most disadvantaged members of society being better off than would be the case if these privileges were not extended to a select few. Given that access to (and participation in) higher education is an unequally distributed social good, the least we must do is recognise that being the recipient of privileges such as obtaining a good degree and securing a professional occupation ought to have certain social responsibilities attached to it. The early twentieth-century theorists of the social trustee model of the professions (Durkheim, 1957; Marshall, 1963; Parsons, 1954; Tawney, 1920) recognised this sense of civic responsibility when they argued that professionals ought to employ their specialised expertise in the interests not just of themselves but of humanity as a whole. This view is repeated by Freidson (2001) who argues that professions are governed by an ideology of doing good work rather than being motivated just by economic reward. It is consistent with how at the beginning of this chapter I defined, following Grimmet and Neufeld (1994), the meaning of an authentic motivation. Harvard professor Howard Gardner also noted that 'good' work, and we might say 'good' professional practice, carries qualities of excellence, engagement *and* ethics (Gardner, 2011). Good work then is not just a matter of efficiently and accurately solving technical problems, that then is to be compensated by certain privileges.

Of course, it is questionable that the motivations of the professional class that had firmly established itself by the twentieth century were always viewed in such a positive light. In his 1906 play *The doctor's dilemma*, Bernard Shaw observed that in the attempt to secure their prestige, power and wealth, all professions were 'a conspiracy against the laity', a view eventually shared by the critical theorists of the professions since the 1970s (e.g., Johnson, 1972; Hoyle & John, 1995; Larson, 1977; Illich, 1977). Larson (1977) eventually coined the notion of the 'professional project', which refers to the collective attempt by an occupational group to secure control of a body of knowledge and to ensure the translation of this resource into economic returns. A growing suspicion that the real motivation of professionals was perhaps less altruistic than self-serving, combined with a new economic order, led to the imposition of strict accountability regimes across the public sector, especially in the UK but also elsewhere. While intended to restore public confidence in the professions, it has been argued that these same accountability measures in reality contributed significantly to its decline (e.g., Ball, 2003; O'Neil, 2002; Ranson, 2003).

New audit and accountability regimes

The evolution of new accountability regimes in the public sector is linked to the prevailing ideology of neoliberalism, a worldview that is now of international scope. Contrary to the welfare state, in which the government assumes principal responsibility for ensuring social and economic security of the state's population, neoliberalism uses a discourse of markets, efficiency, autonomy and consumer choice, with the purpose, and effect, of shifting risks and responsibility from government to individuals. This general neoliberal ideology is associated with a new management philosophy that has emerged in the 1980s, known as New Public Management. Justified to the public by the intent to 'modernise' the public sector, this management philosophy is characterised by a strong market-orientation which leads to increased cost-effectiveness for governments. These new pressures in the politico-economic environment led many organisations to adopt a new way of governance, typically referred to as new managerialism. 'New managerialism' is characterised by a powerful management body that overrides professional skills, knowledge and judgement. It is driven by efficiency, external accountability and standards (Deem & Brehony, 2005) and thus has a disciplinary function that is a threat to authenticity.

In this and the next section I suggest that there is a direct link between the new accountability regimes that have been employed across the public sector, and professional practice increasingly taking on the form of *labour*, a concept Hannah Arendt (1958) discusses in her book *The human condition*. My intent is also to surface the consequences that a professional life practised exclusively as *labour* would entail for practitioners, arguing that such a professional life would be both unsatisfying and inauthentic.

How does Arendt understand the notion of *labour*? Although we tend to use the terms labour and work interchangeably, for Arendt these had distinct meanings. *Labour* refers to the cyclical, repetitive and continuous process of meeting the needs of the moment. The activities associated with *labour* have no clearly defined beginning and end. Through *labour* humans secure their sheer survival. *Labour* leads to concrete products (for example growing food), but these are never lasting as human survival requires their immediate consumption. Although the products of *labour* do not endure, *labour* takes care of our basic needs.

I suggest that we can readily see how certain aspects of professional practice resemble *labour*. At the most basic level we might observe that new clients come and go, as soon as one project is completed another urgent matter needs addressing. The waiting room of the doctor's office is always busy, patients on hospital wards are helped as soon as a bed becomes available, new students arrive at university each year, the phone at the law firm rings permanently, the stacks of case files on the social worker's desk are not getting lighter despite increasingly longer working days. The normal activities of every profession, I want to argue, include aspects of *labour*. Next to these duties requiring immediate attention there are other routine tasks such as proposal development, report writing, the updating of courses or procedures, the recruitment of clients and so forth that need to be completed in cyclical intervals. In the meantime the working conditions (e.g., organisational or policy context) change, requiring professionals to immediately adapt to new processes of work (e.g., professionals increasingly work in large organisations) or domain expertise (Fournier, 2000). The expectation that modern-day professionals ought to be adaptable is often couched in the language of lifelong learning (e.g., Biesta, 2006; Giddens, 1991) and 'flexibility' (Evetts, 2012; Fournier, 2000).

Moreover, a widely reported decline in public trust in the professions, especially since the economic crisis of 2008, has led to ever more stringent accountability regimes and increased 'surveillance', which in turn have resulted in a process whereby ever more quality assessments need to be carried out regularly. What is emphasised is a one-sided sense of accountability through meeting economically efficient targets, which in turn encourages a culture of performativity, compliance and *in*authenticity (Ball, 2003). At one university I am well familiar with, comprehensive quality assurance forms need to be completed each year for each course and each programme, thereby, allegedly, 'ensuring' that targets are being met (although in all likelihood taking attention away from less measurable but more important tasks and responsibilities such as giving feedback to students). It is rare to meet professionals in public sector organisations who do not feel that the essential aspects of their practice are negatively affected by the inordinate amount of time they are required to spend on meeting these cyclical external accountability requirements. In the process of meeting external accountability demands, direction is taken away from what many practitioners feel really matters in professional practice (May & Buck, 1998).

Ranson (2003) draws an important distinction between two versions of accountability. The first understands being accountable as 'hierarchical answerability'. The person or organisational unit is 'held to account', which, in the performativity culture (e.g., Ball, 2003), easily leads to inauthentic or fabricated accounts of practice. Ranson writes, 'Such regimes of accountability deny our agency, turning us into *inauthentic* subjects pursuing and resisting the imposition of extrinsic goods alone' (2003, p. 462, emphasis added). The second version of accountability understands being accountable as giving an account, or as demonstrating 'communicative reason' or 'discursive reason'. In this second version, standards are deliberated publicly and the idea is to strive towards establishing shared understanding and shared accounts of practices and purposes (see Habermas, 1984). This second version, Ranson argues, stands a far better chance of establishing the public's trust in public services. He further argues that 'The preoccupation with specifying goals and tasks distorts the practice of public services as quantifiable models of quality and evaluation increasingly displaces concern for the internal goods of excellence' (Ranson, 2003, p. 460).

While new accountability regimes are controlling and likely lead to inauthentic accounts, there is also another dimension to increased 'control' at the workplace that is far less tangible and potentially much more damaging to individuals. I shall discuss this other dimension in relation to the next aspect of the culture of inauthenticity in professionalism, which is concerned with the changes in professional work and identity.

Changes in professional work and professional identities

Evetts (2009) argues that in the era of heightened 'performativity' (Ball, 2003) increased control over practitioners in organisations works in such a way that the occupational values of professionalism (such as 'autonomy' and 'making informed judgements') are intentionally emphasised (indeed appropriated) to promote the efficient management of the organisation. What happens is that professionals' commitment to achieving targets is thus controlled indirectly; by believing that their deeply-held values are being honoured they actually collude in their own oppression (e.g., Casey, 1995; Fournier, 1999). Perhaps in a rather similar vein, Fleming (2009) and English and Mayo (2012) show that a new cultural politics is at work in many organisations as part of which employees are encouraged to be '*authentic*', thereby ostensibly conveying the impression that workers' views are highly valued while in reality important decisions are made elsewhere. This last point regarding the misappropriation of the notion of 'authenticity' is relevant to the present discussion of *labour* because practitioners feel personally responsible for reaching targets, while the targets themselves (usually defined as *quality* or *excellence* in . . .) are rarely stated in real or absolute terms, and thus are not achievable but remain always something to aspire to. Hence our work is, in a real sense, endless.

To mention just one concrete example to make this last point a little clearer, excellence in supervision of postgraduate students is something every academic values, takes pride in or aspires to, and the university also needs to demonstrate its excellence in this area, in the UK now increasingly by means of postgraduate student surveys. However, as the number of postgraduate students admitted to our institutions increases, many of them being international, with varying levels of proficiency in the English language, the workload associated with achieving 'excellence' in doctoral supervision likewise increases. It is not uncommon for faculty members to supervise eight or more students at a given time. The institution's response, in many cases, given that it is keen to stay a key player in the global competition for students, is not to cut down student intake, nor is it to employ more staff; instead it is to offer more workshops on 'how to be an excellent supervisor'!

In our valuing of (and constant striving towards) 'quality' or 'excellence' in professional practice (in the above example the practice is supervision of doctoral students but it could be any other professional domain), we may remain oblivious to the fact that it actually is wearing us down, and hence we become colluding selves freely participating in our own oppression. Drawing on Antonio Gramsci (1971), Stephen Brookfield discusses this as the phenomenon of hegemony, referring to people coming to happily support the beliefs and practices that actually work against their own best interests. The point here is that we *consent* to these beliefs and practices that end up hurting us; they are not actually foisted upon us. Brookfield (2005) explains that 'The cruelty of hegemony is that adults take pride in learning and acting on the beliefs and assumptions that work to enslave them' (p. 45).

It should go without saying that although all professional practices contain aspects of *labour*, a professional life that was exclusively a matter of *labour* would be utterly unsatisfying and out of character with what it means to be human. It is in this sense that we could say that such a professional life, built around labour, would be 'inauthentic'. Nonetheless, the changing conditions of work in modern society do render professional life increasingly a matter of *labour*. This is not the same as saying that professional activity will ever be *only* labour (nor is it to argue that *labour* as such is necessarily bad or dangerous – this is not what Arendt meant either); the point of this discussion, and its relevance to civic-mindedness in the professions, is that being required to increasingly engage in '*labour*-like' tasks actually takes attention away from the freedom to *act* (a point to be considered in Chapters 9 and 10). But first, let us explore how professional practice construed as *work* changes professional identity.

In contrast to labour, which is integrated with nature, the activity of *work* is geared towards gaining control over and separating from nature (Arendt, 1958). *Work* is not cyclical but has a clear beginning and end. It is associated with producing things (or 'fabrication'), such as tools, that are permanent and can be used and re-used. *Work* is therefore based on a technical rationality characterised by using appropriate means in order to produce predetermined ends. The stable structures produced by work instil a sense of security and confidence in the light of the unpredictability of nature, and thus generate a safe space for humans to live. *Work*, according to Arendt (1958), like labour, is principally a private activity. Although the end products of *work* are often traded in the public sphere, the purpose of the exchange is mainly to serve the private interest of the master builder, not truly public interests.

Our daily engagements with clients, earlier discussed as including aspects of labour, also show aspects of *work*. Think, for example, of an engineer who oversees a complex industrial building project from beginning to end, or even a teacher who is in a position to support a student over a longer period of time and sees him or her succeed in an exam or indeed later in life. Both may perceive their activities as the successful application of certain approaches (means) to a predetermined end (i.e., the functioning pipeline, bridge or high-speed train; the student's success). The activities of all professions include at least some aspects of *work*; yet, as I shall argue in Chapter 9, professional practices are enriched, and I suggest more appropriately construed, if they are practised also as *action*. Indeed our above teacher and engineer, who successfully completed their 'projects', are unlikely to have engaged solely in a process of 'production', i.e., the successful application of 'techne' to a given problem, but in all likelihood relied as well on their capacity to make astute personal judgements, and, ideally, reached their personal judgements not simply in isolation but in dialogue with others.

I suggested in this and the previous sections that the present conditions of public sector service work push professional practice increasingly into the domain of *labour*, while beyond that it is largely construed and practised as *work*. On a different level of interpretation, we might also argue, in reference to an earlier point, that the professions are now largely construed in terms of *work*, that is, the effective provision of technical services based on specialised knowledge (e.g., Brint & Levy, 1999; Brint, 1994).

Changes in the professions and professional identity, as discussed above, must be understood within the context of the knowledge society (UNESCO, 2005), which is also at the same time a knowledge economy (*ibid*.). The aim of the Lisbon Strategy, for example, was to make Europe 'the most competitive and dynamic knowledge-based economy in the world, capable of sustainable economic growth with more and better jobs and greater social cohesion' (Lisbon European Council, March 2000, electronic source). In knowledge-based economies, knowledge is recognised as a valuable commodity to be traded in a global market, as made clear in the following two quotations, the first offering a definition of the knowledge-based economy and the other a rationale for why countries need to strengthen their knowledge economy.

> [A knowledge-based economy] is one in which the generation and exploitation of knowledge has come to play the predominant part in the creation of wealth. It is not simply about pushing back the frontiers of knowledge; it is also about the more effective use and exploitation of all types of knowledge in all manner of activity.
>
> (Department of Trade and Industry, 1998, electronic source)

> Continuous, market-driven innovation is the key to competitiveness, and thus to economic growth in the knowledge economy. This requires not only a strong science and technology base, but, just as importantly, the capacity to link fundamental and applied research, to convert the results of that research to new products, services processes or materials and to bring these innovations quickly to market.
>
> (World Bank, 2002, p. 21)

Within this context of the rising knowledge economy, an interesting phenomenon has occurred: Professions increasingly came to define their principal contribution as providing a service of economic rather than public value (Brint, 1994).

When professional practice takes on the form of *work*, it is also principally a private activity. Although the professional products or services are made available in the public sphere, it is the professional or professional organisation that benefits from the customers' purchase of these services. We see this increasingly with the privatisation of public services and the expectation that public institutions subsidise their operating income through private sources. Again, in the academic profession examples of this can be found in the commercialisation of higher education and advertising of trendy online programmes (many of which do not expect students to come to campus any more) through visually appealing catalogues, the recruiting of more overseas students, partnerships and external consultation with industry, and so on. Of course there are reasons, other than economic, for the recruitment of international students, innovative online courses, the offering of courses abroad and partnerships with 'industry' that make such initiatives worthwhile. These reasons include the enhancement of interculturality on our campuses and in our wider communities, the provision of educational opportunities to people in countries with low capacity at present, and ensuring the relevance of university education and research to the real needs of the community. However, my point is that, viewed from the perspective of *work*, professional practice is an activity carried out to achieve predetermined ends efficiently. While it has social implications, it is not really directed at public but private interests.

In Chapter 9 I shall argue that when professional life is practised as *action*, professionals recognise their civic mission and understand themselves as citizens and part of the wider public, becoming politically engaged, with others, in deliberation, thereby making their appearance in, and possibly a difference to, the world.

In the final section of this chapter I shall, rather briefly, address the relationship between professional practices and institutions. I shall return to this point in Chapter 5 where I discuss professional practices as sites of self-cultivation.

The relationship between professional practices and institutions

Ideal-type professionalism (Freidson, 2001), referring to the professions' control of work combined with a strong commitment to public service based on specialised knowledge, is increasingly called into question by the conditions of contemporary public sector work. These conditions often give rise to value conflicts (e.g., Robinson, 2005): professional values compete against personal ones; those held by the professional may differ from those of his or her employer; and the state itself may compromise its social justice commitments in light of economic imperatives. In fact, most professionals today do not have the luxury of working as independent practitioners. As public sector workers they are vulnerable to the wider policy context as well as the culture characteristic of the organisations employing them. As May and Buck (1998) observe: 'Autonomous decision making, unhindered by pressure from both managers and clients, may well be an ideal closely defended by public sector professionals. In practice, however, it has long been a problematic ideal to attain . . .' (electronic source). Similarly, Brint (1994) concluded that 'From the beginning of the modern era of professionalization, professions . . . were embedded in the hierarchies of large organizations as much as they were organized along the lines of occupational solidarity' (p. 203).

Sullivan (1995) argues that 'the achievements of all committed professionals remain precarious in the absence of strong institutions committed to the same end, institutions whose working secures the integrity of individual dedication' (p. 16). The problem is that the reasons that once drew professionals to a particular practice may be incompatible with the goals of the institution.

The Scottish philosopher and social critic Alasdair MacIntyre offered an interesting account of the relationship between practices and institutions.

The importance of this relationship is highlighted in a longer section in *After virtue* that is worth quoting in full.

> Institutions are characteristically and necessarily concerned with . . . external goods. They are involved in acquiring money and other material goods; they are structured in terms of power and status, and they distribute money, power and status as rewards. Nor could they do otherwise if they are to sustain not only themselves, but also the practices of which they are the bearers. For no practices can survive for any length of time unsustained by institutions. Indeed so intimate is the relationship of practices to institutions – and consequently of the goods external to the goods internal to the practices in question – that institutions and practices characteristically form a single causal order in which the ideals and the creativity of the practice are always vulnerable to the acquisitiveness of the institution, in which the cooperative care for common goods of the practice is always vulnerable to the competitiveness of the institution. In this context the essential feature of the virtues is clear. Without them, without justice, courage and truthfulness, practices could not resist the corrupting power of institutions.
>
> (MacIntyre, 2007, p. 194)

The danger MacIntyre points to has become only too familiar to public sector workers. When efficiency rules and all that counts is the cost-effective attainment of externally set targets, the real reasons, or internal goods, for engaging in the practice may be at risk of being sacrificed. Consider this excerpt from an interview with a social worker describing how the demands placed on professionals by the institution conflict with the values that actually drive their engagement in the practice.

> R: I do get fed up and I think the paperwork can go hang, the people are more important. And then you get someone coming in and saying 'you haven't done your SS1P and you haven't done your care plan and you haven't done your SS610', you know, and you think for goodness sake.
> I: What you're saying is that you still provide some sort of 'old' social work?
> R: Yes, yes I do, I go out, I mean I just go out and see the people and talk to the children and get involved with them because that is far more use than just referring them on.
>
> I feel more de-skilled as each month goes past. The skills that I have is direct work with children and families . . . and I'm really being asked to be a business manager more and more.
>
> (May & Buck, 1998, electronic source)

What saves us from the corruptive potential of institutions, according to MacIntyre (2007), is the cultivation of those virtues that are inherent in all social practices. He argues that as long as we are guided by certain virtues, among them justice, courage and truthfulness, in our professional activities, the practice will not be separated from its internal goods. Yet, how does virtue develop in the light of institutions which, to secure their survival, focus on external goods? Sullivan (1995) observes that 'Professional integrity . . . can only be nurtured, given favourable institutional contexts, among free human agents who come to find an important part of their identity and meaning in the work they undertake' (Sullivan, 1995, p. 195). It is one thing to say that virtues are cultivated as they are practised, or acted upon, and that social practices are characterised by the pursuit of internal goods, the achievement of which depends on virtue (MacIntyre, 2007); it is quite a different challenge to grow virtuous in an environment that is unfavourable to the pursuit of internal goods. A problem of authenticity arises. The authenticity of the practice is at stake.

Final comment

This chapter surfaced 'the culture of *in*authenticity' that has besieged the professions. Four different aspects of this culture were distinguished. Although the picture portrayed here might have seemed bleak at times and too focused on the negative, encouragement towards a striving for greater authenticity was implied in this discussion, and the possibility for public sector workers to develop authentic professional identities was at least intimated. The next three chapters will examine what is involved in the development of authentic professional identities that are framed around both personal and public value.

Chapter 3

Conceptualising ideal graduates through accounts of authenticity

Introduction

In Chapter 1, I argued that in light of the growing 'professionalisation' of the university, as well as the contrasting discourses on the purposes of higher education, it was timely to ask what our vision of the ideal or 'good graduate' was. In this chapter my intent is to take a more careful look at the notion of 'graduateness'. 'Graduateness' refers to the key abilities (or we might say personal qualities, skills and understandings) students are expected to attain over the course of their university experience. To make it more likely that students will achieve certain key outcomes, several colleges, especially in North America, have moved towards abilities-based curricula, at times also referred to as outcomes-based curricula. Alverno College in Milwaukee, Wisconsin has been a leader in this area since the 1970s (e.g., Mentkowski et al., 2000), but Mount Royal College (now Mount Royal University) in Calgary, Alberta is another example of an institution which has followed an outcomes-based curriculum since the 1990s. The idea is that these central abilities or outcomes, more typically referred to as 'graduate attributes' in the UK and Australia, guide learning across the entire institution, irrespective of disciplinary or programme specialisation. For this reason they are also at times helpfully referred to as 'overarching graduate attributes' or even *generic* graduate attributes, although the extent to which they can indeed be considered *generic* is questionable (e.g., Jones, 2009; Kreber, 2009). It is worth mentioning too that many professional programmes in particular have opted for an outcomes-based approach to curriculum design despite the rest of their institution not necessarily having adopted this approach. An example is the abilities-based approach implemented in a baccalaureate nursing programme at the University of New Brunswick in Canada, as described by Thompson et al. (2013).

There is considerable diversity in how overarching graduate attributes are interpreted. Upon analysis of interview data collected from a group of faculty members from different disciplines following the phenomenographic tradition (e.g., Marton, 1981), Barrie (2007) concluded that faculty understand the notion of graduate attributes in four qualitatively different ways. The four increasingly complex conceptions range from viewing graduate attributes as those foundational abilities students must master before they can even undertake university study, to viewing them as '*enabling* abilities and aptitudes, that lie at the heart of all scholarly learning and knowledge, with the potential to transform the knowledge they are part of and to support the creation of new knowledge and transform the individual' (p. 440). The most complex or sophisticated conception, therefore, conceives of graduate attributes as being fully integrated with the academic content of the discipline and infusing university learning generally.

Interest in overarching attributes, or central abilities, is often inspired by the employability agenda (e.g., Coetzee et al., 2012). Nonetheless, a broader vision of the educational purposes of higher education is at times articulated (Bowden et al., 2000), emphasising the need for students to develop the capacity for *continuing learning in a world that is uncertain, having an inquiry-orientation*, and being *capable of contributing effectively to civic life in a global context* (e.g., Hughes & Barrie, 2010). Not dissimilarly, Alverno College's core abilities include: *communication, analysis, problem-solving, valuing, social interaction, developing global perspective, effective citizenship and aesthetic engagement* (Alverno College, 2011). At Mount Royal University the institution-wide clusters of learning outcomes are phrased as *intellectual and practical skills, integrative and applied learning, knowledge of human cultures and the physical, natural and technological world, personal and social responsibilities* (for details see Mount Royal University, 2012). At the University of Edinburgh in Scotland, the three overarching graduate attributes are *enquiry and lifelong learning, aspiration and personal development, and outlook and engagement* (for details see University of Edinburgh, 2011). Of course, Alverno, Mount Royal and Edinburgh represent three rather different types of higher education institutions. Alverno College is a liberal arts college, while Mount Royal University has a stronger orientation to professional learning (albeit not exclusively), and the University of Edinburgh is a leading research-intensive institution. As graduate attribute or ability statements are meant to indicate to future students (and employers) what students will gain from participating in higher education, not just generally but as a result of studying at this *particular* institution, it is not surprising that they attempt to highlight institutional 'distinctiveness'. What all of these graduate attributes (or core abilities or outcomes) have in common, however, is that they have been carefully selected to convey that graduates are well-rounded individuals ready to engage with the key challenges of our times. Note in this context that Alverno College (2011), for example, describes its ability-based curriculum as 'a model of the real world' (electronic source), and other institutions have their own ways of demonstrating the 'real world relevance' of the learning experience they offer.

Recognising the value of these approaches, I suggest that what is lacking in the 'graduate attribute' (or 'core ability' or 'outcomes-based curriculum') discourse is an explicitly theory-based rationale for singling out certain attributes (or core abilities, or outcomes) as being particularly important for our times. Emphasising a lack of a theory-based rationale for the selection of outcomes is not the same as saying that there is no research base confirming how effective the college is in reaching these outcomes. There is evidence from a range of studies carried out at Alverno College, for example, showing that the ability-based curriculum implemented there, and the assessment methods employed, have positive effects on student learning, in the short and long term (e.g., Mentkowski et al., 2000). But how are the outcomes justified in the first place? While existing studies do answer the question 'How well do we do?' or 'Does it work?', they do not answer the question 'What makes them "core"?' or 'Why should we care about these outcomes?' Most certainly, colleagues involved in developing ability-based curricula do not just blindly draw these outcomes out of a hat but consider carefully what the outcomes (or abilities, or attributes) should be. My intent, therefore, is not to suggest that no one has reflected on learning outcomes before but rather that such deliberations tend to be based on common sense (and good intentions), rather than engagement with relevant theoretical literature. Both – common sense and theory – I want to argue are important. Theoretical engagement is helpful not just because it may steer us in an entirely new direction but also, just as importantly, because it may lead us to have even greater trust in our intuitive understanding and approaches.

In this chapter I undertake a philosophical investigation into the nature of 'graduateness' based on two distinct positions on the educational purposes of universities. One draws on European existentialism emphasising how human being is affected and deals with the various challenges of being in the world; the other is grounded in the North American tradition emphasising community engagement and moral commitments. The first position, I suggest, is represented in the various published works by the British philosopher and theorist of higher education Ron Barnett, especially his valuable essays entitled 'Graduate attributes in an age of uncertainty' (Barnett, 2006) and 'Learning for an unknown future' (Barnett, 2004), but also a number of monographs (Barnett, 1990, 2000, 2007); the other position is represented by work advanced by the Carnegie Foundation for the Advancement of Teaching in the United States, and expressed most clearly perhaps in a book entitled *A new agenda for higher education*, written by philosophers William Sullivan and Matthew Rosin (2008). I discuss the differences in these two ideas on higher education, drawing on three distinct yet interrelated philosophical accounts of authenticity I developed in earlier work (Kreber, 2013a). I propose that together these inspire a particularly timely understanding of the nature of 'graduateness' and also offer a philosophically-based rationale for the singling out of certain core graduate attributes or 'outcomes' as critical at this time.

Sullivan and Rosin (2008) suggest that the main educational purpose of higher education is to encourage students' 'participation in meaning-giving practices' (p. 124), fostered through the cultivation of a particular type of reasoning. The authors suggest that higher education has a role to play in helping students appreciate that purpose or meaning in life cannot be found exclusively within oneself (and the furthering of self-interest) but through participation and identification with something that is larger than oneself. Crucial to this participation in the meaning-giving practices of the world is the cultivation of practical reasoning, which combines intellectual ability and abstract reasoning with moral purpose and community engagement. Practical reasoning is neither a matter of simply applying abstract principles nor is it about the development of a skill; practical reasoning is about the development of *a certain kind of person*, 'a person disposed towards questioning and criticizing for the sake of more informed and responsible engagement' (Sullivan & Rosin, 2008, p. xvi).

Ron Barnett also emphasises the importance of higher education to foster not only abstract critical thinking but critical '*being*'. However, for Barnett the key challenge for higher education lies not in students developing moral commitments or becoming more socially engaged, although such qualities are clearly desirable. The core disposition to be acquired through higher education, and one which, according to Barnett, is fundamental or prerequisite to qualities such as moral commitments and social engagement, is an inner capacity to cope with two distinct phenomena of our times: epistemological uncertainty and complexity, which, together, he suggests, result in an existential experience of 'strangeness'.

My intent in this chapter is to attempt a synthesis of the above two ideas on 'graduateness' and show how they are associated with different philosophical accounts of authenticity. My argument will lead me to suggest that key aspects of 'graduateness' include a fundamental disposition and two core qualities. I borrow this distinction between dispositions and qualities from Barnett himself, who argues that dispositions are more fundamental and open the door for possible qualities. Although Barnett once argued that higher education should foster in students the *dispositions* of 'carefulness, thoughtfulness, receptiveness, resilience, courage and stillness' (2004, p. 258), in a later text he saw value in separating dispositions and qualities. Dispositions that seem especially important for higher education to develop, he argued then, include but are not limited to 'a will to learn; a will to engage; a preparedness to listen; a preparedness to explore; a willingness to hold oneself open to experience; a determination to keep going forward' (Barnett, 2007, p. 102). Among the qualities to be developed through higher education he included 'integrity; carefulness; courage; resilience; self-discipline; restraint; respect for others; openness' (p. 202). Although there seems to be only a fine distinction here between dispositions and qualities (note the mentioning of 'openness' in both lists, for example), Barnett contends that qualities describe the particular direction or shape that dispositions might take (Barnett, 2007). A disposition is 'an orientation to engage with the world in some way' (p. 102), while 'qualities find their expression in the student's activities' (p. 103). It is this distinction between the notion of dispositions and qualities that I find intriguing and that I shall build on, not the particular types of dispositions and qualities Barnett himself identified. Although the chapter is quite theoretical and perhaps appears too abstract in places to be immediately useful, I think that there is value in exploring the question of what ought to be core college outcomes, or overarching attributes, from a theoretical basis (here philosophical accounts of authenticity) rather than relying principally on stakeholders' perspectives. I also will conclude this present chapter with brief reference to some implications for higher education pedagogies. In the following chapter, I shall draw linkages between the notion of an authentic identity and civic-mindedness.

Coping with strangeness produced by a condition of 'super-complexity'

Barnett (2004) employs the notion of 'super-complexity' (p. 252) as a shorthand to refer to the multi-level challenges students are exposed to in making sense of their experiences. The notion of 'super-complexity' is particularly helpful for unpacking the deeper meaning of 'graduateness'. Barnett suggests that there are two different challenges students need to grapple with, which stand in a hierarchical relationship to one another. The first is the challenge brought about by the rapid and ongoing advancements in knowledge. What to believe or consider 'true' is constantly being called into question due to these changes, leading to an awareness that the future is unknown or unpredictable. Universities, according to Barnett, have a responsibility to develop in students the capacity to cope with this *epistemological uncertainty*. However, this challenge is made more complex, indeed is made 'super-complex', by the increase in different disciplinary specialisations, producing often incompatible frameworks by which to interpret this knowledge. This super-complexity we encounter not just within the university, where different (conflicting) discourses now compete, but also whenever different viewpoints are expressed on significant social, political or environmental issues. 'This is an age that is replete with multiplying and contradicting interpretations of the world', Barnett observes (2007, pp. 36–37).

Given this 'super-complexity', Barnett contends, the important task of higher education is to cultivate in students 'human capacities needed to flourish amid "strangeness"' (2005, p. 794). Such flourishing, he suggests, can be supported through 'a pedagogy of human being' (Barnett, 2004, p. 247). What is important, Barnett (2005) adds, is that students are encouraged to not only endure the strangeness associated with 'super-complexity' but to become part of it. 'For ultimately', he submits, 'the only way, amid strangeness, to become fully human, to achieve agency and authenticity, is the capacity to go on producing strangeness by and for oneself' (Barnett, 2005, p. 794). This is an intriguing and intuitively compelling statement – but what does producing 'strangeness' *by* and *for* oneself mean?

There are four ideas here that require unpacking. The first is the idea of 'strangeness'; the second that of authenticity, which is made possible through 'strangeness'; the third is the idea that coping with 'strangeness' requires authenticity; and the fourth is the idea that authenticity means producing 'strangeness' *by* and *for* oneself. I will address each of these in turn. I then will show that fostering authenticity through higher education means more than promoting critical thinking skills and abilities; even more than what we typically understand by critical thinking dispositions. It is also, and importantly, a matter of developing a personal disposition towards openness to experience, to questioning, and to change (Barnett, 2005), and of developing the qualities of personal moral commitment and responsible engagement (Sullivan & Rosin, 2008). I will argue that the notion of 'graduateness' as defined in this chapter, underpinned by the above disposition and qualities, can be usefully understood through three perspectives on authenticity: the existential, the critical and the communitarian.

The existential perspective

Strangeness. The notion of 'strangeness' is similar to, but is also stronger than, uncertainty. When we say we are uncertain we typically want to convey that we have not fully worked things out yet, but we want to hold open the possibility that we might do so in the future. 'Strangeness', however, suggests that our previous ways of understanding do not serve us well, or that too many contradictory alternatives present themselves simultaneously. 'Strangeness' makes us feel disoriented and uprooted – homeless. When we experience a situation as strange it typically arouses certain emotions in us. When something feels strange it is usually accompanied by a feeling of uneasiness, disquiet and anxiety. 'Strangeness' therefore is reminiscent of Freud's 'uncanny' (Bayne, 2008). It is what the Germans call 'das Unheimliche'. When something feels strange or '*unheimlich*', we no longer feel at home but pushed out of our comfort zone. The reality of 'super-complexity' produces such strangeness. It is not just intellectual uncertainty; it is an experience that affects us also on a deep level, personally and emotionally. It thus affects the core of our being. However, while deeply challenging, the experience of 'strangeness' does not stifle our development but, paradoxically, is essential for helping us achieve the full potential of our being. Why should this be the case? And why should contributing to even more 'strangeness' be the solution?

Authenticity made possible through strangeness. The modern world is characterised by the reality of rapid and constant change and often conflicting discourses, leading not only to a sense that the future is unknown and unpredictable but, at times, also to a sense of an unfamiliar, uncontrollable present. It would be nice to be able to rely on long-held assumptions, beliefs and conventions that have stood the test of time and continue to provide comfort and security. But doing so is often not an option unless we are willing to deceive ourselves; that is, unless we refuse to acknowledge the discontinuity or dissonance we are experiencing. A sense of insecurity and dissonance brings with it a feeling of 'strangeness'. Yet, it is precisely this experience of strangeness that opens up the opportunity for profound learning as it makes us think about our assumptions and reconsider their validity. To face the reality of 'strangeness', we ourselves must muster the courage to question received wisdom and convention. This is both an emotional and an intellectual challenge. It is the challenge of authenticity.

From an existential perspective becoming authentic implies that we become aware of our own unique purposes and possibilities in life, and thereby become authors of our own life, 'beings-for-themselves', who take responsibility for our actions and stand by our inner commitments (Malpas, 2003; Sherman, 2003). Heidegger saw the great task and possibility of being human in the freedom we have to break free from self-deception or *das man* (often translated as 'the they'), whereby *das man* (or 'the they') refers to our unexamined ways of being (what 'one' does or believes). Broadly similarly Sartre spoke of us living in 'bad faith', thereby referring to our tendency to want to take for granted and leave intact conventional ways of doing things although we are on some level aware that we are deceiving ourselves. The key point to hold on to is that *it is only when we encounter 'strangeness' that we ourselves begin to question what until then we took for granted*. For Heidegger (1962), anxiety (felt as a result of 'strangeness') opens up new possibilities, and it is through anxiety that a person stands a chance to move towards greater authenticity. The very process of reaching authenticity provokes anxiety, but anxiety is also a prerequisite to authenticity. This point will be explored next.

Coping with strangeness requires authenticity. Barnett argues that feeling anxiety is a condition of what it means to be a student and that this is similar to what we feel when we participate in the world of contradictory discourses and ill-defined problems, making us aware of the impossibility of ready-made solutions. What higher education needs to provide is ways of helping students to live with this anxiety or strangeness that is produced by 'super-complexity'. To cope with this 'super-complexity', or with the 'strangeness' it produces, Barnett (2007) argues, student *being* itself has to become more complex. This complexity of *being* is grounded in a willingness to challenge oneself and throw oneself forward towards authenticity. A complex *being* is open to its own possibilities, to its own striving for authenticity. More simply put, in order to engage in the most significant learning necessary for our times, we need to be open to the experience of strangeness – we need to be prepared to accept strangeness, to let strangeness into our lives, rather than hide from it.

Authenticity means producing strangeness by and for oneself. Elsewhere Barnett (1990) argued that

> A genuine higher learning is subversive in the sense of subverting the student's taken-for-granted world . . . A genuine higher education is unsettling; it is not meant to be a cosy experience. It is disturbing because, ultimately, the student comes to see that things could always be other than they are.
>
> (p. 155)

A caring teacher, therefore, will encourage students to challenge themselves, to move out of their comfort zone, to come into themselves, and thus to achieve their own possibilities, or full potential of being. But to do so the student must *want to* challenge him or herself, the student must *want to* grow. The student who cannot accept feedback that points out his or her mistakes is limited in his or her potential for growth. A certain disposition is required.

Being able to contribute to 'strangeness', or producing 'strangeness', means to be able to accept that problems are multidimensional and interdependent and that further research may not simplify but only reveal additional complexity. It is an acceptance that experts themselves may not find the answers to some problems or will disagree on what the best answer is. Being able to contribute to 'strangeness' means being able to participate in these discourses and not feel threatened by them. It means to speak for oneself as there is actually in the end no authority to rest on. Becoming authentic in this way means to have the courage to let go of the need of prior confirmation and contribute one's own alternatives. It means to become the author of one's life, taking into account other voices without being determined by these (Baxter-Magolda, 1999). What is at stake here is something that goes beyond being able to think critically.

Beyond critical (analytical) thinking. All graduate attribute or core ability statements make reference to the importance of critical (analytical) thinking in one way or another. This is not surprising given that 'critical thinking' is widely regarded as the *raison d'être* of higher education. What makes higher education *higher*, is that it involves critical engagement with what is learned. However, critical thinking is often discussed as being distinctive to particular disciplines and contexts (e.g., Donald, 2002; Hounsell & Anderson, 2009; McPeck, 1981). While typically described in terms of cognitive abilities and skills (e.g., Watson & Glaser, 1984), such as identifying assumptions, making (accurate) inferences and evaluating arguments, several educationalists and philosophers of education have highlighted the importance also of certain critical thinking dispositions (e.g., Ennis, 1996; Facione, Sanchez & Facione 1994; Norris, 1992; Paul, 1990; Perkins, Jay & Tishman, 1993; Siegel, 1988). Norris (1992) pointed out that an individual will use the ability for critical thinking only if so disposed. Several specific dispositions have been identified, such as: trying to be well informed, seeking reasons, taking account of the whole situation (Ennis, 1996), or being intellectually careful, being inclined to wonder, problem-find and investigate, evaluating reasons, being metacognitive (Perkins, Jay & Tishman, 1993). Facione, Sanchez and Facione (1994) identified seven dispositions including open-mindedness, inquisitiveness, systematicity, analyticity, truth-seeking, critical thinking self-confidence, and maturity. There have also been attempts at singling out an overarching disposition. For Paul (1990), for example, this is captured in the notion of 'fairmindedness', while Siegel (1988) speaks of 'critical-spiritedness'. Dispositions are seen to make critical thinking possible or influence its direction. We can say therefore that critical thinking involves skills and abilities as well as dispositions, and that all of these are involved in making autonomous rational choices. This readiness to make autonomous rational choices, I want to argue, is different from what is involved in becoming authentic.

When students become *authentic*, rather than merely autonomous, they develop the capacity to make choices that are bound up with their own inner motives (Bonnett, 1978; Bonnett & Cuypers, 2003). They become personally invested in their choices and feel a deep inner commitment to them. It is through developing a commitment to a claim (or larger cause) that students become authentic and thus able to cope with strangeness. In the play and film *Educating Rita* we learn that it is not sufficient for Rita to know how to critique a text through the conventions of literary criticism; the much more profound learning occurs for Rita when she becomes capable of critiquing herself and her real motives. To develop commitment, students have to become self-critical. Barnett (2007), too, suggests that 'Becoming authentic in higher education is none other than the formation of critical being' (p. 160); critical being is not just a matter of having certain *intellectual* dispositions, although these are important, too. The student needs to internalise critical voices, not just repeat them. The student needs to take a stance, and be willing to do so. Authenticity therefore involves, requires, and also brings about, what is typically described as critical thinking (or intellectual) skills, abilities and dispositions, but it goes one step beyond. The person who is becoming authentic is invested and committed to her own choices and this requires a more fundamental disposition: it requires openness to experience and a willingness to engage with 'strangeness'. Confronting and embracing strangeness, rather than trying to hide from it, requires a certain openness to experience, or complexity of being, which we can associate with authenticity. This authenticity, in turn, enables significant learning to occur, whereby we reconsider our assumptions, or previous ways of understanding, and develop a new or transformed perspective on issues, a perspective that is our own. Now, given that the world we live in is rapidly and constantly changing, complexity and uncertainty remain persistent challenges. Authenticity, therefore, is never just a state of being (openness to experience) but something we can choose to strive towards (a willingness to engage with strangeness). As we move towards greater authenticity we draw on our capacity for 'critical thinking'.

So far I have outlined a particular perspective on student authenticity that I would call, rather broadly, an existential one. I suggested that this perspective is closely associated with the work of Ron Barnett, who has written extensively on the importance of higher education promoting in students a disposition of critical *being*.

Authenticity in relation to students has also other meanings, and I now want to suggest that these other meanings chime well with the North American tradition of promoting in students a sense of community engagement and moral commitments.

Broadening the concept of authenticity: towards a synthesis of two ideas on the educational purposes of universities

Next to the existential dimension discussed above, authenticity has two further dimensions that are relevant to this discussion. One is the critical dimension (e.g., Habermas, 1984), the other is the communitarian (e.g., Taylor, 1991).

Although the three dimensions are interrelated, for analytical purposes it makes sense to discuss them separately.

The critical perspective

The critical dimension highlights emancipation from ideology and hegemonic assumptions. It adds to the existential dimension the idea of critical consciousness raising (Freire, 1971; Habermas, 1984). The critical dimension then is informed by critical theory which 'envisages a fairer, less alienated, more democratic world' (Brookfield, 2005, p. 27). Brookfield continues that:

> Critical theory . . . springs from a distinct philosophical vision of what it means to live as a developed person, as a mature adult struggling to realize one's humanity through the creation of a society that is just, fair and compassionate. This vision holds individual identity to be socially and culturally formed.
>
> (2005, p. 27)

Viewed from a critical perspective we move towards greater authenticity as we become conscious of how socially learned truths (ideas we pick up in our various communities and thus uncritically assimilated) influence how we make sense of the world. So rather than equating authenticity with pure self-experience, the critical dimension emphasises that people need to recognise how their views of the world have been shaped by the conditions or structures inherent in the contexts in which events were experienced. Examples of socially constructed assumptions that students might unconsciously hold and could come to question include: Experts have all the answers; There is only one truth; I am not worthy of studying at this university; Only texts from White European Anglo-Saxon cultures are of any value to my learning; I am especially deserving of my privileges, etc. While these assumptions will appear 'obviously wrong' to most readers, the point is that they appear 'self-evidently true' to some students. For a more comprehensive discussion of self-evidently true assumptions see for example Brookfield (2005). There are, of course, also assumptions that are more discipline-specific. To mention just one example, one might think of a student who begins to critically reflect on why certain explanatory frameworks have come to determine how we understand a given problem or discipline, what alternative ways of knowing are concealed by this, and what the implications of this are. It is also worth noting that the critical perspective is not only about arriving at a new understanding (and emancipation from hegemonic assumptions) but is intimately bound up with action.

The communitarian perspective

The communitarian perspective (Taylor, 1991) highlights that it is our engagement in meaning-giving practices in our communities that gives us purpose in life.

What ultimately provides people's lives with meaning, it is argued, is not just the furthering of their self-interests but them contributing to something larger than themselves, a common good, with which they identify. Articulations of 'graduate attributes' often include statements regarding critical thinking and problem-solving skills, but at times, as we saw at the beginning of this chapter, they make reference also to ethical, social and professional understanding; collaboration, teamwork and leadership; and civic life (Hughes & Barrie, 2010).

In their book *A new agenda for higher education*, Sullivan and Rosin (2008) provide a vision for higher education that involves students' and faculty's critical, social and civic engagement with practice and our local and global communities. The core concept they discuss is that of practical reasoning, which links critical thinking to concrete practices and situations. They distinguish practical reasoning from abstract critical thinking in this way:

> 'Critical thinking' means standing apart from the world and establishing reasons and causes. This is a necessary aspect of practical reasoning, but is not sufficient for responsible judgment. Education must also give students access to valued practices for engaging the world more mindfully.
>
> (Sullivan & Rosin, 2008, p. 18)

While critical thinking is part of practical reasoning, the latter is a particular type of meaning making that moves back and forth between the particularities of the situation one finds oneself in and the generality of abstract principles (derived from different disciplinary traditions or newer areas of specialisations) (Sullivan & Rosin, 2008). Practical reasoning involves accurately assessing a given situation and making an appropriate decision, while abandoning the security offered by abstract rules (Dunne & Pendlebury, 2003, p. 198). Since what counts as the best decision in a particular situation is not already given in the form of an established or proven rule or regulative, practical reasoning also requires personal investment in one's choices – we might then say, leaning on Bonnett (1978) and Bonnett and Cuypers (2003), that practical reasoning requires authenticity.

A philosophically-based rationale for identifying core graduate attributes

At the beginning of this chapter I argued that there are two different, albeit complementary, ideas on the educational purposes of universities, and hence on the notion of 'graduateness': One draws on European existentialism emphasising how human *being* is affected and deals with the various challenges of being in the world; the other is grounded in the North American tradition emphasising community engagement. Both ideas are equally important to 'graduateness' and both are usefully conceptualised under a broader notion of authenticity I sketched out here. All three dimensions of this broader notion of authenticity involve a certain sense of criticality; however, the focus is slightly different in each.

The existential dimension of authenticity addresses the development of the *fundamental disposition* of being open to experience and one's own possibilities, and willingly seizing opportunities for change and development arising from these experiences (Barnett, 2004); in other words, a capacity to engage with, and contribute to, 'strangeness'. 'Strangeness' can propel us to question assumptions, which then opens up the opportunity for greater authenticity. The relationship between authenticity and 'strangeness' is reciprocal: By becoming more authentic, *being* becomes more capable of being open to, coping with, and contributing to strangeness; and, it is the achieved readiness or openness to the experience of 'strangeness', risk or uncertainty that helps the individual's *being* become more authentic as significant learning is made possible. The critical dimension of authenticity has a different focus stressing reflection on socially constructed and often uncritically assimilated assumptions of how the world should be. It reflects a moral disposition and commitment to make the world a fairer place. Finally, the communitarian dimension, as I've called it here, emphasises that authenticity involves an appreciation of our social interrelatedness, associating authentic being with participating and identifying with meaning-giving practices within the community. The critical and communitarian dimensions of authenticity are involved, in particular, in developing the personal *qualities* or values of moral commitment and responsible engagement, respectively. As noted, both the critical and the communitarian dimensions are tied to taking action in the community. Perhaps, if one wanted to distinguish further between these two perspectives, one might argue that the communitarian motivation to act is associated with a common good to be served by members of the local community and that the norms and traditions of the community as they have evolved should be respected. In the critical perspective, the conception of the common good as it has evolved within the community may itself be questioned, and advocacy for greater social justice and moral commitment extends to exploring the norms and traditions themselves, asking who is served and who is not by present practices, by what mechanisms of power, and what can be done. Of course, I should add that some communitarian writers have strong Marxist inclinations. The distinction between the two perspectives that is relevant to our present discussion is that the communitarian dimension of authenticity, captured in the notion of responsible community engagement, is a graduate attribute that reflects the graduate's self-understanding (or identity) as a member of the community and the experience of personal and public meaning through forms of community engagement that are aimed at furthering the interests of that community. The critical dimension of authenticity, captured in the notion of moral commitment, is a graduate attribute that reflects the graduate's willingness to seek greater social justice through critical reflection and action. Unlike the existential dimension, the critical and communitarian dimensions have to do more with developing a *particular kind* of person (Sullivan & Rosin, 2008), a person who values community, engagement and social justice. The fundamental disposition of openness to experience (and thus risk and uncertainty) and the qualities (or values) of moral commitment

Table 3.1 Linkages between authenticity and two ideas on the pedagogical purposes of higher education

Three distinct yet interrelated dimensions of authenticity

Existential	*Critical*	*Communitarian*
How human being is affected and deals with the challenges of being in the world	How people become conscious of socially constructed and often uncritically assimilated assumptions Oriented towards creating a fairer, less alienated, more democratic world	How people come to appreciate their social interrelatedness and find purpose in the meaning-giving practices aimed at furthering a common good
Is linked to	*Is linked to*	*Is linked to*
The fundamental *disposition* of being open to experience and uncertainty	The *quality* (or value) of moral commitment	The *quality* (or value) of responsible community engagement
As implied in	*As implied in*	
Barnett (2005) Develop more complex *being* – the capacity for coping with and producing 'strangeness'	Sullivan & Rosin (2008) Develop a *particular kind of person* who can *reason practically*, combining academic ability with moral purpose and community engagement	

Source: Adapted from a table previously published in C. Kreber (2014). Rationalising the nature of 'graduateness' through philosophical accounts of authenticity. *Teaching in Higher Education*, 19(1). doi: 10.1080/13562517.2013.860114

and responsible community engagement thus stand in a certain relationship to one another. The disposition is foundational. In order to become *any* kind of person (here a person morally committed to creating a fairer world and responsibly engaged in the community), the person, of necessity, first has to be open to experience (the existential dimension). *Becoming* requires openness, or complexity of *being*, a point I shall explore some more in Chapter 5.

The notion of 'graduateness' is usefully understood through all three dimensions of authenticity: the existential, the critical and the communitarian. Of course, separating these three dimensions makes sense only for analytical purposes. Achieving one's full potential of being, one might sensibly argue, involves *critically* questioning one's choices and recognising that one's own flourishing hinges on the flourishing of others. Nonetheless, the linkages between our social interrelatedness and moral choices are most central, I want to suggest, to both the critical and communitarian dimensions. Table 3.1 offers an illustration of what has been argued.

Conclusion

I opened this chapter by highlighting the kinds of overarching graduate attributes different institutions have identified as important at this time, citing as examples,

Alverno College in Wisconsin, US, Mount Royal University in Alberta, Canada and the University of Edinburgh in Scotland. I then suggested that a theory-enriched engagement with the question of graduateness would be worthwhile to provide a more robust rationale for the selection of certain attributes, answering the questions 'Why are these core?' and 'Why should we care?'

Based on Barnett (2004) and Sullivan and Rosin (2008) I then identified openness to experience, moral commitment and responsible community engagement as three core aspects of graduateness. How do these attributes compare to those underpinning present outcomes-based curricula? And what are some implications for pedagogy?

Most graduate attribute statements emphasise inquiry in one way or another. Alverno refers to 'analysis and problem-solving', Mount Royal mentions 'inquiry and analysis' under the cluster of theoretical and practical skills, and Edinburgh highlights 'enquiry and lifelong learning'. Essential to real inquiry, we should now note, is openness to experience and a readiness to face the unknown. All attribute statements also mention effective citizenship or social responsibility. Social responsibility cannot be achieved without students constructing an identity grounded in a sense of social interrelatedness and desire to achieve a better world (addressing both the critical and communitarian dimensions of authenticity). I suggest that the three dimensions of authenticity discussed in this chapter point to three attributes that are fundamental (or core) to 'graduateness', regardless of programme choice. Most certainly, the particular ways in which these attributes might find expression in different disciplines and programmes will vary, and there will be many additional discipline-specific learning outcomes that are important also.

There are some general pedagogical approaches all programmes could consider adopting to promote the fundamental disposition and two qualities identified here. Such 'Pedagogies for graduateness' would require students to question and defend their own and others' knowledge claims, as well as apply, but also broaden and challenge, their academic knowledge through experiential learning in the community. Such pedagogies can foster learning for the longer term and also learning that is transformative, leading to a deeper understanding of subject matter and self, an identity grounded in a sense of responsible agency, commitment and authenticity. 'Pedagogies for graduateness' would fulfil five conditions:

1   They provoke students to critically reflect on their assumptions, beliefs and values and thus afford them opportunities to move beyond frames of reference that limit how they make meaning of their experiences.
2   They require and encourage students to take risks, take a stance and 'go public' with their knowledge claims, subjecting these, willingly, to the critical scrutiny of others in an environment characterised by trust.
3   They help students 'to construct themselves as active subjects' (Boud, 2007, p. 18) who make personal judgements about their own learning and consider this an integral part of the learning process.

4   They require students to become personally invested in the issues they are learning about in university courses and consider what these mean to them on a personal level and how they can make a difference to the world.
5   They engage students in experiential ways of learning, requiring them to relate abstract academic content to concrete real-life issues of social relevance.

In the next chapter I will explore civic-mindedness as an overarching professional capability that is grounded in an identity that is authentic.

Chapter 4

Understanding civic-mindedness

The external dimension of civic professionalism

Introduction

The previous chapter offered a theoretical model within which to understand the notion of 'graduateness' based on three different accounts of authenticity. Here my intent is to explore civic-mindedness as an overarching professional capability that is grounded in an identity that is authentic. A focus on civic-mindedness, as a key learning outcome of higher education, is important given observations that it is the professionals educated at our best colleges and universities that are to blame for the current 'unhealthy, inequitable, and unsustainable path' (Cortese, 2003, p. 17; see also Chapter 1), making us question whether we may safely entrust professionals with making decisions about the important matters affecting our lives. Similarly Melanie Walker (2012) comments: 'Indeed the recent financial crisis suggests that it is precisely the moral and ethical dimension of human life, rather than the quantity and level of education which has let us down so badly' (p. 387), highlighting further the need for education to contribute to students' ethical development to work towards a fairer and sustainable future.

In Chapter 1, I suggested that civic-mindedness is a disposition associated with a professional identity that is 'authentic'. An authentic professional identity is distinguished by a motivation to pursue one's own personal flourishing while supporting the flourishing of others. Civic-minded professional identities, therefore, are constructed around personal and public values, common good and social justice. In addition I argued that authenticity also reflects:

- being afforded the opportunity to enact this identity in practice (the latter clearly not to be taken for granted in public sector work); and therefore,
- having a disposition to cope with the state of affairs in which we find ourselves, which is one of *'uncertainty'*, *'unpredictability'*, *'challengeability'* and *'contestability'* (see Barnett, 2000, p. 159).

Whilst the first of the above two points reminds us of the constraints to authenticity that graduates may be experiencing at the workplace, the second reminds us that higher education's purpose is not just a matter of fitting people into predefined societal and vocational roles but of encouraging them to confront the challenges of our times. This will require them to critique and innovate, rather than accept the status quo compliantly.

I begin by highlighting that successful professional practice hinges on the acquired disposition to cope with *uncertainty, unpredictability, challengeability and contestability*, extending the argument to being able to deal with other forms of adversity at work. Despite the importance of students developing this disposition, I suggest that it is rare for teachers to understand their role as change agents, or as promoters of the students' ability to deal with these challenges. I then draw tighter linkages between the three core attributes identified in the previous chapter – *openness to experience, moral commitment* and *responsible community engagement* – and the notion of civic-mindedness. I propose that civic-mindedness is meaningfully conceptualised through these three accounts of authenticity. Openness to experience is the key disposition to develop in students as it enables them to confront the manifold challenges associated with professional practice; yet, equally important are the values of moral commitment and responsible community engagement. In the section that follows I shall argue that the three attributes together represent civic-mindedness, which can be conceptualised as an overarching professional capability. I offer some brief observations on the linkages between civic-mindedness and 'civic professionalism', ending the chapter with a short summary.

Coping with uncertainty, unpredictability, challengeability and contestability

Addressing the various challenges professionals are confronted with in the contemporary world, Barnett (2000) observed:

> Professional life is increasingly becoming a matter not just of handling overwhelming data and theories within a given frame of reference (a situation of complexity) but also a matter of handling multiple frames of understanding, of action and of self-identity. The fundamental frameworks by which we might understand the world are multiplying and are often in conflict. Of the multiplication of frameworks, there shall be no end.
>
> (p. 6)

The multiplication of frameworks, we saw in the previous chapter, Barnett (2000) refers to as 'super-complexity'. The age of 'super-complexity' is characterised by four essential features: *uncertainty, unpredictability, challengeability* and *contestability* (Barnett, 2000, p. 159). While the postmodern undertones in Barnett's writing surely won't escape us, and will not appeal to everyone, I think there are some essential messages here that are important to tease out further in order to reflect more meaningfully on the question of what an authentic civic-minded professional identity might involve. If Barnett is right, and I think he is, our world is a rather messy one to live and work in; and while we cannot simply clear up the mess, what we can do is take responsibility for preparing students for it.

Of the four features Barnett identifies as characterising our present age, that of *uncertainty* is perhaps the easiest to grasp. On the one hand it simply refers to being aware that one's knowledge of the world, and of oneself, is not fixed but subject to continuous change. The vast literature on lifelong learning that has been developing since the 1970s has been making reference to the rapid changes in our economic, technological, political, and cultural spheres (e.g., Aspin et al., 2001; Faure, 1972), a phenomenon typically associated with the by now widely accepted notion of 'globalisation' (e.g., Jarvis, 2007). Knowledge taught in universities today will soon be outdated, we are told; hence the need for learning throughout life. This is one aspect of uncertainty but I don't think it is the most significant.

When he speaks of uncertainty Barnett has in mind not only the cognitive dimension of not knowing but also the *experience* of being uncertain. Being uncertain has an existential dimension. We *feel* uncertain. While I am writing this I am reminded of a conversation I had with a colleague who for forty years had been studying the psychology of learning. He argued that my portrayal of states of uncertainty had clearly not been his experience. For him, he explained, uncertainty of knowledge was something humans (and especially academics) had always lived with and there was no reason for it to bring about a state of unrest, worry or even anxiousness only because we had moved into the twenty-first century. It made me wonder whether there might be something in the language I had employed that is a little misleading. I think, therefore, that it is important to acknowledge and emphasise that uncertainty of knowledge as such is not a recent phenomenon. It has always been with us; it is a fact of human life, or a feature of what it means to be human. Since we have consciousness, we are aware of our uncertainty regarding the future, and thus we can *feel* uncertain. Moreover, rapid advancements and innovations through research call previous hypotheses into question and may lead us to give up on a particular course of inquiry to pursue another. The scientific method is built on the idea of falsifiability.

This being said, I also think it needs acknowledging that especially in contemporary professional life uncertainty is now much more prevalent than it used to be. Importantly, *professional knowledge* is uncertain not just in a sense that we have not yet worked things out (but, given adequate resources and more time, will do so eventually). What is significant is that our feeling of uncertainty today is grounded in a sense that we most likely never *will* work things out completely as too many factors are beyond our control. Terrorism is a key example, and how to protect our planet or cure cancer might be others. Note here as well that some of the most important issues we are in urgent need of addressing call not just for instrumental solutions. We might conclude, therefore, that we are probably more likely to be able to cure cancer at some point in the future than we are to free our society of the threats of terrorism or save our planet from destruction (or solve many of our intercultural conflicts for that matter). Uncertainty is greater today as we are becoming aware of the limits of instrumental knowledge for solving problems involving people's values, agendas, and priorities.

Looked at in another way, uncertainty in professional knowledge arises also in light of the complexity of the situations we find ourselves in as practitioners, requiring us to judge and act in the midst of this epistemological uncertainty. Equally difficult to deal with are uncertain working conditions. Not knowing whether the various policies, budget decisions or software programmes (to mention just a few examples) that determine organisational practices this month will still be the same a month later, whether the clients we are working with today will still be with us tomorrow (or be transferred to someone else, or disappear from the register altogether), or as importantly, whether the job as we know it will still be there for us next week (see Beck, 2000). Professional life is drenched in uncertainty and risk. How to deal with uncertainty is an important issue for programmes to address whose purpose it is to prepare students for professional practice. So what about Barnett's second claim, that the world we live in is one of unpredictability?

Unpredictability is described by Barnett as a concept that is more context-bound than uncertainty. While uncertainty is a general state of human being, unpredictability refers to moments of not being able to form a definite picture of what is going to happen at some point in the future, or what the outcomes of one type of action might be. Unpredictability was identified by Hannah Arendt (1958) as a key feature of the human condition, as we will see in Chapter 9. Unpredictability, therefore, is not a concept that has befallen humankind only since modernity; yet, it is a feature of human life that we perhaps have been slow to accept: think of the rise of the scientific method intended precisely to predict and control events with high levels of certainty. In professional life it is essential to recognise that unpredictability is inescapable, and that we often cannot rely on 'evidence-based practice' of the kind *if we do X then Y will necessarily follow* (e.g., Hargreaves, 1997). Professionals need to recognise the limitations and dangers of these narrow instrumental discourses of evidence-based practice (Biesta, 2007).

Challengeability refers to our present understandings of the world occasionally being revealed to us as not being adequate for making sense of new experiences. Jack Mezirow's (1991) transformative learning theory is based on this recognition of challengeability of our present frames of reference. Personal growth and transformation, as well as social change, are inextricably linked to the fact that our interpretations of issues are challengeable. They can be called into question and replaced by new ones. Challengeability, therefore, harbours the origin and possibility of change. While ultimately challengeability can have positive outcomes, being challenged is not altogether a pleasant experience. Giving up long-held assumptions, beliefs or values, or having them revealed as invalid, can be deeply unsettling and confusing. Yet, it is through such experiences that much significant learning occurs. Preparing students for 'challenge-*ability*' should be a core aspect of professional programmes.

Finally, *contestability* refers to one proposition, interpretation or explanation being confronted with another that appears equally valid and internally consistent but is based on claims that contradict the first. This is not just a matter of different academic discourses or theories opposing one another (to provide just one example of contested discourses from the field of philosophy, is there a core self that one can be true to or are there multiple, fluid and shifting selves?); contestability can be observed also when traditional academic or professional values come up against managerial ones. Should the professional organisation (for instance the academy) ensure it meets its targets so as to stay competitive and protect its survival (within the academy, targets would include high rankings for research productivity as measured by the REF in the UK), or should the organisation instead put greater effort into supporting and working collaboratively with local communities to address the needs identified there? Contestability is the key feature of a work environment characterised by 'super-complexity' (Barnett, 2000). How to navigate one's way through conflicting discourses, when each position is adamant to not surrender to the other? The realities of professional life surely can be mentally and emotionally exhausting. How might we assist students in developing the capacity to deal with contestability?

In view of the above observations I suggest that if civic-mindedness were to be recognised as a core outcome of higher education, it would need to involve a 'disposition to be knowledgeable of and involved in the community, and to have a commitment to act upon a sense of responsibility as a member of that community' (Bringle & Steinberg, 2010, p. 429); yet civic-mindedness would need to go beyond that. The commitment to act upon a sense of responsibility as a member of one's community would need to extend to a readiness to act in civic-minded ways in the light of *uncertainty, unpredictability, challengeability and contestability*. Note in this context that there is now a growing literature on different aspects of adversity experienced at the workplace, especially in the helping professions (e.g., Jackson, Firtko & Edenborough, 2007). The challenges professionals, particularly in the public sector, have to deal with are numerous, including, for example, excessive workloads, lack of autonomy, changing responsibilities, disgruntled customers, strict accountability regimes that take time away from important tasks, policies that are based on values that conflict with one's own, and so much more. Some of these were discussed in Chapter 2 as aspects of 'the culture of inauthenticity'. Surely professional education needs to engage with the question of how professionals can be helped to develop civic-mindedness in the light of such adversity as well as the four challenges Barnett highlighted for us.

In addition, I suggest that civic-mindedness also includes a readiness to challenge existing practices and structures. This is to say that civic-mindedness is not controlled entirely by the political, social and economic forces professionals experience, although these do have an undeniable impact. Genuine civic-mindedness interacts with and occasionally challenges these external forces. At stake here is the key difference between the compliant and critical citizen, or the compliant and critical professional (e.g., Giroux, 2011). Genuine civic-mindedness, I want to argue, involves a preparedness to engage in contestation. This view raises questions regarding pedagogy, starting with how academics understand the purposes of higher education teaching and their role as teachers.

Based on a number of studies, Dan Pratt and colleagues at the University of British Columbia in Vancouver, Canada, identified five distinct teaching perspectives (Pratt et al., 1998), which they labelled Transmission, Developmental, Nurturing, Apprenticeship and Social Reform. A teaching perspective is a combination of beliefs, intentions and actions that characterise one's general outlook on and approach to teaching.

The Transmission perspective is 'based on the belief that a relatively stable body of knowledge and/or procedures can be efficiently transmitted to learners. The primary focus is on efficient and accurate delivery of that body of knowledge to learners' (Pratt et al., 1998, electronic source). Apprenticeship is a perspective whereby 'teaching is the process of enculturating learners into a specific community' (*ibid.*). This perspective assumes that 'learning must be located in authentic social situations related to the application of knowledge' (*ibid.*). The Developmental perspective is rooted in the assumption that 'prior knowledge and ways of thinking form the basis of each learner's approach to any new content and provide a window into their thinking' (*ibid.*). The teacher's task is to learn as much as he or she can about where the student is at, in order to then further his or her cognitive development by building on previous knowledge. The key assumption driving the Nurturing perspective is 'that learning is most affected by a learner's self-concept and self-efficacy. That is, learners must be confident that they can learn the material and that learning the material will be useful and relevant to their lives' (*ibid.*). Finally, the Social Reform perspective seeks to change society in substantive ways and is described by the authors as being

> characterised by the distinctive presence of an *explicitly stated* ideal or set of principles which are *linked to a vision of a better society*. Each ideal is based on a core or central system of beliefs, usually derived from an ethical code (such as the sanctity of human rights), a religious doctrine (such as the sanctity of God's law), or a political or social ideal (such as the need to redistribute power and privilege in society).
>
> (*ibid.*, emphasis in original)

Except for the Social Reform perspective, these perspectives resemble loosely those identified by other researchers (e.g., Fox, 1983; Kember, 1997; Trigwell & Prosser, 1996).

Dan Pratt and his colleague John Collins also developed a questionnaire that higher education teachers can complete to identify their preferred perspective on teaching, known as the *Teaching Perspectives Inventory* (TPI). The TPI has been completed by over one hundred thousand academics from a wide range of disciplines and countries, teaching across different levels (e.g., 1st year, 3rd year, undergraduate, postgraduate, etc.). For several years I used Pratt and Collins's TPI as a self-diagnostic tool to stimulate reflection among faculty at the University of Edinburgh who were participating in a master-level programme intended to prepare them for their various academic practice roles, including teaching. Although there is a developing literature that supports the view that higher education has a role to play in preparing students for social change (e.g., Colby et al., 2003; Cortese, 2003; Nussbaum, 2010; Taylor, Barr & Steele, 2002; Walker & McLean, 2013), it was extremely rare on the programme to encounter academics who felt that preparing students for social reform was one of the core purposes of their teaching, let alone of higher education generally. Pratt, Collins and Jarvis Selinger (2001) acknowledge that the social reform perspective 'represents the views of a small, but important group of adult educators involved in social change movements' (electronic source).

However, the questionnaire (TPI) stimulated lively and, at times, heated debate among course participants, with one group (the majority) insisting that the social reform perspective bordered on indoctrination and that the real purpose of the academy was to promote the autonomous mind through disciplinary ways of inquiry, and the other group (the minority) responding that the real purpose of the academy was to develop the next generation of citizens and that our world was in dire need of reform. Although one might expect a divide along disciplinary lines, such a divide was not always obvious. Of interest here is a study reported by Deggs, Machtmes and Johnson (2008) who used Pratt and Collins's TPI with academics from a wide range of disciplines at a large research-intensive university in the United States to explore whether dominant teaching perspectives varied by discipline. Findings revealed disciplinary differences only along the apprenticeship perspective but not any of the others.

Now, it may be the case that academics teaching from the Social Reform perspective, as described by Pratt and colleagues, are seen to push their own agenda a bit too far, or that the wording of the TPI items pertaining to the Social Reform perspective is somewhat off-putting to most readers. Responses of some academics might also crucially depend on the particular vision of a 'better' society that is advocated. Speaking for myself, I can see myself fully supporting one vision of a changed society but strongly opposing another, and many colleagues may feel similarly, explaining the low scores obtained for that teaching perspective. Nonetheless, what struck me about the discussions we had in class following the completion of the TPI was how few academics thought about the purposes of university teaching beyond the boundaries of their own discipline, or about how, through their own discipline, they might contribute to larger educational goals (see also Stephen Brookfield's astute observations on this that were featured in Chapter 1). It is not so much that colleagues would not want students leaving university after three to four years to be civic-minded graduates ready to tackle the difficult issues confronting our world (which in my mind resonates with the goal of 'seeking to change society in substantive ways'); it is rather that they think the responsibility for promoting this readiness in future graduates lies not with them but elsewhere. But if the responsibility does not lie with the teachers and programme organiser, where is it located? A fundamental problem with the academy is that far too often opportunities to develop the skills, abilities and dispositions necessary to make a difference in our communities arise only in 'voluntary extras' (for example summer courses in service-learning and similar worthwhile activities) that students can sign up for if they wish, but they are not fully embedded across the curriculum. It is for this reason, of course, that abilities-based curricula, and the graduate attribute initiatives discussed in the previous chapter, are so promising. However, individual academics' and/or departments' engagement with these initiatives varies substantially, sometimes not extending much beyond box-ticking following a curriculum mapping exercise. Ultimately, too few academics see their role as agents of social change engaged in preparing students to take on the challenge to become the change agents of the future.

Civic-mindedness: openness to experience, moral commitment and responsible community engagement

In the previous chapter I proposed that 'graduateness' involved a fundamental disposition of *openness to experience*. This openness to the unknown leads us to question assumptions, which in turn opens up the opportunity for *significant* learning (i.e., learning that is transformative) and greater authenticity. Shaun Gallagher (1992) points out that 'an essential aspect of all educational experience, including play, involves venturing into the unknown, going beyond ourselves and experiencing the unfamiliar' (p. 50). This venturing into the unknown is sometimes referred to as 'self-transcendence' (Gallagher, 1992), whereby we let ourselves be immersed or taken up by the new experience. The self that (re)emerges from this journey into the strange or unknown, is a recovered, reclaimed or 'reappropriated' self, a transformed self that has grown from the adventure and thus has become more open to experience (Gallagher, 1992). Barnett (2004) would say that *being* itself has become more complex as a result of encountering strangeness. I associated this fundamental disposition of *openness to experience* with the existential dimension of authenticity which stresses openness to one's own possibilities.

For practitioners to be able to act in civic-minded ways, I now want to suggest, they must have developed the complexity of *being* (Barnett, 2004), or openness to experience, needed to deal with, and actively engage with, uncertainty, unpredictability, challengeability and contestability, and also other forms of work-related adversity. It is one thing to be civic-minded when the conditions are conducive to demonstrating a sense of responsibility as a member of one's community (Bringle & Steinberg, 2010). It is quite another to do so when the conditions press for compliance with the status quo or are otherwise unfavourable.

Openness to experience, a preparedness to engage with the unknown, is a fundamental disposition for professionals to develop in order not to succumb to the many challenges they confront. The idea of *openness to experience* may seem abstract. Yet, the key point is that situations of uncertainty, unpredictability, challengeability and contestability can be reframed as opportunities for learning and growth – but only if we are ready to embrace this learning. This readiness or openness involves having the courage (and perhaps will and resilience) to engage with it. I will have more to say about the nurturing of the virtues in the following chapter; here my point is that each experience we allow ourselves to have also transforms us in some way, and thus makes our *being* more complex. It makes us better able to deal with future situations where we find our views challenged, or when we need to navigate our way through conflicting goals or interpretive frameworks.

Also imperative for being able to act in civic-minded ways are the two qualities (or values) associated with 'graduateness': a sense of *moral commitment* and a willingness to become *socially engaged*. *Moral commitment* is associated with the critical dimension of authenticity which stresses critical reflection on how we arrived at our socially constructed assumptions of how the world should be. The critical dimension is informed by critical social theory and thus 'is grounded in an activist desire to fight oppression, injustice, and bigotry and create a fairer, more compassionate world' (Brookfield, 2005, p. 10). A moral commitment to contributing to a fairer world develops, at least partially, through critical reflectivity (Brookfield, 2005). Critical reflectivity involves, on the one hand, the testing of validity claims and questioning of presuppositions through abstract or analytical reasoning (e.g., Dewey, 1991); but it also involves, on the other hand, learning to recognise how relations of power can distort experiences and how hegemonic forces can make us collude in our own oppression (e.g., Brookfield, 2005). It thereby helps to reveal structural forms of power that serve to sustain social injustices.

Responsible community engagement is associated with the communitarian dimension of authenticity which emphasises recognition of our social inter-relatedness as well as commitment to participating in the community and finding meaning in these practices. Finding meaning in contributing to community develops through practical reasoning (Sullivan & Rosin, 2008). Practical reasoning is reasoning located in practice and oriented towards action. However, it is not about how to perform a particular skill to bring about a certain product; instead, practical reasoning involves reflection on what ought to be done in a given situation and is inextricably connected with notions of meaning and responsibility.

Highlighting how practical reasoning is different from the abstract analytical thinking usually taught in universities, Sullivan and Rosin (2008) suggest that individuals involved in practical reasoning 'use critique in order to act responsibly, as it is the common search for ways to realize valuable purposes and ideals that guides their reasoning' (p. xvi). Practical reasoning then clearly involves critical thinking as typically understood in higher education, but connects it with personal meaning and questions such as what ought to be done here, and, also, how should I live. Moreover, when I use the term *critical* I include in my definition a critical theory dimension. Although there are clearly connections between *critical* reflectivity and practical reasoning (indeed *critical* reflectivity is rooted in practical reasoning but permeates it with ideology critique – Habermas, 1984), it should be clear that not all proponents of practical reasoning espouse a critical theory position (exceptions include Stephen Kemmis's 2012 critical interpretation of the virtue of 'practical wisdom'). It is for this reason that it makes sense to treat the two concepts of critical reflectivity and practical reasoning as separate processes, both important for civic-mindedness.

The three core attributes of 'graduateness' discussed in Chapter 3, therefore, can be conceived of as essential for higher education to foster in students if our aim is to graduate civic-minded professionals. Having established tighter linkages between the notion of 'graduateness', grounded in three dimensions of authenticity, and civic-mindedness, I now want to proceed with my next task, which is to demonstrate why civic-mindedness is appropriately conceived of as a professional capability.

Civic-mindedness: an in-person capability

Chapter 1 and also this present chapter employed the notion of capabilities, making cursory reference to Nussbaum (2000, 2011) as well as Walker and McLean (2013); however, the association of 'capabilities' with core learning outcomes of students on professional programmes is not common practice. What I still need to do, therefore, is to offer a rationale for why professional practice and the core learning outcomes of university graduates (especially on professional programmes) are meaningfully theorised as *capabilities*. This is my purpose in this section.

To begin with, let's resolve the ambiguity surrounding the meaning of capabilities. The term 'capabilities' is often used interchangeably with 'capacities', 'abilities and skills' and even 'competencies'. It is important to clarify, therefore, that when I speak of capabilities in this book I do so in reference to the *capabilities approach*, an approach to social justice pioneered by economist Amartya Sen (2009) and further developed by philosopher Martha Nussbaum (2000, 2011; Nussbaum & Sen, 1993). Sen proposed the capabilities approach as an alternative to standard economic approaches to achieving quality of life, such as those based on Gross National Product (GNP), or straightforward utilitarian approaches that consider how the population, on average, rate their satisfaction. Even Rawls's (1971, 1999) theory of justice, Nussbaum (2000) explains, falls short on one central point: 'that individuals vary greatly in their need for resources and in their abilities to convert resources into valuable functionings' (p. 68). By asking what are people actually able to be or do, the capabilities approach reveals social inequalities, treating each person as an end.

Influenced by both the Marxist and Aristotelian traditions, Nussbaum, in her version of the capabilities approach, argues that capabilities need to be informed 'by an intuitive idea of a life that is worthy of the dignity of the human being'

(Nussbaum, 2000, p. 5), and proposes a list of ten central capabilities. Nussbaum claims that her list is universal, in a sense that it applies across the globe regardless of different cultures and traditions, a claim that has been contested by some feminist scholars. Her list, which she explains is 'the result of years of cross-cultural discussions' (Nussbaum, 2011, p. 76), includes the following ten central human capabilities (each further detailed by Nussbaum): (1) life; (2) bodily health; (3) bodily integrity; (4) senses, imagination, and thought; (5) emotions; (6) practical reason; (7) affiliation (being able to live with as well as towards others and being treated with respect); (8) other species; (9) play; (10) control over one's political and material environment (pp. 78–80). Each of these capabilities, sometimes referred to as comprehensive capabilities, represents a sphere of life over which individuals must have real choices. The central idea is that only if these sets of capabilities are given, that is, only if individuals have real freedom to choose their functioning in these spheres, can we speak of a life of human dignity, or a life that people have reason to value. The distinction between functionings and capabilities is important. While functionings are actual beings and doings, capabilities refer to real opportunities to be in a certain way or do certain things. Drawing on an example used by Amartya Sen, Nussbaum (2011) explains the difference between capabilities and functionings this way:

> A person who is starving and a person who is fasting have the same kind of functioning where nutrition is concerned, but they do not have the same capability, because the person who fasts is able not to fast, and the starving person has no choice . . . To promote capabilities is to promote areas of freedom, and this is not the same as making people function in a certain way.
>
> (p. 25)

Melanie Walker at Free State University in South Africa (previously at the University of Nottingham) and Monica McLean from the University of Nottingham recognised the relevance of the capabilities approach for professional practice and professional education. 'The capabilities approach', they observe, 'conceptualises people living in poverty (and subject to other injustices) as deprived of opportunities to make choices for capabilities and functionings that comprise a healthy and dignified life' (McLean & Walker, 2012, p. 587).

If professionals really are to contribute to people's overall quality of life and serve the public well, as is widely assumed (e.g., Sugrue & Solbrekke, 2011), then they need to make their unique contribution to expanding comprehensive capabilities among individuals in the society in which they live and work (Walker & McLean, 2013). Just which capabilities different professions are best suited to help expand will obviously vary, but there can be no doubt that each has its distinct role to play. Although Walker and McLean located their research in the context of South Africa, where poverty among a large proportion of society is a central social problem and a key concern for government (Walker & McLean, 2013), the key idea that capability expansion in wider society is at the heart of professional practice, I suggest, applies anywhere, including countries that do not face the same social economic disparities as South Africa. Moreover, countries such as Scotland or Canada also have their own unresolved social justice issues, including poverty, that (civic-minded) professionals would want to help address (e.g., Mooney & Scott, 2012; Raphael, 2002).

In numerous publications, but summarised in their valuable recent book *Professional education, capabilities and contributions to the public good: The role of universities in promoting human development*, Walker and McLean (2013) then argued that the notion of capabilities is usefully extended to professional practitioners themselves. As mentioned in Chapter 1, they coined the term *professional capabilities* to signify those freedoms to function that professionals need in order to create a better world through their professional practice, a practice which has as its aim to expand basic capabilities in society. Examples of the '*professional* capabilities' the authors identified as essential for students to develop include: practical reasoning; public reasoning; affiliation; integrity; emotional awareness; informed vision; imagination; empathy; developing relationship and rapport across special groups and status hierarchies; having confidence to act for change; social and collective struggle; resilience; and communicating professional knowledge in an accessible way (see Walker & McLean, 2009, 2011, 2013; McLean & Walker, 2012). These professional capabilities clearly resonate with the notion of civic-mindedness as developed earlier in this chapter.

In conceptualising civic-mindedness as a capability it is helpful to note that Nussbaum actually makes a distinction between *inner* or 'in-person' capabilities and *combined* capabilities, the latter referring to substantial freedoms. While *combined* capabilities are 'created by a combination of abilities and the political, social and economic environment' (Nussbaum, 2011, p. 20), *inner capabilities* are characteristics of a person. Inner capabilities, Nussbaum explains further,

> are trained or developed traits and abilities, developed, in most cases, in interaction with the social, economic, familial, and political environment. . . . One job of a society that wants to promote the most important human capabilities is to support the development of internal capabilities – through *education*, resources to enhance physical and emotional health, support for family care and love, a system of education, and much more.
>
> (p. 21, emphasis added)

This quote is helpful in two ways. First, it highlights the importance of education in promoting inner capabilities generally. Second, it allows us to conceive of civic-mindedness as a(n inner) capability to be developed through professional education. Melanie Walker (2012) also helpfully observes that:

> Education, while by no means the only arena for intervention for the formation of capabilities, might be operationalized to form the kind of human beings who can contribute to shaping the kind of society which values

capabilities, who want to contribute to capability building and a society and public culture which can sustain capability for all.

(p. 392)

Given that capabilities are those opportunities of being and doing that allow us to choose and live in ways we find meaningful or have reason to value, capabilities are key to human flourishing, or, as I want to suggest, to 'authenticity'. As higher education institutions promote the *professional* capabilities identified in Walker and McLean's (2013) research, and the overarching professional capability of civic-mindedness that I developed here, they can be seen as contributing to the students' (future professionals') path towards authenticity; and just the same, as these professionals later engage in helping expand basic capabilities *for all*, they are involved in supporting the authenticity of other members of their communities.

Thus, when I speak of civic-mindedness as an overarching professional capability I am building on Walker and McLean's important and pioneering work in this area. My contribution is to conceive of their so-called 'public-good professionals' (professionals who make decisions about public goods, for example, health care or education, wisely and in the interests of the public) as civic-minded professionals whose professional identity, in turn, I interpret through the lens of authenticity.

Civic-mindedness and 'civic professionalism'

In stressing the importance of 'civic-mindedness' as an overarching professional capability guiding professional practice, natural linkages emerge to the concept of 'civic professionalism' as advocated by Boyte (2004), Boyte and Fretz (2010, 2012) and Sullivan (1995, 2005). Sullivan, who developed the notion of civic professionalism in his 1995 book *Work and integrity: The crisis and promise of professionalism in America*, sees professional practices as providing opportunities for individuals to make something of themselves; that is, to cultivate particular talents and capacities but also to find personal meaning in these practices. This personal development, he argues, is possible through a strong commitment to the community of practice of which the professional is part (for example, nursing, teaching, engineering, law, social work, journalism and so forth). However, the distinguishing feature of *civic* professionalism is that professionals construct an identity not exclusively with regards to their own professional community whose purposes and continuous improvement they feel committed to; rather civic professionals find fulfilment in advancing the well-being of the larger communities they are part of that are meant to benefit from the professional practice. Sullivan (1995) perhaps takes an idealised view when he writes:

> The goal of self-actualization needs to be transcended, or perhaps better, reoriented by integrating individual goals with those of the larger community. The logical fulfilment of this process is a kind of character for who what

happens to those larger communities is as important as what happens to the self, or more so.

(p. 237)

The recent literature on higher and professional learning has highlighted the importance of professional *being* (e.g., Barnett, 2008, 2011; Dall'Alba, 2009; Vu & Dall'Alba, 2011), next to professional knowing and acting. What is proposed in this literature is that professional practice demands *a special kind* of being, a being that is implicated in a struggle towards becoming authentic. This struggle towards becoming authentic involves recognising one's possibilities as a professional. Drawing on Charles Taylor (1991), Barnett (2011) observes that 'All professional life to be worthy of the name has been conducted against a horizon of the ethical; it is there, if at all, that it gains its authenticity' (p. 35). Just what ethical means will be explored more deeply in the following chapter, although some precursors were set already in Chapter 1. Here I would like to make just one point, in an attempt at a synthesis of Sullivan's (1995) and Barnett's (2011) statements: acting ethically involves doing what is good, but good for both the professional him or herself as well as the wider community, the latter including the various publics supported by the profession.

The limits of a professional practice that remains too closed upon itself and inward-looking, rather than being open to its wider community and outward-looking, were recognised by Jon Nixon and his colleagues (Nixon et al., 2001). Focusing specifically on the academic profession, the authors observed that academics for too long had taken comfort in a narrow sense of professional identity based on 'their own "small world" of professional interests' rather than 'the wider public interests of the world "out there"' (p. 237). The authors propose as values that should guide (academic) professionalism those of 'care and affection, of critical engagement and dialogue, of public concern and welfare' (p. 237). Citing from the famous Reith Lectures (broadcast by the BBC each year in the spirit of enriching the intellectual and cultural life of the nation) given by Edward Said in 1993, they espouse a view of professionalism that is 'based not on "doing what one is supposed to do" but on asking "why one does it, who benefits from it" . . .' (Nixon et al., 2001, p. 237). Linked to these considerations is a recognition that professions should develop identities that are not limited to a sense of belonging to a particular professional group but to the larger community which is meant to benefit from the practice. Professionals need to understand themselves also, and perhaps foremost, as fellow citizens whose goals and aspirations are aligned with those of their peers in the broader community. The concept of civic-mindedness developed here resonates strongly with this view.

Final comments

Four objectives were pursued in this chapter. First, I argued that *openness to experience* is an essential disposition for students to develop as it provides the foundation from which to deal with the core challenges characterising professional practice, which include uncertainty, unpredictability, challengeability, contestability, as well as other work-related adversity. Second, I showed that *openness to experience* (linked to the existential dimension of authenticity) is foundational also to the two human qualities or values of *moral commitment* (linked to the critical dimension of authenticity) and *responsible community engagement* (linked to the communitarian dimension of authenticity), and that all three, in the previous chapter discussed as the central features of graduateness, provide for a sound theoretical foundation for the concept of 'civic-mindedness'. Third, I suggested that civic-mindedness is appropriately conceptualised as an overarching professional capability that is rooted in authenticity, and is essential for professionals to acquire if we want them to be ready and willing to contribute to a fairer world. Finally, I intimated that civic-mindedness is the central capability underlying 'civic professionalism', which is distinguished by a strong community orientation. In summary, this chapter focused on the importance of civic-mindedness as an overarching professional capability. Table 4.1 provides a summary of what has been argued.

The next chapter will look into how and why the professional's self-cultivation is necessary to sustain civic-mindedness.

Table 4.1 The linkages between civic-mindedness, capabilities and authenticity

Overarching professional capability	Civic-mindedness	
⬆		
Particular professional capabilities (identified by Walker & McLean, 2013)	e.g., practical reasoning; public reasoning; affiliation; integrity; emotional awareness; imagination; empathy; developing relationship and rapport across special groups and status hierarchies; having confidence to act for change; and communicating professional knowledge in an accessible way	
⬆		
Two qualities/values Associated with the critical and communitarian dimensions of authenticity	**Moral commitment** Stresses critical reflection on how we arrived at our socially constructed assumptions of how the world should be	**Responsible community engagement** Emphasises recognition of our social interrelatedness as well as commitment to participating in the community and finding meaning in these practices
⬆		
A fundamental disposition Associated with the existential dimension of authenticity	**Openness to experience** Openness and capacity to engage with uncertainty and adversity	

Chapter 5

Recognising self-cultivation

The internal dimension
of civic professionalism

Introduction

A meaningful interpretation of 'graduateness', I proposed in Chapter 4, would include students having developed the overarching professional capability of civic-mindedness, the latter grounded in the three attributes of an openness to experience, moral commitment and responsible community engagement. This capability, I further argued, underlies the practice of 'civic professionalism' (Boyte, 2004; Boyte & Fretz, 2012; Sullivan, 1995, 2005), which assumes a professional identity that is civic-minded and 'authentic'. The professional identity is authentic in terms of all three dimensions of authenticity outlined in the previous two chapters. Civic-minded professionals are open to taking risks and confronting challenges, they seek a fairer world and they are acutely aware that what is most valuable in professional practice, ultimately, is not to satisfy only their own goals and aspirations, or those of their professional group, but additionally those of the larger community they are part of. The ideal of civic professionalism is based on a complete integration of one's personal goals, those of one's professional group and those of one's larger community (Sullivan, 2005), resulting in an overriding motivation to contribute to the well-being of the greater community. This chapter now asks what is involved in this integration of diverse and possibly conflicting goals, and explores also critically Sullivan's implied claim that self-actualisation could occur through the professional practices in which we are engaged. For Sullivan, we saw in the previous chapter, the ideal professional, or 'civic professional', considers what happens to his or her 'larger communities . . . as important as what happens to the self, or more so' (2005, p. 237).

It will be undisputed that as professionals we cannot only be self-regarding and pursue our own interests and desires but also need to be other-regarding. Being service-oriented is one of the key criteria defining professions. And yet, we are only too aware that there have been occasions when professionals clearly have been too self-regarding and have pursued their privileges, such as wealth, fame or status, to the detriment of others (see Chapter 2). The financial crisis of 2008 is one tragic example. Another extreme case of selfishness, narcissism or egocentricity is that of the notorious Dr Shipman in the UK, and many more recent disturbing cases from within the clergy, education, nursing, business, engineering and other professional fields, publicised widely through popular media, could be featured. However, while professionals surely can be *too* self-regarding, there are also times when professionals might have erred in the other direction and have been too other-regarding, trying to serve at all cost believing that only to do that is the morally justifiable choice. This second extreme is rarely highlighted, and perhaps is even silently tolerated, given policy and work environments that make little reference to the importance of the professional's own well-being, instead emphasising the expectation of compliance and meeting targets efficiently, and thus of uncompromising service. There can be a real tension then between pursuing what is considered personally meaningful and fulfilling, and serving the needs of others. Yet, it is essential to note that experiencing a healthy level of self-regard by doing what is personally meaningful and fulfilling is not the same as being self-obsessed, narcissistic or egocentric. One can be self-regarding and still recognise the intrinsic worth of other people. Healthy self-regard, therefore, is linked to eudaimonism (see also Chapter 1); too much self-regard is linked to egoism.

Sullivan's notion of 'civic professionalism' is of particular interest as it is located somewhere in between the widely shared perspective of *moral professionalism*, which, as we saw in Chapter 1, highlights one's obligations to others, and a *professional ethics* based on the importance of *the practitioner's self-cultivation*, as developed by Chris Higgins (2011) in drawing on Bernard Williams's (1985) important distinction between morality and ethics. According to Higgins (2011), the flourishing (or self-cultivation) of the practitioner is an overlooked aspect of professional ethics and yet is crucial to arriving at a deeper understanding of the workings and motivations driving good professional practice. Taking inspiration from Charles Taylor (1989), Higgins suggests that while moral professionalism prompts us to ask 'what it is right to do', a professional ethics grounded in the ancient virtue tradition would ask the richer question of 'what it is good to be' (Charles Taylor, cited in Higgins, 2011, p. 21), or, more generally, 'how should I live'. It is helpful to cite Taylor in full here:

> . . . contemporary philosophy give[s] a very narrow focus to morality. Morality it conceived purely as a guide to *action*. It is thought to be concerned purely with what it is right to do rather than with what it is good to be. In a related way the task of moral theory is identified as defining the content of obligation rather than the nature of the good life. In other words, morals concern what we *ought to do*; this excludes both what it is good to do, even though we are not obliged . . . and also what it may be good (or even obligatory) to *be* or *love*, as irrelevant to ethics. In this conception there is no place for the notion of the good in either of two common traditional senses: either the good life, or the good as the object of our love or allegiance.
>
> (Taylor, 1989, p. 79)

It is not insignificant that the professional practice Higgins is concerned with is teaching, since, as we will see momentarily, there are good reasons for arguing that teachers' self-cultivation would be beneficial to the students whose learning they are meant to inspire. However, if professional ethics based on the idea of self-cultivation is to have purchase for other professional practices as well, then it is vital to explore more deeply just how the practitioner's self-cultivation is beneficial to clients as well as wider society. Some readers might feel that this is too instrumental a view. Self-cultivation, they will argue, is an essential good in itself; we do not self-cultivate in order to do something else. I fully appreciate that self-cultivation is a good in itself that deserves to be protected. In his book *The reasons of love*, Harry Frankfurt (2004) likewise seems to be suggesting that self-cultivation, or, as he puts it, self-love or whole-heartedness, is a good in itself. While Frankfurt is not concerned with whether there is any larger moral force associated with self-love, he definitely considers self-love an essential, and a legitimate, focus of care for a happy life. Loving what you do and who you are is a good in itself, he argues, even if it benefits no one. Indeed, he suggests that, in principle, one could be wholeheartedly wicked (which, of course, would not be commendable). Self-cultivation then is important for a good life, and thus is a good in itself; and still, when aiming to assess the purpose and significance of self-cultivation in professional life I think we cannot escape the question of just how self-cultivation is significant beyond the good life of the practitioner.

I can see three possible attempts at responding to the question of how self-cultivation is significant to the good life of the practitioner, and beyond. I shall briefly sketch these out here and will return to them again later in this chapter.

One response is to argue that the self-cultivation of the practitioner is important because it offers a counter force to the many situations of adversity experienced at work. In order to withstand the challenging and often negative forces we are exposed to, it might be said, we need to self-cultivate so that we become more resilient, less easily frustrated and perhaps even more creative with how we engage with such situations. Ultimately, it might be said, our clients are then not negatively affected since as long as we do a good job looking after ourselves, the professional practice will not be disrupted. A second response might be to say that we need to self-cultivate as only then can we promote it in others. A person (a teacher might be the prime example) who is not engaged in self-cultivation is in no position to inspire growth and development in others, it might be reasoned. Similarly, commenting on the relationship between inner self-cultivation and responsiveness towards others, Martha Nussbaum (2010) argues that 'The two typically develop in tandem, since one can hardly cherish in another what one has not explored in oneself' (p. 104). A third response could be that self-cultivation is important as it directly enhances the professional practice itself, and it is through our professional practice that we support clients and enrich our larger communities. While I think all three responses carry weight, I am inclined to lend my strongest support to version three, although it still requires both some further unpacking and elaboration. The key issues to be delved into more deeply include: does self-cultivation influence professional practice, or does professional practice influence self-cultivation, or is the relationship perhaps reciprocal? Moreover, why should the 'cultivated' practice necessarily be a civic-minded practice, or, to put it slightly differently, how, if at all, is self-cultivation relevant to civic-mindedness?

This chapter tackles these questions. I will argue that while civic-mindedness represents the external dimension of civic professionalism (which is oriented towards being responsive towards others, that is, individual clients and the larger communities we are part of), self-cultivation can be conceived of as the internal dimension of civic professionalism (which is oriented towards self-development and the development of the professional practice itself). Why the 'cultivated' professional practice (the one enriched by practitioners' self-cultivation) should be a civic-minded practice is not immediately obvious, and more will need to be said later in this chapter. However, an initial albeit still incomplete argument in support of this claim, coming from three different directions, can be offered at this stage.

The first direction from which an argument could be developed is grounded in the well-known psychological theories of Erikson (1965) and Maslow (1972), who considered civic-mindedness to be an expression of healthy identity development and self-actualisation, respectively. Similarly Smart et al. (2000) argue that

> The ability to consider and care for others as well as for oneself may be considered the culmination of an individual's development. It is manifested in the way parents care for their children, in the way teachers foster their students' intellectual and emotional development, and in the way we as a society support members of our communities and govern our countries.
>
> (p. 4)

According to these psychological theories, civic-mindedness, a responsiveness towards and concern for the nurturing and well-being of others in society, is considered part of a healthy process of self-development.

The second direction from which an argument could be developed is associated with communitarian philosophers such as Charles Taylor (1989, 1991) and Alasdair MacIntyre (2009), in whose work we find an emphasis on the significance of our social interrelatedness (but see also liberal theorists including Terry Eagleton, Martha Nussbaum and Jean Hampton who agree with this point). In Taylor (1989), in particular, we encounter the argument that our answers to the question of 'what makes life worth living . . . are not rendered valid by our own desires, inclinations, or choices, but rather stand independent of these and offer standards by which these can be judged' (p. 4). What Taylor has in mind in this passage when talking about standards is *horizons of significance*, among which, in a later text, he includes, for example, our history, the demands of nature, the needs of our fellow human beings, the duties of citizenship, or the call of God

(Taylor, 1991). In Taylor's view broad issues such as these provide a standard (a *horizon*) against which we need to judge the validity or rightness of our actions and decisions. Discussing specifically what it means to hold an identity that is authentic, Taylor (1991) argues that only if we exist in a world in which any one of these broad issues '*matters* crucially, can I define an identity for myself that is not trivial' (p. 41, emphasis in original). We can now extrapolate from this statement to the identity of professionals. In line with Taylor, we would then argue that, ideally, the self-cultivation of the professional needs to be defined against something significant, something that really matters in life and to our society. In professional life in particular (but also in the life of every person), what 'really matters' would include living well and living well together which entails enabling the flourishing of others (see Chapter 4). To the extent that we are involved in enabling the flourishing of others, we enact our civic-mindedness, an overarching capability that orients us towards civic professionalism (see previous chapter).

The third direction from which an argument could unfold is the ideal of a profession itself, as advocated by the early functionalist theorists of the professions. Whether we are sceptical of this ideal portrayal of professions (e.g., Illich, 1977; Johnson, 1972; Larson, 1977), or whether we genuinely espouse this view (e.g., Tawney, 1920), professions traditionally have been deemed to be more motivated by doing good work than by economic reward (Freidson, 2001). Tawney (1920), and later Durkheim (1957) and Parsons (1954), stressed especially the social value and civic/public purposes of the professions. Professionals, as social trustees, were seen as carrying social responsibility. Although Brint (1994) more recently showed that in contemporary times professionals understand good work increasingly as providing an efficient technical service (see Chapter 1), the original ideal, and the key point I would like to bring out here, highlighted the professions' civic responsibility. Therefore, if we stayed loyal to the original ideal when considering what professional practices – for example, nursing, teaching, city planning, doctoring, social work, engineering and many others – are meant to achieve, *if practised well*, we would identify service to individual clients and larger society as key criteria (in Chapter 8 I will have more to say about the problems associated with the social trustee model based on the idea of doing things *for* others, but I should not get ahead of this discussion). The well-functioning and developed professional practice, we then would argue, is one underpinned by the capability of civic-mindedness, which in turn is imperative for the enactment of civic professionalism.

This chapter will first explore what is meant by self-cultivation, and how self-cultivating activities are different from those we might experience as self-refreshing or, as I shall call them, 'self-maintaining'. It will also show how self-cultivation can occur through activities and practices that have the potential to change us, and Alasdair MacIntyre's definition of a practice as a social activity embedded in a tradition, standards of excellence, internal goods and virtues, offers a useful analytical tool for this discussion. Finally, I shall demonstrate how self-cultivation is intimately connected to community, thereby developing a stronger argument for how self-cultivation hinges on civic-mindedness and thus is foundational to the practice of civic professionalism.

How might we understand the notion of self-cultivation?

The notion of the 'cultivated person' can have elite overtones, especially when being associated with having had exposure to what are considered culture's highest achievements, for instance in the arts, politics, science and so forth. Yet, what I mean by self-cultivation is a little different. While it is indeed possible (some would say likely) that people experience self-cultivation as they engage with certain disciplines or forms of art, for example literary texts, music, theatre or paintings, I would like to submit that volunteering in our communities, caring for one's elderly parent, studying or working in a foreign country, or living through a traumatic or challenging experience can be at least as powerful a self-cultivating force as it is to read a good novel.

'Bildung' is the word used in German to describe what happens as a result of education, especially formal and higher education. While formal education, clearly, is not the only context in which Bildung may occur, it is on the basis of the term 'Hochschul*bildung*' (the German word for 'higher education') that we can usefully explore the meaning associated with this notion. The verb form of the noun Bildung is 'bilden', which on the one hand means being 'built', shaped or educated by others, but, on the other hand, refers to educating oneself. 'Being built or educated' by others implies becoming 'cultured', that is becoming socialised into certain knowledge communities and learning about issues that are considered worthwhile knowing about. In the English language the word 'formation' is typically used to refer to this process of socialisation. But is the 'cultured person' thus understood necessarily cultivated? The cultured person certainly knows a lot of things, and presumably a lot of things that are widely deemed to be important; but it is the cultivated person who has developed him or herself. The cultivated person is not just well-versed in what is considered worth knowing in our society; the cultivated person has personally grown through and from his or her experiences.

The difference between being cultured and being (self-) cultivated is perhaps best captured by Gallagher (1992), who, as we saw in the previous chapter, associated the notion of Bildung not with formation but with *openness to experience* from which the individual emerges as a transformed self. Self-cultivation refers to this second meaning of Bildung as *trans*formation. When Higgins (2011) argues for the importance of self-cultivation in teachers (and we might want to expand the notion of teachers to educators working in contexts other than the school), he implies that teachers cannot be successful in promoting significant learning in students unless they themselves remain open to experience, nurture their own curiosity, and engage in activities that stimulate personal growth (some of these activities will not be related directly to work).

The above point I raised earlier as the second of three possible reasons for why self-cultivation of the practitioner might be significant. The first reason I had given was that engaging in activities that provide a counter-force to things in life that can wear us down, especially the various pressures experienced at work, was important for a healthy life. 'Time out' from the regular (playing tennis with a friend, playing the guitar, going for a walk, spending an hour on the phone with your best friend planning the next holiday, painting your study pink, trying out a new recipe, or even going bungee jumping if you are so inclined, etc.) is critical to experience some relief from the stress associated with the constant duty we may feel towards caring for others, be these clients or the goals of the organisation we work for. Doing such pleasant things, no matter what form they might take for you, is 'self-refreshing' or 'self-maintaining' and protects us from becoming burned out. Engaging in self-maintaining or pleasurable activity will make us more content and probably easier to be around. Yet self-cultivation and self-maintenance are not the same. Conflating the two prevents us from recognising that self-cultivating activities involve self-development and are not always perceived as pleasurable at the moment, although, of course, they may be. To be self-cultivating means more than to refresh; it means to experience 'the free flourishing of one's powers and capacities' (Eagleton, 2007, p. 96). When we experience self-cultivation we release some kind of potential in us.

Moreover, we should also recognise that the same activity can be self-cultivating for one person yet not so for another, and of course, pleasurable for one person and not so for another, and yet more self-cultivating for the person for whom it was less pleasurable. My friend might take pleasure from cycling up a mountain on our biking trip through the Scottish Hebrides while I wished I had never been born, yet both of us might feel doing so was worth it in the end. The experience might qualify as self-cultivating for me to the extent that I feel I have grown in endurance perhaps, or have become more open to engaging in similar adventures in the future. For my friend, although she developed these qualities and dispositions already some time ago, the experience might still have been further self-cultivating in other ways (or perhaps simply self-maintaining).

The above argument seems to be saying 'there is value in engaging in self-cultivating activities (some pleasant, some not so pleasant) as people who do so are eventually happier and in a better position to have positive effects on others, and as a result the rest of the world will be better off'. There is something compelling in this statement, but it does not yet get at the real point of how and why self-cultivation should be essential for professionals. The fact that I feel good and might have learned some important things after having cycled through Scotland for the summer (or improved my tennis serve, read a gratifying novel and taught myself how to grow strawberries, etc.) might make my life more enjoyable and me a less sour grape and more pleasant to be around; however, it is not immediately obvious why any of this should make me a better dean, teacher, nurse, engineer, city planner, doctor, accountant, social worker, dietician, journalist or lawyer. Is there not still something missing in the argument for there to be a persuasive case to be made for the significance of the practitioner's self-cultivation to professional practice?

Let us then briefly summarise the three points that have been made so far. First, a wide range of activities, many of which not necessarily involving academic learning in higher education, can be self-cultivating. Second, self-cultivation is not the same as self-maintenance, or self-refreshment, but involves self-development. Third, not all activities that give us pleasure will have self-cultivating consequences; and, not all self-cultivating activities are pleasurable. Indeed, it deserves special mentioning that many of the most significant experiences in life, and those that ultimately might make us a better person, typically are among the hardest to live through (for example, coping with a serious illness, suffering the loss of a person who assumed great importance in one's life, giving up on a project around which until now one has defined one's identity and self-worth, being thrown into poverty due to war, a natural disaster or economic crisis, reaching the limits of one's physical endurance, etc.). The point that hasn't been clarified in full is how the experiences that I perceive as self-cultivating should be of any relevance to my life as a professional (see the third of three reasons I offered earlier in support of the claim that self-cultivation of the practitioner was significant). It might be commented that the person cannot be separated from the professional role he or she assumes (I am still the same person regardless of whether I am in my role as educator, researcher, dean, wife, daughter, friend, tennis partner, cycling pal, etc.) and consequently what the person experiences in one domain of life has consequences for another. While this might make intuitive sense to us, there is value in taking a more careful look, first, at how or why experiences we perceive as self-cultivating in a domain unrelated to professional practice should influence our practice as professionals; second, at how professional practices themselves can be self-cultivating; and third, at why self-cultivation should enhance our capability of 'civic-mindedness'.

A helpful answer to the first and second question can be found in Alasdair MacIntyre's (2007) theory of practices, and especially the connection he draws between participation in different practices and personal life narrative.

Practices as sites of self-cultivation

MacIntyre argues that people are involved in a wide range of social practices and we develop as individuals through these practices. He understands practices as particular kinds of social activity because they have a history and are thus associated with certain traditions. Practices are not static. We become socialised into communities of practice with their norms and particular ways of doing things, but once that socialisation has been achieved we can develop the practice further. It is the tradition that offers guidance on what excellence means, in terms of the end product and how it is to be reached. Winning a game of chess by cheating, for example, does not meet the standards of excellence associated with the practice of chess. Getting good at a particular practice, be it chess, tennis, agriculture, architecture, nursing or social work to list just a few further examples, therefore, means to achieve the standards of excellence that are associated with the practice in question. Critical for the achievement of these standards of excellence are certain qualities or dispositions, or as MacIntyre puts it in good Aristotelian fashion, human powers of excellence, or *virtues*. He further argues that all social activities that fulfil his criteria of a practice necessarily rely on 'the virtues of justice, courage, and truthfulness' (MacIntyre, 2007, p. 191), but he does not consider this list of virtues to be exhaustive for each practice in question. What precisely he means by a practice he explains as follows:

> By a practice I . . . mean any coherent and complex form of socially estab-
> lished cooperative human activity through which goods internal to that form
> of activity are realised in the course of trying to achieve those standards of
> excellence which are appropriate to, and partially definitive of, that form
> of activity, with the result that human powers to achieve excellence, and
> human conceptions of the ends and goods involved, are systematically
> extended.
>
> (MacIntyre, 2007, p. 187)

We learn the meaning of the virtues (or the human powers to achieve excellence) through the different practices we engage in, but it is at the level of our individual life narrative that we integrate these virtues into something that guides us as persons. So while being courageous, truthful, or just takes on different concrete forms in different practices we participate in, we integrate our understanding and proper enactment of these virtues within our lives. For example, in a tennis tournament I might decide that it is the right (or just) decision to follow the rule 'if both serves go into the net the point is lost', while in my practice as teacher I consider it the right (or just) decision to deviate from the rule 'if the essay is not turned in by 4.00 pm on the Tuesday, 10 per cent will be deducted from the grade, and another 10 per cent each following day', as I know something about the circumstances of the particular student who was not able to submit by 4.00 pm that leads me to conclude that the general rule of employing some kind of penalty is not the right (or just) response in this case. In both circumstances I feel my actions were right (or just). This evolving understanding of what is right (or just) will guide me in other situations where the circumstances will again be similar or different to these situations. Virtue then develops through practices but they need to be integrated at the level of my individual life narrative. The third level (next to individual life narrative and practices) by which our moral understanding, and thus the development of virtue, is affected, according to MacIntyre, and which feeds down into how we interpret what is good at the level of our individual lives, is the history, culture and norms of the society we live in. This third level is similar to Taylor's (1991) notion of horizons of significance, which, as we saw earlier in this chapter, provide a standard for judging the validity or rightness of our actions and decisions.

So how is this helpful in answering the question of how self-cultivation is relevant for professionals? To the extent that the non-professional practices we are engaged in serve to develop certain virtues in us, we are justified in saying, first, that these practices are self-cultivating, and second, that they also may have a positive influence on us as professionals. This is so because what we learn in one practice feeds into what we learn in another. It is through our individual narrative of life that we integrate the virtues. We approach our practice as the person we are, while the practice also changes us. Thus some things important for professional practice we learn through the particular *professional* practice we have chosen as our career (e.g., nursing, social work, education, engineering, accounting, doctoring, city planning, etc.); other things that turn out to be important for the professional practice in question we learn from other self-cultivating activities unrelated to our profession.

What is essential about *self*-cultivation is captured in the prefix *self*. If we understand the self as a mosaic of many fragmented selves (and it can feel that way at times), we will be less inclined to appreciate that essential qualities or dispositions learned through involvement in one practice may feed into our engagement with another practice. Yet, if we understand the self as striving to make meaning of our life as a whole, we will be more inclined to accept that we are constantly aiming to integrate our experiences from different practices to achieve some sense of wholeness. Self-cultivation is about developing the whole person; about striving towards making meaning of life; about seeking authenticity. Activities that are self-cultivating have the potential to develop powers, or dispositions, qualities or strengths (or *virtues*), in us, that achieve this larger purpose. According to William Sullivan (1995), well-functioning practices allow professionals to 'find an important part of their identity and meaning in the work they undertake' (p. 195). MacIntyrean practices are particular kinds of social activities as they, by definition, have the potential to be self-cultivating.

This being said, I suggest that there are potentially self-cultivating activities that do not qualify as practices as MacIntyre defines them. Even engaging in a mundane task such as doing the dishes may develop my attitude toward detail, or if you will the virtue of accuracy, or attentiveness; or, of course, it may not develop anything really but makes me simply stare complacently out of the kitchen window humming my favourite songs until the bloody job is finished. Weight-lifting may exercise only my biceps (which then could hardly be considered *self*-cultivation), yet, it may exercise also my sense of endurance, my courage to challenge myself to higher levels, and so forth. Much more importantly, as indicated earlier, many experiences we have in life that involve significant learning, and thus self-cultivation, are not 'practices' in MacIntyre's sense at all (think of coping with a serious illness or accident, losing a significant person, working through a difficult situation exceeding one's hitherto anticipated limits cognitively, physically, or emotionally). The activities we might engage in that could have self-cultivating effects are unpredictable, and, as noted, they do not have to be practices of the kind MacIntyre has in mind. And yet, the *practices* (in MacIntyre's sense) in which we are engaged have a high potential of being self-cultivating, and feed into our larger narrative of life. Practices make us who we are. We thus can speak of the making of the professional through practices, including the particular *professional* practice we have chosen as our 'career'.

Our professional practice then can be a site of self-cultivation; yet, if it is *not* in some way self-cultivating, if it is *not* contributing to a sense we have of 'making something of ourselves' (Sullivan, 1995), then we need to critically assess this situation. One reason why a practice may not be experienced as self-cultivating could be that we chose the wrong profession, one too far removed from our own values and sense of self. Parker Palmer (1998) tells the moving story of Eric, a college teacher who for many years was unhappy in this profession. He did not see himself as fitting in and his values clashed with those of the high-status profession (and institution) he had entered into. He ended up not being good with students, always inclined to put them down by letting them know that they did not fit in either. College teaching, for him, had not been the right choice. Palmer (1998) writes:

> The self is not infinitely elastic – it has potentials and it has limits. If the work we do lacks integrity for us, then we, the work, and the people we do it with will suffer. . . . Eric's self was diminished by his encounter with academia, and choosing a different vocation might have been his only way to recover integrity lost.
>
> (p. 16)

Importantly, then, what is self-cultivating, or life giving, for one person may lack integrity for another; and while professions to a certain degree make us who we are, we also need to acknowledge that two people practising the same profession may not experience the same sense of self-cultivation or fulfilment through their professional practice. It is critical, though, for professionals to find some personal meaning in their practice, as otherwise not only the professional but the entire community will suffer. Apart from internal reasons, I now want to argue, there are also external reasons that may prevent our professional practice from becoming sites of self-cultivation, as we shall see in the next section.

The practice corrupted by institutions

The idea of self-cultivation of the practitioner suggests that the self-actualisation, fulfilment or happiness of the professional should matter somehow; and yet, duty towards others, at times to the detriment of oneself, is how the purpose of professional life is typically portrayed. Surely, serving people in need and engaging in altruistic acts is 'good' and many of us take satisfaction from engaging in such good deeds. Putting things this way, serving others does not seem contrary to but rather supportive of self-cultivation. The moral philosopher Jean Hampton (2007) raised a number of insightful points about the relationship between self-cultivation and service that are relevant to this discussion. Emphasising that self-cultivation (i.e., personal flourishing, or the pursuit of one's personal desires) was critical to a life well lived, she further argued that self-cultivation is based on authentic desires. Personal desires that were not authentic, but nonetheless pursued by the individual, did not contribute to self-cultivation but rather self-negation. Note now that we might find it indeed self-cultivating to live a life of service, or altruism. Yet, altruistic acts are authentic only when doing the act is in harmony with our personally chosen and authentic desires. In an important section of her essay Hampton (2007) reasoned that

> Service to others is morally acceptable only when it arises from an authentically defined preference, interest or project undertaken by someone who pursues her legitimate needs as a human being and who accepts a Kantian conception of human value.
>
> (p. 62)

Hampton suggests that too often we fail to extend the Kantian conception of human value to ourselves. She further observed that 'Self-sacrifice cannot be commendable if it springs from self-abnegation' (p. 67). Aware that our mistakes can be found more often in the other direction (namely our selfishness), she conceded:

> I do not want to deny that many of us who are privileged err in the other direction, and serve ourselves too much and others too little. The art of living well is to know how to balance competing moral obligations – some of which are to yourself.
>
> (p. 71)

Of particular importance to our discussion of the professional's self-cultivation are her reflections on the meaning of self-authorship or self-cultivation:

> Self-authorship involves more than autonomous choice: it involves a decision to develop traits, interests, and projects that not only are consistent with meeting your objective human needs but are also ones *you* want, and not ones that others prefer you want (and perhaps try to persuade you to want).
>
> (p. 60, emphasis in original)

The key issue here is that of adaptive preferences in contrast to authentic preferences. Reasoning from a Marxist perspective, Nussbaum (2011) speaks of adaptive preferences to point to desires (or preferences) people might have acquired given their limited options that are ultimately not in support of their real interests. The notion of adaptive preferences is relevant here in that as professionals we might accept, perhaps a little too often and rather uncritically, that putting the needs of others above our own, not the least the needs of the organisation we work for, should be the overriding motivation for us. This expectation that what we ought to do is serve unconditionally is informed by the notion of 'moral professionalism', discussed at the beginning of this chapter when it was contrasted with the richer notion of professional ethics.

Stephen Brookfield (2005), leaning on Italian socialist Antonio Gramsci's notion of hegemony, speaks of hegemonic assumptions as being those that we accept and fully buy into, since the contexts in which we work reinforce these assumptions on a daily basis. We then lose awareness of how acting according to these assumptions is wearing us down. We essentially give ourselves up without noticing it, still holding the assumptions that cause us personal harm in high regard (see Chapter 2).

Catherine Casey's (1995) incisive case study of work patterns in a large organisation showed how the changing conditions of contemporary work affect how people behave at the workplace, and the strategies they develop (consciously and unconsciously) to cope with new policies, procedures and expectations. Casey speaks of employees who take on an identity, or coping strategies, as 'colluded selves' (next to co-workers who become 'defensive selves' and 'capitulated selves'). The transformation into colluded selves is especially worrying as these are employees who fully buy into the organisation's objectives. They are dependent, compliant, easily managed and open to manipulation. They are seen by the organisation as the ideal employees. 'Colluded selves', using Brookfield's language, voluntarily participate in their own oppression.

Hampton (2007) reveals those communities as selfish that expect others to take on a life of service that is of instrumental value to them but detrimental to those carrying out the service. Specifically, she observes: 'Many of our commendations of what look to be altruistic behaviour may be more self-serving than we realise' (p. 67). A sense of duty, she further argues, is very different from a sense of wishing to help others in response to a sense of connection we feel to these others on the basis of our common humanity (a point we will revisit momentarily).

It is vital then to distinguish authentic from inauthentic desires and appreciate that self-cultivation is rooted in authentic desires. Sullivan (1995) argues that 'the achievements of all committed professionals remain precarious in the absence of strong institutions committed to the same end, institutions whose working secures the integrity of individual dedication' (p. 16). While practices have the potential to be self-cultivating, institutions have the potential to either support or obstruct this process. 'An adequate conception of professional ethics', Sullivan furthermore remarks, 'must therefore move from the question of individual meaning and vocation through consideration of social and institutional contexts within which these arise and develop' (p. 206). Institutional contexts, therefore, should be examined more closely for their potentially corrupting force. I'm going to suggest that when the practice is supported by strong institutions, it is less likely that inauthentic desires are being promoted (MacIntyre, 2007).

Institutions, according to MacIntyre, sustain practices; yet they 'are character-istically and necessarily concerned with . . . external goods' (MacIntyre, 2007, p. 194). External goods are competitive by nature and include things such as wealth, prestige and status. In Chapters 1 and 2 we have seen how professions can become too far oriented towards these external goods to the detriment of the internal goods of the practice. Internal goods are distinguished from external goods by being inherent to the practice and achievable only through the practice in question. To illustrate this point, the good internal to the practice of teaching has been conceptualised as 'some responsibility for the development of students as whole persons' (Noddings, 2003, p. 249), and the good internal to the practice of nursing has been defined as 'the satisfaction of helping others' (Sellman, 2000, p. 28).

Professional practices have a tradition. Things are done a certain way. Participating in a practice involves both accepting and creatively continuing (and building on) this tradition. As previously intimated, MacIntyre does not think that the standards set by tradition should be followed without critical awareness or 'blindly'. Traditions, he argues, 'offer an authorized starting point from which the task of critical interpretation and successive interrogations begins' (MacIntyre, cited in Serrano del Pozo & Kreber, 2014, electronic source). Dall'Alba, although basing her work on Heidegger rather than MacIntyre, also usefully comments:

> While social structures and traditions of practice frame what we do and how we see ourselves as professionals, they also provide openings for a range of ways of being professionals in our contemporary world. As we engage with these structures and practice traditions in the present, we carry forward the past in anticipating possible ways of being.
>
> (Dall'Alba, 2009, p. 32)

The point is that traditions are important for practice but do not altogether determine practice. A tradition is what allows us to proceed in reason. However, a problem might arise under two conditions. First, to the extent that the practice does not question its own tradition, a practice may become dogmatic and constraining (Nussbaum, 2012). Nussbaum is critical of any interpretation of tradition as an authority we accept unquestionably only because it provides some guidance or existing order. Second, and this is my point here, to the extent that institutions lose their function as bearers of traditions, practices may become corrupted preventing both the practitioners' self-cultivation as well as the well-being of clients and larger society. Practitioners and organisations (which qualify as institutions) then may become principally oriented towards external goods; or, as we have seen in the discussion of 'adaptive preferences', practitioners may commit fully to the organisation's goals, irrespective of how these might deviate from the traditional standards of excellence. They then might develop inauthentic desires (Hampton, 2007) which ultimately will lead not to self-cultivation but self-negation.

So far in this discussion a case has been made in support of the claim that the practitioner's self-cultivation is important. I showed that involvement in a wide range of social activities, including professional practices, can have self-cultivating consequences. I further demonstrated how self-cultivation can benefit the practice in question and, by extension, individual clients and larger society. Finally I argued that practices can become corrupted, thereby pre-empting self-cultivation. The point I have not dealt with explicitly, although pointers were given in reference to Taylor as well as the early functionalist theories of the professions, is how self-cultivation is linked to civic-mindedness. This last point I shall now turn to in the final part of this chapter.

Self-cultivation: the internal dimension of civic professionalism

Why should self-cultivation make us more civic-minded? I already argued that involvement in certain activities, especially professional practices, can significantly contribute to self-cultivation in the sense that there is an opportunity, through engagement in such practices, to develop certain virtues. I now want to suggest that civic-mindedness, in the previous chapter theorised as an overarching professional capability, can also be considered a virtue, and that this virtue can be cultivated through participation in professional practices that are free of corruption. The virtue of civic-mindedness is vital not only for professional practice but also for citizenship more generally. Recognising our social interrelatedness and enacting a sense of social responsibility is important for both the realm of professional work but also our lives as citizens in our local and global communities.

Hampton (2007) pointed out that altruistic acts, or we might say acts we carry out based on the virtue (and capability) of civic-mindedness, are morally acceptable only in so far as they do justice to the person performing the act. Thus altruistic acts are authentic, and as such self-cultivating, to the extent that we feel unified with those whom we hope to benefit through these acts. What the benefactors 'regard as good for themselves is what will be good for those with whom they are unified' (Hampton, 2007, p. 64). It is here where we see a direct link between self-cultivation and civic-mindedness. Following Taylor (1991), Sullivan (1995) argues that the search for meaning and integrity of professional identity takes place in a community, thereby bringing us in dialogue with others who are part of our social world. 'Because the self is so thoroughly social', Sullivan writes, 'the important questions of life, including our most intimate issues of identity, are questions of how best to respond to the larger ongoing conversations which make up our social world' (Sullivan, 1995, p. 205). In this section Sullivan again emphasises that self-cultivation (or the search for identity) occurs in dialogue with others, that is in a community. Self-cultivation demands recognition of our social relatedness and common humanity. Reconsider Terry Eagleton's argument outlined in Chapter 1. For Eagleton (2007), the fulfilment, or, we might say, self-cultivation, of each person is the foundation for the flourishing of the other.

For ultimately, there can be no well-being unless we look out for one another. The other needs to be recognised as 'what brings me into being', Eagleton writes (p. 97).

I suggest that developing civic-mindedness is an aspect of self-cultivation and this is supported through the professional practice in which we are involved. While civic-mindedness constitutes the external side of civic professionalism, self-cultivation constitutes its internal side. Both sides are important.

Final comments

This rather long chapter argued that there are many activities or experiences that can be self-cultivating, but MacIntyrean practices, especially professional practices, carry an exceptionally high potential for self-cultivation, due to their inherent standards of excellence, internal goods and the virtues needed to attain these. Professional practices, according to the traditional social trustee model (Durkheim, 1957; Parsons, 1954; Sugrue & Solbrekke, 2011; Tawney, 1920), are meant to support the well-being of society. The well-functioning professional practice, therefore, is one underpinned by the capability (and as I also argued, the virtue) of civic-mindedness. However, professional practices can become corrupted by the institutions that are supposed to sustain them. This corruption can lead to external goods such as wealth, prestige or status being emphasised at the expense of the internal goods. I finally argued that civic-mindedness and self-cultivation are related. Self-cultivation occurs in dialogue with others, or in community, thus implying civic-mindedness (e.g., Eagleton, 2007; MacIntyre, 2007; Sullivan, 1995; Taylor, 1989, 1991) and acting in civic-minded ways can be self-cultivating (Hampton, 2007). Yet, altruistic acts, when performed out of an unhealthy sense of duty or civic-mindedness rooted in hegemonic assumptions, may be self-negating, and thus inauthentic, rather than self-cultivating. Such self-negating effects were associated with harmful institutional contexts that encourage adaptive rather than authentic preferences (Hampton, 2007; Nussbaum, 2011).

How has the argument of this book unfolded so far? Following the first two chapters which outlined the broader contemporary context of professional practice, Chapter 3 explored what might be essential aspects of 'graduateness'. These were defined as openness to experience, moral commitment and responsible community engagement. Chapter 4 demonstrated that these three dimensions of 'graduateness', together, provide a sound theoretical foundation for the concept of 'civic-mindedness', which then was identified as the overarching *professional capability* (see Walker & McLean, 2013) imperative for the practice of civic professionalism (e.g., Boyte & Fretz, 2012; Sullivan, 1995). This present chapter developed a case for the importance of the practitioner's self-cultivation or personal flourishing (Higgins, 2011). It discussed factors that might promote self-cultivation and those that may obstruct it, and showed how self-cultivation is linked to the overarching capability and *virtue* of civic-mindedness. I further argued that while civic-mindedness constitutes the external side of civic professionalism (e.g., Boyte & Fretz, 2012; Sullivan, 1995), self-cultivation constitutes the internal side, and that both are important.

The present chapter focused on the service side of civic professionalism. However, in Chapter 8 we will move away from an exclusive concern with providing services for others, and explore the potential of a more politically motivated sense of professionals' civic engagement. Before we can get there, though, it is necessary to consider different types of knowledge and different types of emotions relevant to professional practice. The next chapter distinguishes between professional knowledge that is instrumental, communicative and emancipatory in nature, while the one following takes a closer look at the role of emotions.

Chapter 6

Valuing different types of professional knowledge

Introduction

Some readers will have chosen to turn to this present chapter because they inferred from the title that it might be the most pertinent; and it may be the only one they manage to look at. If this applies to you, you are wondering 'Will reading this be worth my time? Will it be useful?' Educating for 'civic-mindedness' is laudable, you may be thinking, but unless it can be shown that this is achievable whilst teaching students all else they need to know in order to function well in the particular profession, it is just a nice idea with little relevance to teachers on professional programmes.

Making a discussion of professional knowledge worthwhile to people from across a wide range of professions has its challenges. Not only is a single author unlikely to be a specialist in the various domains of expertise different professions have carved out for themselves, but the challenge to be perceived as contributing something useful might be even greater if the author is an educationalist. I base this claim on the observation that when discussing educational issues, here professional learning in higher education contexts, educationalists naturally draw on the scholarship relevant to their subject area. However, the scholarship relevant to education is often as alien to engineers, accountants, lawyers, social workers, nurses, and others, as the scholarship of any of their respective fields is to the educationalist. While initiatives linked to 'the scholarship of teaching and learning' (e.g., Hutchings, Huber & Ciccone, 2011; Kreber, 2001, 2013a) have met with some success in bringing people from a wide range of disciplines together to talk intelligently about higher education pedagogy, it needs acknowledging that there is a learning process involved in conversing meaningfully across disciplines, including the field of education. Note as well that education itself is a multi-disciplinary field of study, involving the traditional disciplines of philosophy, sociology, psychology, history and more recently also linguistics, computer science and instructional technology, finance, management and others. Given this diversity, it is not surprising to find that even educationalists tend to have trouble talking to one another across specialisations (what do the theories of Albert Bandura, Michel Foucault, Aristotle and Marc Prensky have in common?).

I conjecture that one reason why books and conferences on education, especially those characterised by a more sociological and philosophical orientation, are at times considered irrelevant, perhaps even patronising, by colleagues from other disciplines (especially those with a strong scientific orientation), is that the language, concepts and methods distinctive to the field (or particular sub-field) of education are unfamiliar. Well-intentioned efforts to translate this academic discourse into everyday language with the purpose of enhancing understanding do not always succeed, however. What occasionally happens then is that very important matters of concern to education, such as those associated with improving our social relations, our communication with and understanding of others, and our caring for the social and natural environment, are perceived as 'unscholarly' endeavours and thus trivial. This is so because matters such as these are unsuited for 'scientific inquiry'. Indeed, the more scientific educational scholarship appears to be, that is, the more it is based on empirical evidence, understood as research findings obtained by following standardised procedures to establish the effectiveness of a particular method ('if you do X then Y will happen'), the greater the likelihood for it to be taken seriously and earn the respect of colleagues in other parts of the academy. At first sight this seems only fair; after all, we do need to know which approaches are most effective. Yet, in education (including professional education) we are not just concerned with establishing effectiveness but also with the desirability of actions and their consequences (Carr, 2000; Biesta, 2007). The purpose of this present chapter is to show the difference in the nature of professional knowledge aimed at each of these goals, effectiveness and desirability, and to explore how this knowledge is acquired.

To provide some context to this chapter's concern with different types of professional knowledge relevant to civic professionalism, I shall briefly summarise what has been argued so far. A case has been made in previous chapters for the importance of students developing the overarching *professional capability* (and also *virtue*) of civic-mindedness (e.g., McMillan, 2015; Bringle & Steinberg, 2010), as this was shown to be an essential attribute underpinning 'civic professionalism' (e.g., Boyte & Fretz, 2012; Sullivan, 1995). A *civic-minded graduate* is defined by Bringle and Steinberg (2010) as 'a person who has completed a course of study (e.g., bachelor's degree), and has the capacity and desire to work with others to achieve the common good' (p. 429), and I developed the concept further, especially in Chapters 3 and 4.

Specifically, I suggested that civic-mindedness is grounded in an authentic professional identity, characterised by openness to experience (associated with the existential dimension of authenticity), moral commitments (associated with the critical dimension of authenticity) and responsible social engagement (associated with the communitarian dimension of authenticity). I added that civic-mindedness could be nurtured through curricula and pedagogies that have the potential to be transformative; transformative of students, learning communities and larger society. In the previous chapter I argued that civic-mindedness constituted the external side of 'civic professionalism', oriented outwardly towards giving and being responsive to others (or, alternatively, towards commitment and duty). I then made a case that a professional life that was exclusively oriented outwardly, or towards service, could be potentially damaging to the individual practitioner as well as our larger communities. As professionals we cannot be only giving and responsive but also need to consider our own desires and aspirations. As such it is critical that we engage in activities that are self-cultivating.

Among a wide range of activities that could have self-cultivating forces are those that fulfil MacIntyre's (2007) criteria of a practice. Professional practices (Serrano del Pozo & Kreber, 2014) especially carry a particularly high potential for self-cultivation given their inherent standards of excellence, internal goods and importantly the virtues required to attain these. Assuming supportive institutional contexts, I suggested that professional practices could themselves become sites of self-cultivation. Arguing from the perspective of philosophers who stress our common humanity and social interrelatedness, pointing out that our personal flourishing presupposes the flourishing of others (e.g., Eagleton, 2007; Nussbaum, 1998, 2004b), I then brought to the surface the vital linkages between self-cultivation and civic-mindedness. What distinguishes 'civic professionalism' from other interpretations and enactments of professional practice is that practitioners integrate their own personal goals and aspirations and those of their professional group with those of the larger community (Sullivan, 1995). It is in this way that the identity of the practitioner is bound up with what is considered good for the community. Civic-mindedness is sustained by the practitioner's self-cultivation. While civic-mindedness characterises the external side of 'civic professionalism', self-cultivation represents the internal side.

Types of professional knowledge

About twenty years ago, Michael Eraut (1994) described the knowledge needed for professional practice as an under-conceptualised field. He then introduced a knowledge map distinguishing between propositional knowledge, personal knowledge (including pre-propositional impressions or experiential knowledge), and finally process knowledge. The latter he subdivided into five categories: acquiring information, skilled behaviour, deliberative processes (planning and decision-making), giving information and several meta-processes for monitoring one's own behaviour (each of these individual aspects of process knowledge he further sub-categorised as well). Eraut (1994) gave each of these knowledge areas, together with their subsets, quite extensive treatment in his book. Once the domains most relevant to his analysis had been identified, he commented:

> Finally there are some areas of knowledge which are more than impressions yet different again from propositional or process knowledge. These include

moral principles and knowledge embedded in literature and the arts, *the particular characteristics of which I do not propose to address.*

(Eraut, 1994, p. 103, emphasis added)

Eraut's (1994) taxonomy is helpful not the least in that he encourages us to consider the question of professional knowledge more carefully. There is some, albeit limited, overlap between Eraut's model and the one I am going to employ. Not unexpectedly, we both recognise the importance of propositional knowledge, process knowledge and personal knowledge in professional practice. Apart from this similarity, I shall in this book be more concerned with the types of knowledge Eraut chose not to address. Moreover, in the model I shall introduce, the categories of personal and moral knowledge become blurred, which is a function of espousing a particular view of moral knowledge relevant to professional practice. Rather than asking '*what it is right to do*', I argued with Higgins (2011) and Taylor (1989) that a richer question to pose is '*what it is good to be*'. As noted earlier, the first question is distinctive of 'moral professionalism' based on principles and a duty to serve, while the second question embraces a view of professional ethics that considers not only the well-being of clients and/or larger society but also that of the individual practitioner. Process knowledge and propositional knowledge are also not treated separately in the classification I am following. In essence I shall propose in this chapter that there are three broad types of knowledge especially important for professional practice. Drawing on the work of German sociologist Jürgen Habermas (1971), I refer to them as (1) instrumental, (2) interpretive (or communicative) and (3) emancipatory knowledge (see also Cranton, 1998; Mezirow, 1991).

Civic-minded professional practice, I submit, relies on all three types of knowledge. To be sure, any professional practice requires knowledge of how to perform professional services effectively based on specialised scientific theories and technical and procedural know-how; yet, at least equally important for civic-minded practice is theoretical and personal knowledge of values, norms and culture that enables mutual understanding and interpretation of situations and events. Moreover, given that a civic-minded professional practice is oriented towards contributing to a fairer world, an essential type of knowledge for practitioners to develop is that which is liberating or emancipating of distorted assumptions and beliefs underpinning one's convictions. While domain-specific skills and scientific knowledge continue to be important for professionals, so is a general disposition to question and critically reflect on the ideals, norms and tradition informing practice, as well as one's own ethical conduct.

Before discussing the nature of the three types of knowledge essential for professional practice, it is helpful to consider a particular challenge confronted by higher education, one articulated especially thoughtfully by MacIntyre. I first introduce 'MacIntyre's challenge' and then respond to it on the basis of the three types of knowledge that are central to this chapter.

MacIntyre's challenge

In an article discussing explicitly the role of education in contemporary society, MacIntyre (1987) focused on the tension between preparing people to fit into predefined social roles and educating them to think independently. Rather than seeing this tension as one that could be resolved creatively, he argued that the two educational purposes are fundamentally incompatible in our age due to the decline of an educated public or common general culture. The observation that the existence of such a general culture can no longer be assumed in our contemporary world presents an irresolvable dilemma for MacIntyre. At the core of his argument is the consideration that since the eighteenth century, by which time society had become larger, more complex, and increasingly in need of different types of knowledge and skills to secure its economic advancement, the key discipline of moral philosophy, which up to that point provided a foundation from which to perform public debates, had become disjointed from its social functions, just as the new social and/or professional functions that the new social order required had become disjointed from philosophy. What is lacking in today's society, MacIntyre (1987) argues, is a common philosophical foundation: a set of presuppositions and standards of justification that could enable rational public debate. Knowledge has become fragmented, with each new body of knowledge having its own theoretical frameworks and standards, often incompatible, prohibiting any discipline to consider how it contributes to, or is relevant to, the work of another.

The most significant problem, according to MacIntyre, is 'the lack of resources possessed by our culture for securing rational agreement on what it would be relevant and important for members of a contemporary educational public to share in the way of belief, in the way of perspective, in the way of debate' (1987, p. 28). He observes, 'The link . . . between the particular responsibilities of particular social roles and the ability to appeal to principles about the general good and to participate in debate about these principles has been broken' (p. 24). Knowledge has become so fragmented that questions of utmost social concern such as those addressing 'good and the good . . . the relationship of justice to effectiveness or the place of aesthetic goods in human life, about the tragic, the comic and the farcical not only in literature, but also in politics and economics' (p. 25), are either posed only by specialists within their particular domain or are raised in forums that are not guided by any principles and standards, which then make a genuine debate impossible. As a result, thinking has become the task of the specialists who are in charge of certain social or professional roles.

Given that there is no general culture within which to justify or test one's claims, MacIntyre asserts, the possibility of learning to think for oneself has disappeared, leaving education to be concerned principally with the task of training people to fulfil specific social roles. MacIntyre concludes his essay by asking how a community that satisfied his conditions of an educated public could be reinstated through the educational system, yet claims that curriculum reform does not present a way out of the dilemma. Indeed, while he personally seems to see some potential solution in a revisiting of Greek philosophical and political texts, he is under no illusion that this proposal would be unrealistic. He states rather gloomily: 'The concept of an educated public has no way of taking on life in contemporary society. It is a ghost haunting our educational systems' (p. 34).

MacIntyre's essay is intriguing and thought-provoking on a number of levels and of particular interest in relation to this chapter's concern with professional knowledge. I agree with his view of the centrality of a vibrant public sphere where issues important to our communities can be openly debated; however, I find myself disagreeing with his general scepticism that the opportunity for debate has been lost for ever. Barnett (2004) too recognises that we live in the age of super-complexity, where many different interpretive frameworks compete for recognition, but emphasises the importance of preparing students for this complexity, a view I find myself more readily in agreement with (as discussed in Chapter 4). I also agree with MacIntyre that the two purposes of education, promoting independent thinking and preparing people to fulfil certain social roles, are in tension; however, I suggest that this tension can be lessened by infusing professional study with the critical spirit of the humanities (Nussbaum, 1998, 2011; Sullivan & Rosin, 2008). Indeed, one would hope that most academics charged with preparing students for work think about the relationships between university, work and wider society more broadly, and do not just aspire to fit people into predefined roles. The German professor of higher education Ulrich Teichler, for example, raises as one of the core questions to be confronted by universities:

> To what extent should higher education deliver the competences which seem to be *on demand* on the part of the employment system, or to what extent should higher education prepare students to *become active agents of innovation* and change in the world of work.
>
> (Teichler, 1999, p. 170, emphasis in original)

To become active agents of innovation and change, students must be provided with opportunities to think *for themselves*.

I furthermore agree with MacIntyre (1987) that 'one only can think for oneself if one does not think by oneself' (p. 24); yet, I disagree that we have lost the ability to think with others to arrive at decisions that are both informed and rationally justifiable within our community. I agree with MacIntyre (a point he articulated in *After virtue*) that the idea of a social practice offers both the backdrop and fertile ground for the development of a decisively practical rationality that is appropriately concerned not just with technical but moral questions (MacIntyre, 2007); yet, as already noted in previous chapters, I propose that professional communities themselves may be viewed as practices in the MacIntyrean sense (Serrano del Pozo & Kreber, 2014) with their standards of excellence informed by tradition, internal goods and virtues. According to this argument it is through participation in these practices that professionals acquire not only the cognitive and technical skills on which their profession relies but also the way in which decisions are made, and why, and importantly, come to appreciate the ideals informing the profession and consider how things could be done differently.

Below I propose the three types of knowledge – instrumental, communicative (or interpretive), and emancipatory – as a particularly useful framework for professional knowledge, and a helpful response to the core challenge MacIntyre outlined for us.

Instrumental knowledge

Instrumental knowledge allows us to control and predict our environment. It is the expertise, rooted in scientific knowledge that is made up of specialised knowledge and skills, needed to perform tasks associated with predetermined outcomes. Examples include how to design a bridge that lasts, land an airplane, carry out heart-surgery, provide therapy for a patient who has just undergone a hip replacement, help a former inmate reintegrate into society, counsel someone who is going through bereavement, test and treat people and animals for certain diseases, help recent immigrants become integrated in society and get their academic achievements accredited, re-structure a city's public transport or emergency services, give an injection, win a law case, invent a new computer software (or hardware), construct a proposal for the greening of a city, develop a sound business plan, inform the public about news that is relevant to them and thus enabling of democratic citizenship, plan the infrastructure for a new major airport, teach English as a second language, remove a tooth with as little pain as possible, and so much more. The need for instrumental knowledge seems endless and unquestionable. Such expertise includes both knowing how and knowing what (Ryle, 1949) but with a particular emphasis on technique informed by scientific knowledge. This knowledge is instrumental in nature as it is the instrument to achieve something else. It is productive and goal-oriented.

To be sure, as we shall see momentarily, technique, and the scientific knowledge that underpins it, is certainly not all that is required in any of the examples of professional activity featured above. Moreover, while with some (for example, heart-surgery or building a bridge), technique and scientific knowledge will be dominant, with others (for example helping a former inmate reintegrate into society or informing the public about news that is relevant to them and enables them to participate in democratic decision-making) it will play a far lesser role. Importantly, though, instrumental knowledge is the kind of knowledge that in most professional education programmes is considered core knowledge and fundamental to the curriculum. With the discourse of evidence-based practice becoming ever more dominant (the idea that what we do as practitioners should be based on research findings, ideally, based in controlled experiments), we see this type of knowledge being valued increasingly also in fields that hitherto were grounded in knowledge which, while specialised, abstract and associated with action (and inter-acting with others), is not necessarily 'instrumental' in the same way.

Instrumental knowledge derives from a technical human interest in control over one's environment and thus the prediction of events. Hannah Arendt (1958), we saw in Chapter 2, associated the human activity of *work* (which she distinguished from the activities of *labour* and importantly *action*) with instrumental knowledge. Instrumental knowledge is associated with the '*homo faber*' (that is, 'man the maker') who controls the environment with tools (Arendt, 1958). Instrumental knowledge is knowledge that allows us to do a good job, whereby 'good' is conceived of as the efficient production of the desired end. In the *Nicomachean ethics* Aristotle discussed this as the intellectual virtue of 'techne', which guides productive activity (or 'poiesis') (Thomson, 1976). Brint's (1994) and Wilson et al.'s (2013) observation that professionals tend to conceive of good work increasingly as the efficient provision of professional services, suggests that the instrumental aspects of their professional knowledge have become the dominant knowledge domain for them.

Instrumental knowledge has led to enormous achievements throughout history (think of the breath-taking architectural achievements of ancient times for example) but especially to new inventions since the industrial age. Advancements and innovations in science and technology have saved many lives and made our lives more comfortable. Simple pleasures such as being able to read in bed after sunset or wake up to the smell of hot coffee induced by the turn of a switch, or being granted prolonged life as a result of a pacemaker, new kidney, or drug that ensures a certain quality of life, are privileges we can enjoy in developed countries that have been made possible through the progression of instrumental knowledge. Instrumental knowledge, however, also has its downside. The exclusive emphasis on technological and scientific innovation has raised ethical concerns, with the atrocities carried out following the invention of weapons of mass destruction and developments in genetic engineering being prime examples (Habermas, 1984). We do not even have to go this far though to recognise that patient care, teaching, nursing or social work are not merely a matter of following protocol, or accurate procedure, but require of us to be able to connect and communicate with each other as people. And while it might be interjected that what I am saying here may be important for the so-called people (or caring) professions (Bondi et al., 2011), but is irrelevant to professions such as emergency management, engineering, accounting or health inspection, I would like to challenge this claim. All pro-fessions, we have seen throughout this book, carry social responsibility which extends to their individual clients as well as larger society. This responsibility cannot be fulfilled through exclusive reliance on instrumental knowledge.

I was writing the first draft of this chapter one week after we read in the news that a German co-pilot of a passenger plane which was on its return flight from Barcelona to Düsseldorf allegedly denied the pilot, who had briefly stepped out, access to the cockpit, then put the plane into a descent only to intentionally crash it into a mountain in the French Alps, killing himself together with all other 150 people on board. If this official account of events is true, the plane did exactly what the co-pilot instructed it to do. This example is so horrible that I almost didn't include it. And yet, I came to the conclusion that what this tragedy shows is that there are important forms of professional knowing that are based on something other than technical rationality. Even if the co-pilot suffered from a serious mental illness such as depression, which for many would call the notion of 'acting rationally' into question, my point is that as horrible as the action itself was, the knowledge of how to order the plane into descent leading to its ultimate demise is instrumental knowledge. But suppose now the conspiracy theories were true, and the co-pilot was framed for suicide and mass murder to cover up a major technical dysfunction of the Lufthansa/Germanwings Airbus 320 that led it to plummet to the ground. What would that tell us about professional knowledge? Would fabricating 'evidence' (or hiding evidence) and thereby intentionally misleading the public with the intent to control and predict the public's future behaviour, not also be utterly unethical, and indeed despicable? While most of us have a stronger reaction to mass murder than to mass deceit, surely, mass deceit, or any betrayal, is not behaviour we would wish to tolerate in professional practice.

My purpose in discussing this is not to suggest that instrumental knowledge (based on means-ends reasoning) is evil; rather my point is that instrumental knowledge does not protect us from ethical misconduct. The problem with instrumental knowledge is that it does not ask, and therefore does not respond to, questions of ideals, values or ethics. It is not interested in whether something is desirable, or ethical; it only asks '*Does it work?*' Instrumental knowledge in isolation, and in the absence of other personal qualities, dispositions and types of knowing, then is insufficient for professional practice. In the above example, the co-pilot (if he intentionally caused the plane's destruction) or the airline officials (if they intentionally misled the public into believing in the safety of the plane in order to control the public's future participation in air traffic) would lack certain dispositions, and hence types of knowledge intimately bound up with character, that are imperative for professional practice, as they exclusively employ instrumental knowledge.

Professional knowledge then cannot be exclusively of an instrumental nature. Some of the most difficult problems professionals have to confront, namely how to communicate with others to make their ideas understood and understand others, how to persuade, or be persuaded, that one course of action is better than another, how to engage in meaningful debate across different perspectives, and so forth, cannot be successfully approached from the perspective of instrumental knowledge. Think of the interactions between a doctor and patients, a teacher and students, a social worker and clients, two external affairs ministers from different countries and cultures, an engineer responsible for a contentious project (for example the building of a new airport close to a prime recreational area or biosphere reserve) and members of the community affected by the project with their values and priorities. In order to come to an understanding, the two parties need to agree on some fundamental norms or values that would guide their interactions and reasoning. The knowledge they need is interpretive or communicative in nature.

Communicative knowledge

Interpretive or communicative knowledge arises from a deep practical interest in reaching an understanding with others, and hence working with and living peacefully with one another. While the empirical-analytic sciences are the tool for instrumental knowledge, interpretive (and hence also communicative) knowledge relies on agreed upon norms and values within a community from within which an understanding can be reached. For Taylor (1991) these norms and values constitute the 'horizons of significance' discussed earlier, and for MacIntyre (2007) they are located not only at the level of society or (larger) culture but also at the level of different social 'practices', which for him include for instance games, productive practices (e.g., fishing or agriculture), established intellectual and artistic pursuits, or social projects (e.g., family, community projects, etc.) (Miller, 1994).

These shared values and norms on whose basis decisions are reached offer insight into the 'practical rationality' (MacIntyre, 2009) underlying communicative knowledge, compared to the technical rationality underlying instrumental knowledge. According to MacIntyre (2007), practices, and we can reasonably conceive of professional practices as a form of MacIntyrean practices (Serrano del Pozo & Kreber, 2014), have their own rationality as they are based on knowing what applies 'characteristically and for the most part' (p. 104), or as Dunne (2005) put it, 'about what would count as satisfactory or at least not entirely unacceptable' (cited in Serrano del Pozo & Kreber, 2014, p. 104). Importantly, according to MacIntyre, the practical rationality underlying practices is grounded in certain virtues that allow access to the internal goods of the practice and attainment of standards of excellence. The cardinal virtue, that enables the proper ordering and application of all the other moral virtues that sustain particular practices, such as truthfulness, justice and courage (but perhaps also resilience, preparedness, patience, pride, solicitude, attentiveness . . . and we might add civic-mindedness as a virtue), is *phronesis* or practical wisdom, a virtue closely tied to character which describes the 'capacity to judge and to do the right thing in the right place at the right time in the right way' (MacIntyre, 2007, p. 150). Practical knowledge therefore arises through practice, or experience, and reflection on that experience. It involves, as Dunne and Pendlebury (2003) argue, making a judgement appropriate for the situation, while abandoning the security offered by definite rules and regulations.

Although Aristotle discussed phronesis, or practical knowing, initially as an intellectual virtue, he actually conceives of it as both an intellectual and moral virtue that guides us in our development, ordering and enactment of the moral virtues. Practical knowing, or phronesis, is thus a particular form of professional knowledge tightly linked to character and critical for making 'good' professional decisions (see Bondi et al., 2011; Kinsella & Pitman, 2012; Robinson, 2005; Strain, 2005). Practical knowledge develops through engagement in practices and thus experience (Kemmis, 2012), and as MacIntyre (2009) further explains, 'Practical reasoning is by its nature, on the generally Aristotelian view that I have been taking, reasoning together with others, generally within some determinate set of social relationships' (p. 107). For him, these relationships exist in practices. Practical knowing develops through the norms and traditions that have developed within and now are guiding the practice, and is crucial for the further development of the practice. It should be clear as well that what MacIntyre calls practical reasoning, and what we here call communicative/ interpretive knowing, is also crucial for a society and/or professional group to draw upon in order to decide on its aspirations or ideals. When we ask questions such as 'what kind of society is a decent society', 'what are the characteristics of a decent or good profession', and 'what principles should it be based on', it is not instrumental knowledge but communicative knowledge that helps us answer these.

While a big part of communicative or interpretive knowledge is practical knowing as discussed above, it also includes theoretical knowledge that is non-scientific. For example, one of the teachers Colby et al. (2003) interviewed on their suggestions on how to develop in university students moral reasoning and civic engagement emphasised that it would be essential for students to learn about *political* theory and philosophy, and the assumptions different models make about community participation. Knowledge associated with political theory and philosophy is theoretical discipline-based knowledge although it is not scientific. Both instrumental and communicative knowledge, as I use these terms here, then include abstract knowing (or as Eraut would say propositional knowing) and process knowledge (instrumental versus practical reasoning), while communicative knowledge includes as we saw earlier, in addition, personal knowledge rooted in character.

For Habermas (1984) the norms and values guiding mutual understanding are inherent in the 'lifeworld', which he understands as the pre-reflective world we take for granted and which forms the background of our convictions. He writes:

> Subjects acting communicatively always come to an understanding in the horizon of a lifeworld . . . formed from more or less diffuse, always unproblematic, background convictions . . . [it] serves as a source of situation definitions that are presupposed by participants as unproblematic . . . The lifeworld also stores the interpretive work of preceding generations.
>
> (Habermas, 1984, p. 70)

In a frequently cited essay written in 1977 in which Habermas engages critically with the work of Hans-Georg Gadamer, he identifies what he perceives as the limitations of the purely interpretive sciences, commenting that, 'in grasping the genesis of the tradition from which it proceeds and on which it turns back, reflection shakes the dogmatism of life-practices' (Habermas, cited in Dunne, 1993, p. 183). Reflection that shakes the dogmatism of life-practices is known as *critique* or *critical* reflection, and the knowledge resulting from critical reflection on traditions or structures, and grasping how they have evolved and continue to influence, is emancipation or empowerment. This is the third knowledge domain that I suggest is imperative for professional practice, especially if the professional identities we hope students will be constructing are those that strive for authenticity (see also Chapter 1).

Emancipatory knowledge

Emancipatory professional knowledge is knowledge that challenges blind compliance with the status quo, the latter being determined either by tradition (see Nussbaum, 2012) or contemporary regulations and imperatives. Habermas argues that it is through a process of critique practised through critical discourse, assuming a set of ideal speech conditions, that ideology, and thus also structural violence, could be revealed. Structural violence, for Habermas, refers to the systematic distortion of communication whereby 'those involved form convictions subjectively free from constraint, convictions which are, however, illusionary' (Habermas, 1977, p. 2). However, the point is that the communicatively generated power may, as soon as it is institutionalised, become an oppressive force and be used against them. The notion of adaptive preferences discussed in the previous chapter is again of particular relevance here.

Emancipatory knowing, then, goes beyond communicative knowing as it reveals how one's own experience, that is one's assumptions, values and views of the world, has been shaped by the conditions or structures inherent in the contexts in which events were experienced. Emancipatory knowledge works on different levels. On the one hand, it may lead to recognition of one's own oppression (Freire, 1971) and adaptive preferences (Nussbaum, 2011), yet it may also lead to a changed understanding of the purposes and ideals of one's professional practice. The latter could come about as a result of asking substantial questions such as who is served by our present practice, as well as *'who gains—who loses, by which mechanisms of power'*, *'is this desirable'* and *'what can be done'* (see Flyvbjerg, 2001, p. 162, emphasis added). Questions such as these are essential for phronesis to not remain the prisoner of tradition. The virtue of phronesis or practical knowledge then itself becomes infused with a critical rationality (Flyvbjerg, 2001; Kemmis, 2012). 'Phronesis', or *'critically inspired* phronesis', plays a crucial role in professional practice. It is 'phronesis', formed in the course of our life-history and as a result of responding to the contingency and unpredictability of our environments by means of critical reflection, that can guide us in recognising the appropriate way of engaging the moral virtues in particular situations (e.g., what does acting in a just or fair way mean in this situation?). To be clear, though, 'phronesis' cannot provide us with a guarantee that we have indeed identified 'the best' course of action (it is precisely not 'techne'). 'Phronesis' is better understood as a disposition of discerning what the right option under the uncertain circumstances might be, and being ready, and mustering the courage, to then act on this understanding. This discernment of appropriate action (and choosing between at times conflicting possible actions) is the purview of 'phronesis', and critically inspired phronesis.

Emancipatory knowing, and thus critically inspired phronesis, involves critical self-reflection on the underpinning sources of our values and opinions. Emancipatory knowing is the foundation for developing an authentic professional identity. An authentic professional identity is constructed around purposes of personal and public value, around common good and social justice, and involves being afforded the opportunity to enact this identity in practice. It thus also involves being able to cope with uncertainty, as well as 'unpredictability', 'challengeability' and 'contestability' (see Chapter 1).

Emancipatory knowledge in professional practice then prevents the practice from becoming too inward-looking and too reliant on tradition. In Chapter 4 we saw that professional practices are prone to be too inward-looking and principally concerned with their own internal development. Becoming more outward-looking and concerned with the public interest is a transformative process that relies on critical reflection and emancipatory knowledge. The related point I would like to emphasise at this stage pertains to the disciplinary knowledge base professions traditionally have considered to be the foundation of their practice. Given that the most pressing problems humanity and our planet face require inter-disciplinary rather than uni-disciplinary solutions, there is an urgent need for professions to critically reflect on the extent to which they need to broaden their knowledge base for it to become more relevant and suitable for addressing these concerns. This broadening, however, inevitably means to collaborate with other disciplines or professional groups, thereby making the boundaries between jurisdictions more permeable. Larson's (1977) analysis of the linkages between the professions' protected jurisdiction, social status and wealth, would suggest that professions, especially high-status professions, would be reluctant to share their knowledge and thus give up their specialisation. A truly civic-minded practice, however, might place greater value on the public good than the profession's loss of power.

A further question associated with emancipatory knowing relates to where important or legitimate knowledge is seen to reside. Is it found exclusively with the professional or professional group (and hence the academy that teaches and the professional organisation that accredits this knowledge), or also in members of the public who are affected by professional decisions (see also Taylor, 2014)? I shall revisit this point in Chapter 8 where we consider the possibilities of democratic professionalism. Emancipatory knowledge 'helps adults realize the ways dominant ideology limits and circumscribes what people feel is possible in life', writes Stephen Brookfield (2005). Looking ahead to Chapters 8 to 10 we might say that it is emancipatory knowledge that leads professionals to become aware of the disabling power they exert over citizens by making decisions *for* them, and it is emancipatory knowledge too that citizens develop as they themselves seize the opportunity to become civic agents.

MacIntyre (1987) argued that preparing people to fit into predefined social roles and educating them to think independently were incompatible goals. While this is probably the case, it is far from clear that professional education is (or should be) purely a matter of fitting people into predefined roles. In this chapter I proposed that it is important for professional education to not only be concerned with instrumental knowledge (that, by extension, would also lead to people fitting into predefined roles) but also to foster communicative and, importantly, emancipatory knowing. Not only should graduates develop the Socratic ability to reason about their beliefs (Nussbaum, 1998, 2006), they should also learn to reason critically about their own practice, with its internal goods, standards of excellence and tradition. Put differently, students need to learn to reason critically about the practice's purposes and ideals.

The key virtue to be developed is a critically inspired 'phronesis' or practical/ emancipatory knowing, that guides decision-making (and thus the exercise of other moral virtues) in practice. Civic-mindedness and self-cultivation both rely on the development of phronesis. The development of this capacity occurs in dialogue with others and across different points of view. It is important then as well that the 'practice' is guided not just by the goals and aspirations of the professional group but is defined in dialogue with other professional groups and importantly the larger community served by the practice (a point to be taken up in Chapter 8).

Final comments

This chapter considered three types of knowledge, instrumental, communicative and emancipatory, arguing that all three are important for civic-minded professional practice. While some of this knowledge can be acquired by 'being told', much of it is developed only through involvement in the practice itself. Domain-specific procedural skills as well as domain-specific abstract knowledge (scientific theories but also political, philosophical or social theories) continue to be important for professional practice; however, it was argued that a more interdisciplinary knowledge base, and hence stronger collaborations among professions (and disciplines), would more effectively address the challenges modern societies are confronted by. Importantly, it was observed that much of the knowledge needed for professional practice is not based on a technical rationality but on a practical and importantly critical rationality. Knowledge associated with practical and critical rationality is largely, albeit not exclusively, grounded in dispositions. These dispositions, or motivations, are necessary for achieving understanding, agreement with others and identifying distorted assumptions, both in relation to oneself and the ideals of the professional practice one is part of.

So far in the book is has been claimed that civic professionalism (an approach to professional practice whereby one's own goals and aspirations, and those of one's professional group, are integrated with those of one's broader community) is built upon the professional's self-cultivation and civic-mindedness. This chapter showed that civic professionalism is also informed by three types of knowledge. These in turn are important for attaining the core graduate attributes of openness to experience, moral commitment and social engagement, which enable civic-mindedness (see Chapters 3 and 4). The next chapter will build on this discussion and explore specifically the importance of emotions in professional knowing and the role of emotions in sustaining a professional practice that is civic-minded.

Chapter 7

Cultivating political emotions

Introduction

While instrumental knowledge remains an important element of the professional curriculum, the previous chapter demonstrated that meaningful engagement with professional practice is dependent also on the essential contributions of communicative and emancipatory knowledge. The present chapter now goes one step further arguing that knowledge (instrumental, communicative and emancipatory) alone is not a sufficient basis for good professional work but that certain emotions are involved.

Emotions are implicated in professional practice in a variety of ways. Much has been written about the complexity and uncertainty associated with many contemporary public sector work contexts that cause feelings of insecurity and anxiety, and the emotional resilience needed in practitioners to cope with the various forms of adversity they may encounter (see, for example, the comprehensive review of pertinent studies compiled by Jackson, Firtko & Edenborough, 2007). Emotions are also part of transformative or emancipatory learning, as when we come to terms with the often deeply troubling realisation that the values and assumptions that guided us up to this point no longer hold up to critical scrutiny (e.g., Brookfield, 1987; Felton, Gilchrist & Darby, 2006; Kreber, 2012). Transformative learning can be a traumatising experience owing to emotions such as fear, loss and grief (e.g., Scott, 1997). Similarly, Dirkx (2006) argued that the process of moving towards greater authenticity requires us to acknowledge, confront and work through our emotions. Emotions then clearly come into play in a range of ways in professional learning and practice.

Nonetheless, the consideration of emotions in the professional curriculum is still not the norm; and if communicative and emancipatory forms of knowledge were perceived by some readers as 'fluffy stuff' to be teaching in higher education, then the same readers will have a similar or even stronger reaction to suggestions that higher education should concern itself with the teaching of emotions. Langstraat and Bowdon (2011) observe in this context that the academy is characterised by

> a broad attitude of disdain or anxiety surrounding the conflation of education and emotion, an attitude partially rooted in a positivistic tradition that casts

emotion as immeasurable or so unwieldy that meaningful discussion of our affective lives is deemed off limits in the public space of the classroom.

(pp. 5–6)

The claim regarding immeasurability, however, has been challenged by recent research. Studies in neuroscience and evolutionary psychology, conducted with humans as well as nonhuman animals, combined with the development of new imaging technologies, have yielded persuasive evidence that emotions are directly linked to reactions in our brains (e.g., Nussbaum, 2013), findings which might render consideration of emotions in the curriculum a little more palatable to some people. Already in her earlier work Nussbaum (2004b) commented on the cognitive nature of emotions:

> If we think of emotions as essential elements of human intelligence, rather than just supports or props for intelligence, this gives us especially strong reasons to promote the conditions of emotional well-being in a political culture: for this view entails that without emotional development a part of our reasoning capacity as political creatures will be missing.

(p. 3)

However, this chapter is not about any type of emotions implicated in professional practice; it intentionally focuses on those that have been shown to be relevant to political engagement, or the enactment of civic-mindedness.

Treating knowledge and emotions separately, as in discussing them in two separate chapters, is somewhat artificial. We have already seen in the previous chapter that some forms of knowledge are rooted in personal dispositions and ways of making sense of situations that are intrinsically linked to a desire to act. The recognition of injustice, brought about through critically inspired phronesis (i.e., critical practical knowing or wisdom), would, presumably, cause the agent to act on this knowledge. Nonetheless, the question of whether knowing (for example, recognising a breach of justice) is indeed enough to prompt us into action is worth exploring more deeply. After all, we *know* we live in a world characterised by blatant injustices. We *know* that we enjoy privileges that are not accessible to the majority of people living on this planet. We hear and read about atrocities committed in the world daily, of people dying because they have no food or shelter. We see people less well off than us regularly also in our own localities. What does it take to make us act on what we *know* is unjust? Why does Angelina Jolie appearing on television demonstrating concern about social injustices, for instance by appealing to states to urgently act on the Syria and Mediterranean refugee crises, move us into action more so than pictures of unspeakable cruelty and poverty?

In discussing this issue I will draw strongly on the ideas of Martha Nussbaum who, in a coherent body of work publicised through several monographs written over the past thirty years (e.g., *The fragility of goodness* 1986, *Cultivating humanity* 1998, *Hiding from humanity* 2004a, *Upheavals of thought* 2004b, *Developing capabilities* 2010, *Not for profit* 2011, and most recently *Political emotions* 2013), has provided a full and sophisticated account of how and why emotions matter in promoting greater social justice in the world, and how we might foster them through education. Yet, I will also consider an alternative to Nussbaum's proposed 'pedagogy of compassion' by considering a perspective that argues that what keeps us trapped in our cocoon of privilege, and prevents us from acting towards greater social justice, is fear of engaging with our own emotions and suffering, and the suffering of others (Kahane, 2009).

This discussion of emotions in relation to professional practice goes beyond predominant approaches to teaching professional ethics which tend to be rooted *either* in an ethics of principles (deontological or utilitarian approaches) *or* an ethics of character (drawing on the Aristotelian virtue tradition). A theory of emotions based on cognitive appraisals we make draws on both traditions, realising the importance of emotions to sustain us in our rationally agreed upon values or principles.

In this chapter I suggest that higher, and specifically professional, education has a vital role to play in the cultivation of emotions in future civic-minded practitioners that sustain them in working towards greater social justice. In previous chapters civic-mindedness was described as a willingness to act in the interest of society rather than in pure self-interest or the interest of the professional group or organisation one is part of. However, I shall argue especially in Chapters 8 to 10 that civic-mindedness is not solely informed by a philosophy of altruism. While altruism, or a desire to serve individuals and the community, surely is important to professional practice, a more comprehensive (and more inclusive) conception of civic-mindedness incorporates in addition a desire to nourish the civic-mindedness, or civic or political engagement, of others. It is in this way that civic–minded professionals do not just help individuals and communities but also work against systemic issues of social justice. As Rosenberg (2000) argued, what should be avoided is acts of 'false generosity . . . acts of service that simply perpetuate the status quo and thus preserve the need for service' (p. 33). Professionals seeking to contribute to greater social justice, I shall suggest later, subscribe to the additional or larger purpose of working with others and empowering others. As Heidegger might have put it, these professionals do not simply 'leap in' for the other but 'leap ahead' of the other; they do not solve problems *for* others (though surely this is important in some cases) but work *with* others to help these others to solve problems themselves (see on this point also Dall'Alba, 2009, in the next chapter).

Yet, we might further reason, if citizens themselves assume a much stronger role in making decisions on issues affecting their lives and that of their communities, then it also follows that the emotions implicated in civic-mindedness are arguably important not only for professionals to acquire but for all members of society. Professionals might then also be conceived of as facilitators of public engagement and/or informal community education (a point to be revisited in

Chapters 8 and 9). As part of this facilitating role they could contribute to the cultivation of appropriate public emotions in society – appropriate emotions being those that serve to sustain us in enacting our ideals or principles that we arrived at through reason. Thus this chapter asks, what kinds of emotions are required in professional practice (and community engagement) to sustain us in seeking greater social justice?

The cognitive structure of emotions

For Nussbaum (2004a, 2013) emotions are not actually separate from knowing, but constitute an important part of how we know. Emotions are rational judgements we make. Thus construed, emotions can be developed through reflection – the point Nussbaum highlights. One particular emotion that is critical for a democracy aimed at creating greater social justice in the world is that of compassion, which often grows out of the closely related emotion of empathy. Empathy is defined by Nussbaum (2013) as 'the ability to imagine the situation of the other, taking the other's perspective' (p. 145). However, empathy alone is not enough to secure social justice as even a sadist could feel empathy and yet take pleasure from inflicting pain on others. Compassion goes beyond empathy and refers to 'a painful emotion directed at the suffering of another creature or creatures' (p. 142). It is compassion not just empathy that moves us into action.

Next to recognising the cognitive nature of compassion, Nussbaum (2004b, 2013) furthermore proposes that we can discern a particular structure to the cognitive appraisals that we make. The structure of the emotion of compassion is such that it is based on four 'judgements' or thoughts that we hold.

The first thought, or judgement we make, is that we consider the plight of others to be serious; i.e., we accept that something bad has happened to this person (or animal), that the situation the person (or animal) is in is one that is far from trivial and that we would not wish for ourselves. The second thought, or judgement, is that we do not hold the individual responsible for it, but realise that the situation he or she is in is not of his or her own doing, is not his or her fault, but the outgrowth of larger forces he or she is not in control of (for instance, we might blame a stealing person for parts of the situation, but ultimately not for what brought the situation about). The third thought we hold is that we recognise that the plight that has befallen others could, at least in principle, be a real possibility for ourselves. However, and this is key, Nussbaum is also aware, and many empirical studies she reviewed for the purposes of building her argument confirm this, that it is a natural reaction to feel compassion and concern towards those close to us, but not towards those distant from us. The idea of 'similar possibilities' registers for us much more easily if we recognise ourselves in the other, than if the other is perceived as very different from ourselves. How to bring people distant and very different from ourselves (in terms of lifestyles, values, language, cultures and traditions) into our 'circle of concern' is the fundamental challenge to be addressed if we are serious about wishing to bring about greater social justice. The point is that good principles or well-grounded aspirations do not necessarily move us into upholding them. Having good principles is important, but how to act according to them remains the challenge. The fourth and final point Nussbaum (2013) mentions is eudaimonistic thought, the idea that we appraise the world (or here the situation of other persons and animals) from our own standpoint, or our own evolving conception of the good life; put differently, we do so in relation to how the situation of others is related to our own flourishing and own important life projects.

Eudaimonistic thought, according to Nussbaum (2013), implies that this person, or these people, 'count for me: they are among my most important goals and projects' (p. 144). In our striving towards eudaimonia it is natural that we would fear anything that would threaten it. Yet, why should the suffering of another threaten my own eudaimonia? The argument by which this question can be answered is precisely the same as that we already encountered in Chapter 5 when we explored the relationship between self-cultivation (the pursuit of personal flourishing) and civic-mindedness (our responsiveness to others). It is a natural reaction to feel grief when we perceive the loss of a person whom we recognise as having played an important part in our life project (e.g., a mother, a person we are romantically involved with, our best friend, etc.), or when we see this person to be suffering. We neither want to lose this person, nor do we want to see this person in pain as we recognise him or her as essential to our own eudaimonia. In other words, this last thought or judgement that Nussbaum highlights as being imperative to the experience of compassion refers to us recognising our common humanity, mutual vulnerability and social interrelatedness. It is a movement in priority from 'my life' to 'our lives', from 'me' to 'us'. Remember the important distinction between eudaimonism and egoism already highlighted in Chapter 5. In eudaimonistic thought others do not just have instrumental value for us; they are not just means to our ends. Unlike egoism, eudaimonism does not deny the intrinsic worth of others. Yet, learning to appreciate the contribution a person very distant and different from me makes to my eudaimonia is the challenge that a good society (and we might extend this to say a decent profession), one serious about contributing to greater social justice in the world, needs to confront urgently. Nussbaum (2013) argues that poetry and public symbols are especially important for fostering such appraisals, and I shall return to this point a little later.

The central question Nussbaum (2013) is asking in her work is *how a good or decent society, one with good principles and aspirations, can become stable and live up to its well-grounded principles in the light of it being driven by greed, anxiety and self-interest. What makes us sacrifice self-interest?* Her answer is that good principles get enacted only if we care about them; thus we need the emotions to stabilise our principles. We need to learn to care about solidarity, diversity and social justice.

A society that is serious about social justice, Nussbaum (2013) is saying, has to be a compassionate society; it cannot be founded solely on good (well-grounded) principles and respect for others. Good principles and respect are important but what is also needed is a deep commitment or love for these ideals. Hence she writes, 'Love is what gives respect for humanity its life, making it more than a shell . . . it is needed in all imperfect societies that aspire to justice' (Nussbaum, 2013, p. 15). Emotions are public or political in the sense that they stabilise, sustain and support us in our shared ideals. They move us into doing what we know we ought to do. Nussbaum (2013) defines political love as intense attachment to things outside of the control of our will (see also Frankfurt, 2004). In other words, if justice or a decent life for all cannot be built on 'respect for humanity' alone, or cannot be guaranteed on the basis of our will (the rational side of human nature), then we need to nurture it through love.

In order to cultivate 'political love', based on empathy and compassion, we need, at the same time, to hold in check those opposite emotions that threaten our aspirations to be a decent and just society. These opposite emotions include fear, shame and disgust (Nussbaum, 2004a, 2013). These, Nussbaum argues, have their origins in the sense of shame, fear and disgust we feel about aspects of ourselves, our own vulnerability and fragility, leading us to want to denigrate others, which we do by projecting on to others all these negative emotions. And what better target is there for disgust, hate and fear than those individuals and groups in our society who are the most different from us and the most vulnerable (for example, the homeless, the long-term unemployed, people with disabilities, old people, people from other cultures and ethnic backgrounds with different customs and traditions, people of a different faith, women, gays, lesbians and transgender people, etc.). Nussbaum offers the following interpretation of how the projecting of shame and disgust works:

> Human beings are deeply troubled about being human – about being highly intelligent and resourceful, on the one hand, but weak and vulnerable, helpless against death, on the other. We are ashamed of this awkward condition and, in manifold ways, we try to hide from it. In the process we develop and teach both shame at human frailty and disgust at the signs of our animality and mortality . . .
>
> . . . both emotions (read shame and disgust) are associated with forms of social behaviour in which a dominant group subordinates and stigmatizes other groups. In the case of disgust, properties pertinent to the subject's own fear of animality and mortality are projected onto the less powerful group, and that group then become a vehicle for the dominant group's anxiety about itself. Because they and their bodies are found disgusting, members of the subordinated group typically experience various forms of discrimination.
>
> (Nussbaum, 2004a, p. 336)

The idea of cultivating emotions is not unproblematic and should not be embraced uncritically. History shows that emotions surely can be made to serve questionable if not atrocious ends (the situation in fascist Germany during the era of National Socialism comes to mind as one prime example). What we need then are *appropriate* emotions and critical engagement with these as well as the ideals they help to support. Critical engagement would include, first, recognition of plurality (the idea that we each may hold different conceptions of the meaning and purpose of the good life), and second, reflection on whether despite this plurality we can identify some key principles of good practice and the emotions needed to sustain them. Cultivating appropriate emotions therefore should not be read as forcing homogeneity thereby taking freedom away from people (a point Nussbaum, 2013, emphasises in her book as well).

Nussbaum's ideas regarding what constitutes a good or decent democratic society I want to suggest have profound implications for civic professionalism. Civic professionalism, at least in the way that I have operationalised this notion in this book in reference to Harry Boyte and others, has a strong social justice orientation and, as we shall see more strongly in the chapters that follow, is rooted in the democratic ideal of participatory decision-making. The question that concerns us then is very similar to the one that Nussbaum asked about the state or society. Slightly rephrasing her central question, we might ask '*How can a good or decent profession, one with good ideals and principles, as expressed in codes of practice and taught in ethics courses at university, become stable and live up to these principles, thereby contributing more strongly to social justice, in the light of the various forces that make this difficult including greed, anxiety and self-interest?*'

However, we might actually be able to do a little more than that. Rather than relying on existing codes of practice, it should be possible for us, notwithstanding our differences, as members of a professional community to come to an agreement, through deliberation, of what our profession, when practised at its best, should stand for. If professions associated with the distribution of important public goods (e.g., think of education, justice, health, access to information, security, food and shelter, the beauty and life-giving force of the ecological environment, etc.) do not recognise it as one of their fundamental purposes to ensure that these public goods are distributed fairly in society, then, surely, there is a problem in the professions. Yet, once we can agree, through deliberation, on what it is we wish to stand for, that is, on our ideals, the next stage would involve reflecting critically on what it would take to actually put our valued project into practice. And what it takes, I propose, again in taking inspiration from Nussbaum (2013), is cultivating *love for our principles and ideals, and empathy and compassion for others*. For students to develop the overarching professional capability of civic-mindedness, professional education ought to provide opportunities for future practitioners to experience (learn to feel) love for the ideals of their profession and empathy and compassion for those most in need. This involves cultivating 'the ability to see full and equal humanity in another person, perhaps one of humanity's most difficult and fragile achievements' (Nussbaum, 2013, p. 3).

Fostering love, compassion and obligation to others

Let's reconnect with the earlier question of why news broadcasts of Angelina Jolie making a case for greater social justice move us into action more so than the obviously desperate situation of the suffering people in Somalia or Syria? (I am being facetious here. I'm actually not suggesting that Angelina Jolie, in particular, moves everyone in this way, although I admit that I respect her commitment to social justice; some of us have this reaction way more so when we hear about Martha Nussbaum's work in India, David Beckham's support of UNICEF, or Bob Geldof's concerts for Amnesty International, to mention just a few of the numerous examples that could be featured.) My reason for focusing on celebrities is to highlight the importance of identification. We actually do not really know Jolie, Beckham or Geldof any better than we know the suffering people whose faces we see portrayed on the daily news who are fighting for their lives in overfilled boats next to the Greek or Italian coast. And yet, what we actually see is an anonymous mass, not individuals; and even if we are confronted with the picture of a crying child in Syria, we know little about this particular child. The point is that even if we don't actually make a habit out of reading the tabloids, we can hardly escape the latest news about Jolie, her children, her husband, her medical issues, her cinematic career, let alone what sunglasses she was sporting when leaving the airport. The 'good' some celebrities do in the world moves us because their popularity creates the illusion of us actually knowing them. We hear about their stories, we know (or rather *we think* we know) the particularities of their lives. They make us reflect on why we always think we are too busy to do something (if they can in the midst of their busy lives, shouldn't we be able to do so too?). The very fact that charities often try to associate themselves with a celebrity is based in this natural reaction people have towards those they 'know' and admire. We identify with those close to us (and these celebrities, in a somewhat distorted way perhaps, have become 'close' to us). Suffering people in other parts of the world move into our 'circle of concern' via the work of the celebrities whom we at some level, whether we acknowledge it or not, admire. My purpose here is to connect with one of Nussbaum's central arguments, namely, that to become more compassionate towards others, we need to nourish our narrative imagination, grounded in the particularity of the case (and our reactions to celebrities provide us with some first clues about the workings of narrative imagination).

'A pedagogy of compassion'

Narrative imagination, as Nussbaum consistently stated in a series of publications, refers to 'the ability to think what it might be like to be in the shoes of a person different from oneself, to be an intelligent reader of that person's story, and to understand the emotions and wishes and desires that someone so placed might have' (Nussbaum, 1998, pp. 10–11; 2006, pp. 390–391; 2010, p. 96). Narrative imagination then is important for being able to empathise with the plight of others and feel compassionate towards them. Nussbaum (2010) argues that narrative imagination can be promoted through 'pedagogies of compassion'. Through literature and film, and other forms of art, students would gain direct contact with the particularities of others' lives or circumstances. By cultivating this deeper understanding of what a situation feels like from the perspective of another person, we develop a stronger sense of closeness and hence concern for this person. Journalists exploited precisely this idea when they, at least momentarily, shocked the world into action by the horrible pictures of a young Syrian boy washed up on the shores of Turkey and the heart-breaking story of his distressed and broken surviving father. People around the world, regardless of culture, could identify with the pain associated with losing a child in such a tragic way, and it hit home the message of who the anonymous victims are in this senseless war: ordinary people, with hopes and love for their families; people like us.

Maxine Greene (1995), although writing from an Arendtian perspective which is, as we shall see in Chapter 9, a little (but not too) different, also emphasises that 'encounters with the arts have a unique power to release imagination' (p. 27), arguing that cultivating the imagination through education is especially important as 'imagination is what, above all, makes empathy possible' (p. 3). In a later section of her book she explains:

> It may well be the imaginative capacity that allows us also to experience empathy with different points of view, even with interests apparently at odds with ours. Imagination may be a new way of decentering ourselves, of breaking out of the confinements of privatism and self-regard into a space where we come face to face with others . . .
>
> (Greene, 1995, p. 31)

Hoggan and Cranton (2014) discuss how engagement with written narratives that depict the situation or plight of others may lead learners to experience changes in themselves, such as the development of a new perspective through critical reflection. Although writing with the purpose of demonstrating the value of arts-based pedagogy (especially reading fiction) in promoting transformative learning in university students more generally, Hoggan and Cranton's study shows the powerful effect narrative can have on fostering people's imagination and, by implication, empathy.

Nussbaum (2010, pp. 45–46) offers seven broad recommendations for a curriculum aimed at educating for democracy and global citizenship. These include developing (1) the capacity of students to understand the viewpoints of others, (2) an understanding of our innate vulnerability and thus mutual inter-dependence, (3) the capacity to experience concern for others including those who are the least like us and the most distant from us, (4) resistance to thinking of minorities as somehow 'lower' or less worthy than ourselves,

(5) actual knowledge about other groups to fight stereotypes, (6) accountability for one's opinions and actions, and (7) the ability to think critically.

In Nussbaum's larger body of work we find essentially two distinct proposals for how appropriate emotions might be cultivated. The first is the one we have been discussing so far, which relates to the formal curriculum (e.g., Nussbaum, 1998, 2010). The second relates to what one might call the informal curriculum, or an approach based on public art and 'symbols' (e.g., Nussbaum, 2004b, 2013). I shall turn to the second of these proposals now before offering an alternative (or expansion) to Nussbaum's approach to 'pedagogies of compassion' more generally.

A pedagogy of 'public emotions' (or 'the informal curriculum')

It is with regards to the informal curriculum that Nussbaum's latest book makes its distinct contribution. Appropriate political emotions, she argues, can and ought to be cultivated publicly, and among the examples she includes are books, films and life performances that expose us to tragedy and comedy (tragedy leading us to realise that bad things can happen to good people, thus making us aware of the fragility of goodness (see also Nussbaum, 1986), and comedy leading us to overcome shame at our vulnerability), public celebrations/festivals, memorials, and even the layout and opportunities offered by public parks for people from different walks of life to come together and interact with one another. Through engagement with the 'messages' received through engagement with these symbols or 'media', she argues, we are reminded of our ideals and learn to live together in a society of difference. Nussbaum's symbols (or as I put it 'media' – in a sense that they are the media through which we are reminded of our ideals) have their place also in university-based professional education (or simply higher education) and continuing professional education. We send, and receive, important messages through the symbols we employ on campus, including the festivals we hold, the anniversaries we choose to celebrate, the way we set up our campus to celebrate the diversity of students and staff who inhabit it (for instance, what faith or other 'identity-based' groups are recognised on campus or what type of food is served in food courts), the accessibility of our campus to the general public, the awards we publicise as our main achievements and so much more.

A particularly powerful symbol is that of the 'living campus' or 'living school' (e.g., O'Brien & Adam, in progress; O'Brien & Howard, in press). By turning the campus (or school) into a vast lab where sustainable practices can be experienced first-hand on a daily basis by students and staff (as well as the public), the 'living campus' reminds the community of its ideal of searching for sustainable solutions. The authors explain the idea of 'living campus' this way:

> Living Campus recognizes the college grounds, building envelope and infrastructure as a learning lab and develops integrated projects that provide

authentic learning opportunities for students. These projects can redefine existing academic and organizational boundaries, positioning Dawson [the campus they are talking about] as a relevant, engaged, innovative and responsible leader, not only within the educational systems, but society as a whole. Through Living Campus, first-hand experience in and with Nature is encouraged, as is the use of technology to build learning capacity. It represents an important counterpoint to the representation of Nature that is often portrayed in popular media . . .

(O'Brien & Adam, in progress)

Although the 'living campus' notion is strongly connected with environmental sustainability, one can easily see how the basic idea would extend to social sustainability. The linkages drawn by O'Brien and Adam between sustainable happiness, well-being for all and living campus are especially important. In their paper O'Brien and Adam argue that 'living campus' fosters hope among members of the community, forges relationships across diversity or status hierarchies, encourages collaboration, models and fosters systems thinking, supports sustainable, healthy living, brings life into education and learning, fosters nature-embeddedness and positive emotions, and develops the capacity to make choices.

Symbols, when employed responsibly, can thus play an important role in uniting people towards common ideals (such as the celebration of diversity, social justice and sustainability). At the same time, it would seem equally important that the professional associations and professional workplaces continue this important work by reminding each other of, and critically interrogating from time to time, the ideals they stand for. I suggested in Chapter 4 that since all public sector professions are associated with important public goods, they all also have a social justice remit. I therefore would argue that appropriate emotions need to be nurtured not only through formal education but also by the professions themselves. Just as political leaders might recognise their responsibility for cultivating appropriate emotions to sustain the ideals of a decent society, namely those associated with upholding or working towards social justice, and programme leaders at universities might recognise their responsibility to do this, so should leaders of professional associations and workplaces. Cultivating emotions should not happen as part of a 'hidden curriculum' through which students or practitioners simply get socialised into holding certain values. Cultivating emotions needs to be done responsibly through constant critical engagement with our ideals and the question of what constitute *appropriate* emotions needed to bring these to life.

'A pedagogy of contemplation'

Nussbaum's 'pedagogy of compassion', we have seen, is based on 'narrative imagination'. Through imagining the lives and plights of others with the help of stories portrayed in literature and other forms of art, students would cultivate the ability to experience empathy and compassion, which would move them into action. However, we may want to ask whether imagining the severe situation of others is really in and of itself enough to help us develop compassion, or whether our own already existing emotions are perhaps what is holding us back in our ability to act on the injustices we observe in the world. The idea that students first need to become aware of and then come to terms with their own emotions is discussed by University of Alberta professor of political science David Kahane (2009). Drawing on his personal experience of teaching a third year course on 'Obligation, Compassion and Social Justice', Kahane proposes an alternative to both *pedagogies of reason* (based on outlining the facts and then identifying arguments or principles based on reason as to why a certain action should be followed) and *pedagogies of sentiment* (based on engaging with particular cases to imagine more vividly what the situation of others is like – a version of this approach being advocated by Nussbaum). He argues persuasively that although getting a better sense of the actual living conditions, experiences and also perspectives of people in other parts of the world is certainly important, this knowledge is not sufficient to prompt us into action to seek greater social justice. Teaching for 'global citizenship', he contends, 'also requires that students be supported in contemplative practices of dissociation from their own and others' suffering' (Kahane, 2009, p. 49). The contemplative practices he proposes include meditation, free writing, as well as careful or 'sacred' reading (p. 56) and seeing (i.e., close engagement with photographs).

Kahane takes as his starting point the same problem that Nussbaum identified. He asks why it is that although we know about the suffering of others (and how little it would actually take for each of us to make a significant difference to this, for instance choosing to order regular coffee rather than lattes and donating the $2 saved each time to a good cause), we fail to act on this knowledge. He writes:

> (instead) I manage, like most privileged global citizens, to proceed relatively untroubled in a lifestyle that is unconscionable by my own standards. As decent people, we nonetheless find it hard to take strangers' welfare seriously in making choices, and indeed to hold an awareness of others' suffering and our capacity to ameliorate it.
>
> (Kahane, 2009, p. 50)

This leads him to ask what it is that is holding us back in drawing these others into our 'circle of concern'. Kahane (2009) offers a tripartite explanation. He argues that the reason we remain largely passive when confronted with the extreme suffering of others is rooted not in self-interest but, first, in inchoate fear ('if I let this suffering in . . . it will destroy me', p. 52), second, in a need to recoil from our own suffering (to distance ourselves from emotional intensity), and third, in us being able to soothe the pain associated with our own suffering and that of others through many habits of privilege, including those of consumption. The core to the problem is then revealed as an alienation from our own internal worlds. Kahane then suggests that engaging in contemplative activities such as free writing, meditation, music or poetry helps students connect with their own inner fears and motives. Letting these inner fears and motives be, letting them surface, he sees as an important prerequisite of students being able to let the situation of others get close to them. He comments that contemplative pedagogies 'can help students to understand the habits of thought, judgement, and reaction that keep them trapped in the cocoon of their own privilege' (Kahane, 2009, p. 59).

Although I discuss Nussbaum's 'pedagogy of compassion' and Kahane's 'pedagogy of contemplation' as being separate approaches, one can readily appreciate their complementarity. In considering both views, we might conclude that the development of authentic professional identities grounded in the overarching capability of civic-mindedness involves not only cultivating compassion for others but also mustering the courage to confront one's own fears. Nixon's (2007) interpretation of authenticity (discussed below) is helpful for making this point.

When we follow a desire to promote basic capabilities in others (e.g., helping others in being able to live a healthy and safe life; being able to stimulate the senses, imagination and thought through education, etc. – see Chapter 4), and thus seek justice for others by raising others' claims to recognition, Nixon (2007) argues, we act on the emotion or virtuous disposition of compassion. Compassion can be thought of as the outward-facing side of our authenticity. When we follow a desire to seek justice for ourselves, by raising our own claims to recognition, we act on the virtuous disposition of courage. Courage is the inward-facing side of our authenticity (Nixon, 2007). Courage, I argued in Chapter 3, is central to authenticity and is most strongly expressed in the graduate attribute of 'openness to experience' and uncertainty. In that chapter I also commented that '*To face the reality of "strangeness", we ourselves must muster the courage to question received wisdom and convention. This is both an emotional and an intellectual challenge. It is the challenge of authenticity.*' Kahane's (2009) observations would suggest that what we need to confront is not just received wisdom and convention but also our own fears associated with human suffering and vulnerability, and our tendency to soothe these fears through withdrawal and consumption. In order to promote social justice we must develop the courage to face our own fears (the inward-focusing dimension of authenticity) but also compassion towards others (the outward-facing dimension of authenticity).

Final comments

This chapter emphasised the positive emotions of love, empathy and compassion but said nothing about justified anger. Ruitenberg (2009) observes that 'Educating the political emotions requires the development of a sense of solidarity, and the ability to feel anger on behalf of injustices committed against those in less powerful social positions rather than on behalf of one's own pride' (p. 277).

Although it was not stated explicitly, civic-minded professionals who seek greater social justice in the world should be 'justifiably angry' at the injustices done to others. The ideas of justified anger and compassion are very close; we would not experience justified anger if we were not compassionate.

Civic-mindedness, which I conceptualised as an overarching professional capability, grows out of both the knowledge of what needs to be done (drawing on the instrumental, communicative and emancipatory knowledge domains) and the emotions of love for our ideals of a community-engaged professionalism aimed at greater social justice, and empathy and compassion for those in need (including justified anger) which prompt us into action.

The chapter discussed three different ways of cultivating 'political emotions'. We can either distinguish 'formal' from 'informal' approaches (i.e., Nussbaum One and Kahane as distinguished from Nussbaum Two), or 'pedagogies of compassion' from 'pedagogies of contemplation' (i.e., Nussbaum One *and* Two as distinguished from Kahane). Adopting the first way of categorisation, I should clarify that by 'formal approaches' I mean the different, yet complementary, suggestions made by Nussbaum and Kahane of how students, through the formal curriculum taught in universities, may be moved towards wanting to make a difference in the world. Narrative imagination and contemplative practices were discussed as means for cultivating a desire to act in just ways through the formal curriculum. 'Informal approaches' (or approaches external to the formal curriculum) refer to approaches that work through public symbols in our communities that serve to remind us of our ideals, and bring us together around these ideals while cultivating positive and appropriate emotions.

I would like to end this chapter by reiterating an earlier, albeit crucial point. I had argued with Nussbaum (2013) that appropriate emotions were needed for sustaining our ideal of social justice, with this ideal itself being grounded in good reason or principles. Yet, cultivating emotions should not be conflated with breeding homogeneity and blind acceptance of values. It is important for the community to develop a culture of deliberation and reflect critically on both its ideals and the emotions needed to stabilise these. Love, empathy and compassion are needed to stabilise our aspiration to be a decent profession. I now want to extend this argument and suggest that these emotions are important to develop not only for professionals but also other members of the community. This idea, although not further explored in the present chapter, is the logical consequence of a professional practice that is democratic in spirit. To the extent that decisions on important matters of public concern are made not just by professionals but also other members of the public, it seems vital that the public has had opportunities to not only decide on its ideals but also to cultivate the emotions necessary to support them in upholding these ideals. In the chapters that follow I shall further develop the idea of professionals being not just social trustees but enablers of democracy and facilitators of public decision-making.

Chapter 8

Enabling democracy

The role of those with specialised knowledge in modern democracy has been an unresolved issue since public intellectuals began to confront it in the Progressive Era . . . What is it to serve the public without an adequate understanding of the public?

(Dzur, 2008, pp. 4 and 274)

Introduction

The idea of civic professionalism connotes professionals' commitment to a broader public, engagement in civic life and fulfilment of important functions that benefit the larger community. So far in this book I have emphasised especially Sullivan's (1995) argument that for civic professionalism to work, professionals need to construct an identity around common purposes, thus integrating their personal goals, and those of their professional group, with the needs and aspirations of the broader community they are part of. The previous two chapters looked first into the types of knowledge and reasoning and then the emotions necessary to sustain civic-minded professional practice. Chapters 3 and 4 showed how civic professionalism is being underpinned by the three core graduate attributes of openness to experience, moral commitment and responsible community engagement, reflecting the existential, critical and communitarian perspectives on authenticity, respectively. These in turn support the advancement of particular professional capabilities in practitioners (e.g., resilience, public reasoning, emotional awareness, informed vision, confidence to act for change, etc.) that culminate in their overarching capability of civic-mindedness. Much has been said on the preceding pages as well about how civic professionalism relies on the interaction between self-cultivation of the practitioner (Chapter 5) and the practitioner's civic-mindedness (Chapter 4), the latter characterised as responsiveness towards others and thus a desire to expand basic capabilities in and for others, thereby helping create opportunities for people to live healthier, happier, or simply better/fairer lives. Figure 8.1 offers a visual representation of these relationships, but also includes additional aspects of civic professionalism that will be the subject of this present chapter.

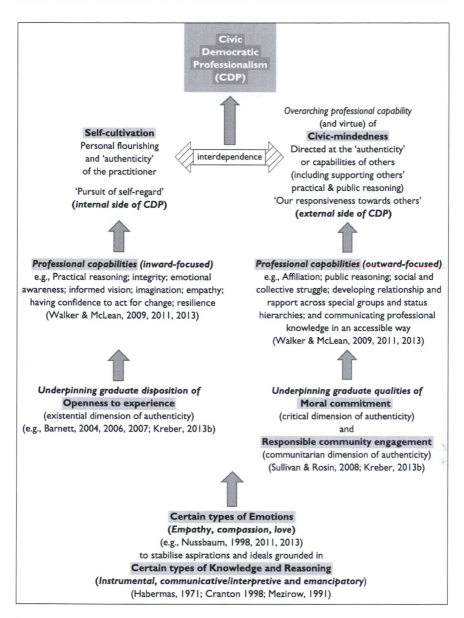

Figure 8.1 The building blocks of civic democratic professionalism

In this current chapter I shall focus on a particular version of civic professionalism, one that moves beyond Sullivan's model and gives citizens a much stronger voice in decisions typically made *for* them. My key purpose is to explore the possibility of professionals moving away from viewing their role principally as providing solutions *for* others and instead as creating opportunities that enable the public to participate more directly in finding solutions themselves on important issues affecting their lives. In short, this chapter is concerned with the potential role of professionals as enablers of democracy (Dzur, 2004, 2008). I shall further argue that enacting professional practice in ways that 'enable democracy' constitutes an example of informal 'community education', and thus qualifies as a form of social activism.

Professionals as enablers of democracy

Professionals being enablers of democracy and, by implication, facilitators of community education is a powerful idea, but how widespread is this civic spirit among the professions? Brint's (1994) sociological and political analysis of the role of professions in American society from twenty years ago revealed that they, including the so-called intellectuals (for example university professors of politics, history, sociology, literature, etc.), had withdrawn from public life. While they saw their responsibility in 'educating sensibilities' (p. 211), for instance through the periodicals they publish in, the contributions they made to our societies lacked political impulse. Writing for the educated public, they failed to present an adversary culture and provided little social criticism in the form of delineating alternatives to the existing social, political and economic order. Brint argued, therefore, that they served only minimally as society's social and cultural conscience, as was once envisaged by the social trustee model, which, in the early twentieth century, had idealised professionalism as a guide to a better society.

The social trustee model (at times discussed as functionalist theories of the professions) is associated, for instance, with Durkheim (1957), Marshall (1963), Goode (1957), Parsons (1954) and Tawney (1920). These theorists stressed that the professions fulfilled socially useful functions which needed to be protected from market forces. For Tawney (1920), professionals were 'men who carry on their work in accordance with rules designed to enforce standards both for the better protection of its members and for the better service of the public' (p. 92). Marshall (1963) and Goode (1957) highlighted the professions' altruism, Parsons (1954) stressed their orientation towards the community, and Durkheim (1957) emphasised their important mediator role between individuals and the state.

Brint (1994) concluded his analysis of the professions by commenting that in 'the age of experts' where professionalism is principally defined by 'its ability to bring negotiable resources to the labour market in the form of credentials and technical knowledge' (p. 204), it was unlikely

> that the professions, as they move in the direction of legitimation through expertise, stand as a likely vehicle for this revival (of a *political* liberalism that disrupts and makes uncomfortable demands for achieving a better and fairer

society [sic]). However, some of the earlier community-minded forms of professional idealism remain relevant to it, and the institutions promoting the autonomy and social responsibilities of professional knowledge are certainly relevant as well.

(p. 212)

Indeed, the literature on civic professionalism (e.g., Boyte & Fretz, 2012; Sullivan, 1995, 2005) that has emerged over the past twenty years essentially seeks to show how the professions might still rise to the professional ideal envisaged by the early functionalist theories of the professions. In particular, Sullivan's model of civic professionalism that I discussed in this book can be conceived of as being still quite closely aligned with this early twentieth-century social trustee model of the professions (Dzur, 2008).

Social trustee professionalism is based on an economy of trust. 'The public places trust in the professional to self-regulate and determine standards of practice, while the professional earns that trust by performing competently and adhering to the socially responsible normative orientation' (Dzur, 2008, p. 98). While the social trustee model is certainly socially responsible in its intention, Dzur criticises it for failing to recognise the significance of including members of the public, who are directly affected by professional action, in the process of defining what their social interests are. He argues that the radical critics of social trustee professionalism, writing in the 1970s, already had realised the dangers of professional task monopoly when they asked 'what the relationship is between professionals and the ability of members of the lay public to recognise and act on their interests' (Dzur, 2008, p. 83). The danger that radical critics such as Ivan Illich (1977) and his colleagues had identified was that of a disabling function of the professions. Professions were seen to be disabling as they took away from ordinary citizens the opportunity to decide for themselves. All weighty decisions on significant matters affecting their lives were made by the professional elite.

Since the 1970s, growing dissatisfaction with the bureaucratic and technocratic management of matters of public concern has become a crucial factor in the public's diminishing confidence in public services. Moreover, customers, empowered by the easy accessibility of previously hard to obtain information through the internet and other sources, have begun to question what they perceive as a paternalistic attitude of professionals, which has led to the perception among members of the public that professional authority is resting on shaky grounds (Fournier, 2000). Events like the economic crisis of 2008, and widely publicised abuses of public trust by some individuals and powerful organisations in other professional fields, notably the health care sector, journalism, and the clergy, have cast further doubt on whether the professionals we rely on really have our, and the world's, best interests at heart. Making the same point, Dzur (2008) observes that media-reported abuses of power in the professions have led to a culture that is 'skeptical of authority and distrustful of privilege' (p. 247). While Dzur agrees that the paternalistic attitude of the professions needs to be challenged, he still recognises the social and political significance of the professions. However, he assigns to them a distinctive function in society, arguing that the professionals' essential role should be to empower lay citizens to become participants in the process of making decisions on issues associated with vital social interests, decisions typically made only by professionals. In Dzur's model, citizens then are not just customers but real participants in the practice and the democratic process. He therefore envisages a role for professionals focused on helping citizens to organise themselves.

Dzur's (2004, 2008) notion of democratic professionalism emphasises the role of professionals as enablers of democracy and public deliberation. He grounds his work, on the one hand, in the democratic idea of task sharing in certain levels of government and civil society, as advocated by Alexis de Tocqueville in the first half of the nineteenth century (for instance lay participation in the justice system, as in the form of the jury), and, on the other hand, in Dewey's notion of professionals promoting 'social intelligence'. Boyte and Fretz (2010) point out how John Dewey emphasised the importance of professionals sharing their expertise with the lay public and employing it to address problems of wider social concern. Indeed, journalists, educators and social scientists had a decisive role for Dewey in encouraging not only lay participation but teaching habits of thought associated with scientific thinking. Dewey saw a key role for social scientists in encouraging community engagement and facilitating public decision-making. Crucially, however, democratic professionals, for Dewey, were not organisers of the public – their role was only to facilitate public understanding thereby helping the public to organise itself. The educative role of the professions lay in professionals challenging the public's scepticism or wariness in relation to new perspectives, to counter prejudice, and so forth. According to Dewey and Tocqueville, professionals ought not to hold task monopoly. Dzur (2008) argues that 'democratic professionals' show openness to being *informed by* the public and collaboratively seek solutions that are grounded in the community's own concerns, thereby becoming agents of social change.

Democratic professionalism thus needs to be understood as an alternative to both the social trustee model of the early twentieth century and its radical critique of the 1970s (Larson, 1977). The features that make democratic professionalism distinct from these two models, according to Dzur (2008), include:

- Professionals are committed to knowledge and to the co-direction of professional services.
- Social duties flow from training and experience but also from public collaboration; lay-people are viewed as citizens with a stake in professional decisions.
- The ideal role of the professional in society is one of sharing authority and knowledge through task sharing.

- Professional ethics should be overseen by professionals and lay-people.
- The political role of the professions is an enabling one as they become an intermediary in the realm of middle democracy (for further details see Dzur, 2008, p. 130).

Dzur (2008) concludes that 'Dewey's democratic professionals are not, therefore, best seen as leaders or organisers of the public; they respond to social problems in a way that facilitates the organisation of the public' (p. 119). In fact, his disagreement with Sullivan is most strongly expressed in the following statement: 'It may be necessary, therefore, to sharpen focus and reject, as least as a primary expectation, the idea that professionals serve as general civic organisers pursuing social purposes *for* the public' (p. 133), as this would diminish the possibility of non-professionals to act as good citizens. In short, Sullivan's (2005) civic professionals are concerned with supporting the public interest as the professionals perceive it; Dzur (2008) believes that the public needs to recognise itself what the public good is.

Perhaps Dall'Alba (2009) is making a similar point at the level of individuals, rather than communities. Grounding her analysis of professional practice in Martin Heidegger's (1962) notion of care, in particular the distinction he draws between 'leaping in' and 'leaping ahead', she argues that being with others can take away care from the other (care here understood as responsibility for pursuing one's own possibilities in life). By 'leaping in' for someone, by taking over the other's responsibility, we might actually dominate the person we hope to help, thereby making him or her dependent on us. By contrast, when we as professionals 'leap ahead' we give authentic care whereby the other person can choose among his or her possibilities and thus take responsibility. The person is taken seriously and the person's own belief or confidence in his or her capability to care for him or herself is nourished. At the level of community rather than individuals, this distinction between 'leaping in' and 'leaping ahead' is often articulated as doing things *for* the public (leaping in) versus doing things *with* the public (leaping ahead). Boyte and Fretz (2012) likewise suggest that, 'In contrast with practitioners applying a technical emphasis, civic professionals are those who work with citizens, rather than acting on them' (p. 95), and Saltmarsh and Hartley (2012) add that 'Democratic engagement seeks the public good *with* the public, and not merely *for* the public, and as a means of facilitating a more active and engaged democracy' (p. 20, emphasis in original).

This particular interpretation of civic professionalism is reflected in how professionals engage with their practice. For civic, or here civic democratic, professionals, the work they are engaged in is a meaning-giving practice with personal, social and political significance. Their self-concept as citizens infuses the work they do, and while they certainly do make use of their technical knowledge and skill and thereby contribute something of value, this is not all they do. Insofar as they facilitate opportunities for public dialogue and participatory decision-making among community members on important issues affecting their lives, they are also involved in a form of adult community education thereby not just developing their own but other people's civic spirit.

Democratic professionalism then is a *particular form* of civic professionalism. It is concerned with task sharing, and citizen participation in decision-making. It values professionals' knowledge and expertise but realises that important expertise lies with the public itself and mobilising and encouraging this public expertise is an important task of professionals. Democratic professionalism is the logical consequence of a civic professionalism that is true to its premises. Democratic professionalism is *civic-minded* in that it acts in the interests of society but recognises that these social interests, and appropriate responses, must be negotiated with the public.

Democratic professionalism is also based on self-cultivation, which, we argued in Chapter 5, occurs in dialogue with others, or in community (e.g., Eagleton, 2007; MacIntyre, 2007; Sullivan, 1995; Taylor, 1989, 1991). Self-cultivation, we saw, demands appreciation of our social interrelatedness and common humanity. It demands recognition that our own flourishing is dependent on others, and hence hinges on their flourishing. In democratic professionalism self-cultivation is protected also in another way. When professional decisions are opened up to public deliberation there is also less of a chance for the professional practice to become corrupted by being driven by the institutional goals of wealth, status, and prestige, which ultimately may work against the practitioner's self-cultivation and the flourishing of the practice. Since in democratic professionalism there is no assumption or expectation that professionals solve matters for others, one would also not expect to find acts performed out of an unhealthy sense of duty culminating in adaptive preferences that can lead to self-negating practices (see also Chapter 5).

However, shared decision-making and public deliberation may indeed imply a trade-off, as professionals' own decisions might on occasion be more just, more accurate and/or more efficient than those favoured by the broader community. Dzur argues that in the interest of democracy, the value attached to shared decision-making with the public should nonetheless take priority over the value of efficiency and technical effectiveness.

The role of professional expertise and knowledge

What might democratic professionalism look like? Is it just an appealing abstract notion or can it already be observed in some professional fields? Imagine the profession of teaching underpinned by the assumptions of democratic professionalism, or nursing, or journalism. Consider your own professional field. How open is it to embrace shared decision-making?

How do professionals in your field understand their role in relation to clients and society? Is there a sense that ordinary citizens have legitimate expertise to bring to the decision-making process or are they seen as vulnerable and in need of professional expert help? Is the relationship between professionals and society hierarchical, and hence paternalistic, or is it more even and collegial? You might make the very reasonable point that years of university study and practical experience in the professional field have led you to develop expertise and wisdom that provide you with a deep understanding of how issues are best addressed, an understanding that is not common for lay-people to acquire despite increased access to information through the internet and other sources. The point is a valid one. However, it is important to remind ourselves that Dzur (2008) is not suggesting that professional expertise does not count any more, or that professionals do not serve a valuable function in society; rather he defines this function in a 'new' way. Reconsider the opening quote of the present chapter:

> What is it to serve the public without an adequate understanding of the public?
>
> (Dzur, 2008, p. 274)

The consequence of decision-making that remains uninformed by the public is either that the decisions to be implemented will not be very effective as they have been forced upon people who may not consider them relevant, or, and this is Dzur's larger point, it fosters a culture in which the public remains passive and unengaged with its own community's affairs as decisions are made *for* them. This, of course, is precisely the critique presented by Ivan Illich and his colleagues who in the 1970s highlighted the disabling function of the professions. The real function of professionals in society, according to the perspective of democratic professionalism, is to provide opportunities or spaces for the public to debate issues of concern and explore solutions and make decisions together. The professionals' expertise is there to inform and help the public to understand issues more deeply and from a variety of perspectives, and appreciate why making decisions about these issues is often complex, and perhaps also why certain decisions that were made in the past did not have desired consequences. Importantly, though, in democratic professionalism information does not flow only one way. Democratic professionals make a point to be informed by the public. They do not assume they know where the shoe pinches (to paraphrase Dewey) but think those who are wearing it are in the best position to describe the problem. Moreover, just as Sullivan's (1995, 2005) civic professionals, democratic professionals understand themselves not just as members of a group of professionals but also as members of their larger community; the community's concerns are, therefore, also their concerns.

In its intent to strengthen public engagement by reviving the genuinely civic and democratic purpose professionals once were seen to fulfil (Dewey, 1927), Dzur's model of democratic professionalism can be conceived of as a creative response to the weakening of the public sphere noted by many commentators (e.g., Putnam, 2000; Taylor, 1991). However, as Nancy Fraser (1992) pointed out, the public arena is weakened not because there is no opportunity for engagement in deliberation and opinion formation but because these processes occur without any real power to make decisions attached to them. Therefore, in cases where the power to make decisions lies ultimately with professionals, it is all the more important that these professionals speak not *for* but *on behalf of*, that is in representation of, the public.

Dzur's model of democratic professionalism then carves out a new role for professionals in society as facilitators of public deliberation. The public is to have its say in the decision-making process and the professional's role is to assist the members of the public in organising themselves and also to represent their interests. In this model the 'professional community of practice' is opened up to lay-members who become legitimate participants in the practice (Wenger, 1998), whose knowledge and experience in relation to the issues of concern are valued and built upon.

Challenges to democratic professionalism

Democratic professionalism, of course, is idealistic and there are serious challenges to be overcome for this model to spread more widely. One challenge we encountered already when we considered studies reporting on how professionals tend to conceive of their roles (Brint, 1994; Wilson et al., 2013). Viewing one's professional practice as the efficient provision of technical services is evidently very different from viewing one's professional practice as civic engagement and social activism. However, the challenge does not only lie with professionals and how they construe their roles. As noted earlier, according to the model of democratic professionalism, professional practice can be conceived of as a form of community education aimed at empowering the public. While most of us would deem empowerment to be desirable on one level, the question remains whether people necessarily cry out to be empowered and take care of their own as well as others' community's affairs. The radical critics of the 1970s certainly wanted to see greater participation of the public in the decisions affecting them, but they also realised that decades of paternalistic social trustee professionalism were changing people's attitudes towards civic engagement. When decisions are always made for us, especially within an ideology where this is portrayed and experienced as the way it should be, it is hard to appreciate that non-participation in decision-making may ultimately work against our own interests. It becomes a form of adaptive preference (Nussbaum, 2000, 2011), a concept discussed in Chapter 5.

To bring the discussion to a more concrete level, let's look at two examples that many readers will be able to relate to: (a) our students, and (b) our own professional development as academic practitioners. Is it your experience that students in your courses typically cry out to be empowered, set their own learning goals, identify appropriate learning sources and decide on the criteria against which to assess their learning? Or is it, perhaps more often than not, the case that they would rather have you tell them what to do (as after all, you are the teacher and you know best)? How about our own preferences when it comes to professional development? Have you ever been asked by your 'supervisor' to write out your own professional development plan? If so, what is or was your first reaction to that? Maybe you immediately and genuinely embraced the opportunity and recognised its value. Yet, I still remember the days when this was a new and unfamiliar approach and while it was rationally construed as reasonable, or valuable, on one level, it was not considered all that appealing on another. It seemed to take time away from more important tasks. Would not a lot of time be saved if someone simply told us what we need: 'Take this course on team leadership and conflict resolution, this one on budgeting, this one on teaching and this one on research. Do as advised and your career will flourish.' So what is the problem here?

The point is that although we deem empowerment to be very desirable on one level, we do not always cheer at it. There certainly are occasions when we resent seeing autonomy taken away from us, but there are just as many occasions when we resent seeing it forced upon us. Importantly, whenever we *are told to do* something, be it to act more autonomously or to comply with regulations, it carries the risk of us simply going through the motions. We do as asked, but do not think much more about it. When students do simply as they were told without indications of genuine personal investment on their part, we sometimes refer to it as them adopting a 'surface approach to learning' (e.g., Entwistle, Tait & McCune, 2000). We might also speak of them as taking a strategic approach, if there is evidence that their main intention is to achieve a good mark by being well organised, managing their time well and being alert to assessment demands. Yet, what we actually want to see is them adopting a deep approach to their learning whereby they are intrinsically motivated and keen to seek meaning for themselves, relate ideas to one another, develop sound questioning skills, consider the reasons behind arguments carefully, demonstrate a real interest in ideas, and so forth.

The issue to be aware of then is that we do not necessarily resist being told what to do; to the contrary at times we prefer it this way. This is so despite us being fully aware that simply 'doing as told' interferes with adopting a 'deep approach' and taking care of your own learning and development. We do know that taking a deep approach and being responsible for our own learning and development would be the more mature response, and yet, at least in some parts of our lives, we might still prefer following instructions as this is easier and less time-intensive. A simple example from ordinary life may illustrate this point. Yesterday a repairman came to my house to take a look at a shower door that had collapsed. After assessing the situation he asked me 'So you will provide the new door?' and I responded 'I was hoping you would do that', to which he replied in return 'But I do not know what it is you want – there are many different types and brands out there, and they vary in quality.' My immediate reaction was to think to myself 'I really don't want to have to deal with this right now', and then I heard myself say 'But I think you know best', to which he, very reasonably, responded 'It's your bathroom.' It was an enlightening situation in that I so gladly would have seen him taking control and relieving me of the chore of spending time on learning about different shower doors and choosing one; and yet, I think he also rightly pointed out that I should take responsibility for what I want. While this particular incident took place in the private arena and thus was *a*political (note that democratic professionalism, of course, is concerned with the public arena where citizens and professionals together become involved in social activism around issues of public concern – in other words democratic professionalism is concerned with the political potential of the professions), the example nonetheless shows how we, at times, quite happily abdicate responsibility to others who we assume will make the right decisions for us. 'Not wanting to be bothered' and 'wanting to trust and rely on others' expertise' are natural human reactions given the busyness of our lives, but they also constitute a real challenge to democratic professionalism.

Democratic professionalism, despite its appeal, then undoubtedly has its challenges. One key challenge, as noted, lies in how to mobilise members of society into becoming more involved in taking responsibility for (and we might as well say 'a deep approach to') decisions typically made by professionals in relation to important public goods such as education, health, food, housing, safety, justice, the beauty and life-sustaining forces of the ecological environment, among others. The success of democratic professionalism then is contingent not only on professionals' identity (whether they understand themselves as enablers of democracy or as efficient providers of technical services) but is subject also to the very natural human inclination of feeling, at times, quite comfortable with others making decisions for us.

That's one side of it. Yet, as intimated earlier, there are occasions when we very much resent being told what to do, and while some people will always want to play a more active role and participate as much as possible in any decisions affecting their lives, others may resent lack of autonomy only in moments when they perceive the decisions that were made for them to impact negatively on their lives. As I am writing this I am reminded of the government plan to have healthier meals in British schools (a similar initiative was recently endorsed by Michelle Obama in the United States, causing strong opposition in some circles). While many parents might actually have welcomed the change in school meals, others were so outraged by this new initiative that they drove to their kids' school during recess and passed junk food over the fence just to make their point (G. Fraser, 2005). If their children want to enjoy a burger and a coke for lunch, followed by a doughnut for dessert, they should have it – and parents should be allowed to give it to them! The issue of concern here, at least in the first instance, is not what is and what is not a nutritious lunch; the issue causing concern is the way, and by whom, decisions on such important matters are made. Many parents feel that the state or education authority, let alone individual schools or teachers, should not make decisions on what they consider to be family choices.

Yet, the issues around healthier eating are complex. Eating disorders among young people are increasing and constitute a serious health concern; more-over, poverty is a reality even in wealthy countries such as Canada or the UK and too many children start the school day hungry (and studies have identified a correlation between poverty and poor quality food). On one level then it is only reasonable for schools to somehow try to educate about nutrition, advocate for heathier ways of eating and provide better food plans. Nevertheless, having such decisions made by either the government or schools (note that schools may also be rather critical of what they perceive as failed government policy as we have seen in the Obama example) without involvement of the wider public is undemocratic, and hence it is not surprising that it would cause rebellion. At the same time it is important to realise that a democratic approach would carry the risk of a less impactful, fair or efficient decision being reached. That's the trade-off.

Imagine for a moment a democratic discussion around school meals. Many parents would likely agree that meals high in vitamins, protein and fibre and low in salt, fat and sugar are a better choice than those with opposite compounds. And yet, let's assume, for the sake of argument, that despite open debate on the issue, which may qualify also as a form of informal community education, participants vote in the end in favour of leaving the decision up to individual parents (also perhaps for the very good reason that food budgets vary greatly from one family to another). In response to the debate, some parents from now on will make different choices, while others will not or cannot. Although shared decision-making in this case would not lead to a massive shift in the types of food to be consumed at school, it would have brought about some changes. Importantly, the democratic process followed would justify what is perhaps a less ideal outcome. In a perfect world, where the public spaces in which issues were being debated were characterised by equal standing of all participants and all arguments were given a hearing and tested for their validity (Habermas, 1984), the best argument would presumably emerge through consensus, enhancing our confidence in the soundness of the outcome being reached – maybe a ban on all junk food and sugary drinks in schools including vending machines, or reduced prices for less popular but healthier choices, or as suggested in the above example, the decision to leave the final decision to parents, or yet again something else. Regardless of the actual outcome attained, the essential value of democratic professionalism lies in the idea of active participation of citizens in decisions concerning their lives – hence in allowing the public a voice and respecting citizens' agency.

My purpose in this discussion has been to highlight the central aspect of democratic professionalism, showing how it offers a strong and viable alternative to the social trustee model. At the same time my intent was to draw attention to some of the real challenges that Dzur's vision entails, which include: (1) professionals entering practice not necessarily having adopted an identity as enablers of democracy; (2) the public possibly being reluctant to be involved in decision-making; and (3) in cases where the public is keen to be involved, or can be mobilised, the final decision being reached, on the grounds of information sharing and debate, not necessarily being the one professionals themselves might have made based on their specialised knowledge and experience.

Linkages between democratic professionalism and capabilities

In Chapter 4 we saw that capabilities allow us to choose and live in ways we find meaningful or have reason to value. A flourishing life, or, as I said previously, an authentic life, is built around capabilities, or the opportunity to grow, and choose for oneself, in important areas of life. Nussbaum (2011) suggested that a just society would guarantee people choices in certain areas of life, allowing them to function in a truly human way. Capabilities are understood as real opportunities to choose among certain functionings or ways of being. The capabilities (or areas over and within which choice, growth and development should be possible) Nussbaum identified include, as previously noted: (1) life; (2) bodily health; (3) bodily integrity; (4) senses, imagination and thought; (5) emotions; (6) practical reason; (7) affiliation (being able to live with as well as towards others and being treated with respect); (8) other species; (9) play; (10) control over one's political and material environment (Nussbaum, 2011, pp. 78–80).

Democratic professionalism resonates strongly with the purpose of expanding capability in society (Nussbaum, 2000, 2011; Nussbaum & Sen, 1993). Following Walker and McLean's lead, I discussed in Chapter 4 that the capabilities approach is relevant to professionalism on two levels. Higher education's role is to develop in students particular *professional capabilities*, which ideally include practical reasoning; public reasoning; affiliation; integrity; emotional awareness; informed vision; imagination; empathy; developing relationship and rapport across special groups and status hierarchies; having confidence to act for change; social and collective struggle; resilience; and communicating professional knowledge in an accessible way (see Walker & McLean, 2009, 2011, 2013; McLean & Walker, 2012). These particular *professional capabilities* culminate in the *overarching capability of civic-mindedness* (see Figure 8.1), whose internal side is self-cultivation. Civic-minded professionals, I argued in Chapter 4, understand their central mission as seeking greater social justice by helping expand basic capabilities among other members of society. An important basic capability that Nussbaum (2000) emphasises is that of practical reasoning (point 6 in the above list), which she defines as the ability 'to form a conception of the good and to engage in critical reflection about the planning of one's life' (p. 79).

I now want to suggest that civic professionals who are also *democratic* professionals, through task sharing and joint decision-making, make a particular contribution to capability expansion through the opportunities they offer for citizens to engage in practical reasoning. As they open up their professional practice to members of the community and facilitate spaces for public deliberation (and task sharing) on important matters associated with public goods, they allow for the capability of practical reasoning to be enacted and offer opportunity for its ongoing cultivation. And it is not only *practical* reasoning that is facilitated in this way but also *public* reasoning. The latter, while not labelled such in Nussbaum's list, is implied in several of her capabilities, especially in (4) 'senses, imagination and thought', (7) 'affiliation', and (10) 'control over one's political environment'.

Having made a case for democratic professionalism in this chapter, it is time to ask what democratic professionalism might look like in practice. Below I shall provide just three examples but I continue the discussion in Chapter 10.

Examples of democratic professionalism

According to Dzur, the possibility of democratic professionalism is limited to certain kinds of professions. He explicitly speaks of 'some professions' (Dzur, 2008, p. 247), or 'a number of professions' (Dzur, 2004, p. 6), and the ones he makes direct reference to include journalism, law, health care and public administration. I would agree that some professions lend themselves more readily than others to an enactment of practice that is truly democratic (indeed, the problem with public sector professionalism is precisely that the agency, so fundamental for democratic engagement, is taken away from the practitioner). Nonetheless, I also believe, as I argued elsewhere (Kreber, 2015), that all professions (including occupations typically not classified as professions but rather as vocations) carry at least some potential of incorporating a political dimension into their work, although with some it will necessarily be more limited.

A profession where we can easily appreciate how a democratic approach might unfold is journalism. Discussing specifically how universities could prepare future journalists for democratic professional practice, Haas (2000) comments that professional education should:

> teach students how to (a) gather information on issues of concern to citizens, and learn about their particular views on and experiences with these issues, (b) write stories that stimulate citizens to critically reflect on the issues involved and engage others in conversations about those issues, and (c) offer citizens opportunities to publicly criticize news coverage of given issues, and then to publicly respond to those criticisms.
>
> (p. 38)

It is evident in this example how a truly democratic spirit pervades the practice. Democratic journalism, with an emphasis on task sharing and public debate, recognises the public's knowledge and provides citizens the opportunity to exercise their agency. In democratic journalism both professional journalists and citizens (lay journalists) inform the community. Haas suggests that if we want journalists to act in this way we need to teach students on professional programmes how to do it.

Concerned specifically with the teaching profession and by implication teacher education, Armstrong (2006) argues that teacher education should become a more democratic practice. He suggests that a democratic professional approach to teacher education would involve 'critical questioning of the contested social and political interests that inform educational policy and practice' which 'entails asking questions about whose interests are served by particular ways of conceptualising educational value and practice' (p. 9). He adds that:

> to ask questions and to explore how, as a community of participation and dissent, we might help each other, and those wider communities with whom we work, requires the existence or the creation of an intellectual space for dialogue about what it is that we do.
>
> (p. 9)

Armstrong emphasises the importance of creating opportunities for students on professional programmes and teacher educators to engage in dialogue with the communities of policy and practice with whom they work, so as to develop greater agency in the face of tightened government regulation. While this is clearly commendable and an example of developing a more democratic professional practice, it is unclear to what extent Armstrong sees the general public (including parents and others interested in the role of education in society) participating in the dialogical processes he has in mind. The questions he proposes as being critical for us to engage in with regards to education are excellent; nonetheless, in highlighting the inclusion of student teachers, teacher educators, teachers in schools and educational policy makers in the dialogue he envisages, it would appear that he places little emphasis on lay-people's participation in the debate.

We might also readily appreciate how the philosophy of democratic professionalism could guide members of the academic profession (i.e., university-employed academics). As public or democratic intellectuals they would share their scholarship and research with their broader communities (that is ordinary citizens rather than other subject specialists) for the purposes of stimulating public debate (Small, 2002). Boyte and Fretz (2012) remark in this context that in order to have a stronger impact on their communities,

> Higher education professionals will also need to make their work more public, in multiple ways . . . more infused with robust democratic and public purposes. Faculty members, staff, and students will need to engage with the community as equals and pursue solutions to community issues, not as a theoretical exercise but as a path to becoming agents and architects of a flourishing democracy.
>
> (p. 99)

To achieve this would necessitate a different kind of communication than that academics are typically used to when sharing their work with other members of their own disciplinary, or interdisciplinary, communities. It would entail seeking out new outlets for the work and also adopting a different genre from the traditional academic research presentation or essay. Most academic publications that appear in top-tier journals are utterly impenetrable to anyone not having been socialised into the disciplinary jargon so lavishly employed there. It is refreshing to see, therefore, that the use of blog posts (see for instance Giroux, 2011) and publicly accessible websites is becoming increasingly common among academics intent on breaking down the wall between town and gown. Next to going public through the mode of writing, public intellectuals could also make use of alternative media, such as interactive radio and TV shows, exhibitions, dance or theatre (e.g., Keen & Todres, 2007).

While it seems only sensible for academics to follow Boyte and Fretz's (2010) suggestion to share their work more widely with the public and in multiple ways, I shall explore, in Chapter 10, some of the challenges faced by academics committed to doing this.

Final comments

This chapter discussed the differences between democratic professionalism and the social trustee model of the professions, the latter conceiving of citizens as dependent on and needy of professional expertise and services. It showed how democratic professionalism is built around the idea of professionals and lay-people engaging in information sharing, public deliberation and joint decision-making. I also suggested that civic professionalism, construed in this way (namely as *democratic* professionalism), constitutes a type of informal community education. Civic/democratic professionals are enablers of democracy aiming to empower citizens to make informed decisions on important matters of public concern. I noted some of the potential challenges associated with democratic professionalism, including the professional's own understanding of their role (that is, their professional identity), the public's reluctance to become engaged, and the possibility that the decision reached through democratic processes may not be the one that professionals themselves would recommend. I concluded with examples of what democratic professionalism might look like in three different professions.

In the next chapter I shall argue that our understanding of what the practice of 'democratic professionalism' *could* mean is enriched by engaging with the political philosophy of Hannah Arendt. The individual concepts underpinning Arendt's theory of *action* allow for a deeper appreciation of both the challenges involved and the need for greater democracy (or *action*) in and through professional practice.

Chapter 9

Reasoning publicly – connecting with community

> Inability to think is not the 'prerogative' of those many who lack brain power but the ever-present possibility for everybody – scientists, scholars, and other specialists in mental enterprises not excluded.
>
> (Arendt, 2003, p. 187)

Introduction

The previous chapter engaged with Dzur's (2008) vision of democratic professionalism which draws heavily on the progressive tradition, especially the legacy of John Dewey. We saw that Dewey attributed a strong educative function to the professions, which by practising and demonstrating critical inquiry based on the scientific method, would help liberate citizens from dogmatism and tradition. In his book *How we think*, first published in 1910, Dewey outlined the problem of prejudice and wariness of the unorthodox he observed among members of society that he thought the scientific method would address. He commented:

> Certain men and classes of men come to be accepted guardians or transmitters – instructors – of established doctrines. . . . inquiry and doubt are silenced by citation of ancient laws . . . *This attitude of mind generates dislike of change, and the resulting aversion to novelty is fatal to progress.* What will not fit into the established canons will be outlawed.
>
> (Dewey, 1991, p. 149, emphasis added)

Dewey thought that by professionals practising the 'scientific method', for example social scientists or journalists presenting social issues from a variety of perspectives to encourage public debate, ordinary citizens themselves would be drawn into the scientific process or critical inquiry, which in turn would open their minds, enhance their power to make informed decisions, and thus strengthen democracy and the public sphere. As Dzur (2008) puts it: 'Dewey's contribution . . . was to conceptualize the democratic professional, the applied social scientist, the engineer, the teacher, and the reporter who worked *with* rather than *for* the public, who *facilitated* public understanding and practical abilities rather than *led* the public' (p. 5, emphasis in original).

In this chapter I shall suggest that Dewey's concern with strengthening the public sphere resonates with Hannah Arendt's call for freedom through 'action'. Action for Arendt happens whenever ordinary citizens come together to openly deliberate issues of public concern taking into consideration all different standpoints. Dewey's emphasis on the 'scientific method' strikes us, at first sight in any case, to not chime easily with Arendt's concept of 'action', which is based on a practical (not instrumental) rationality. 'There could hardly be a philosopher with views more abhorrent to Arendtians than Dewey', writes Robin Weiss (2011, p. 184). But what does Dewey actually mean by the 'scientific method'?

In advocating the scientific process Dewey emphasised the importance of: (a) a willingness to submit claims to public examination, (b) collaboration, (c) experimentation, and (d) argumentation through fact and analysis. Arendt (1968b) argued that facts and strict scientific standards were counterproductive to politics in so far as they preclude debate. She comments:

> The trouble is that factual truth, like all other truth, peremptorily claims to be acknowledged and precludes debate, and debate constitutes the very essence of political life. The modes of thought and communication that deal with truth, if seen from the political perspective, are necessarily domineering; they don't take into account other people's opinions, and taking these into account is the hallmark of all strictly political thinking.
>
> (Arendt, 1968b, p. 241)

Arendt's own view on validity of argument in the realm of politics is based on the notion of intersubjectivity. Opinions gain intersubjective validity through the outcome of collective debate where the standpoints of others are taken into consideration. She calls this form of thinking 'thinking with an enlarged mentality', a mode that calls upon our imagination and capacity to think representatively. In an article comparing Dewey to Arendt, Weiss (2011) showed that they both believe in the need to rescue the public sphere and in the importance of a vibrant and deliberative democracy. Although there are clear differences in the processes they consider to be within the realm of the political, there are also considerable similarities. The section in Weiss's (2011) article entitled 'Science and Politics' is especially instructive and pertinent to this chapter. Although we might expect Dewey to be especially hooked on scientific truths, Weiss argues that both Arendt and Dewey recognise the danger of 'scientific truths' coercing deliberation. If one looks carefully at their respective positions, Weiss (2011) contends, it is clear that neither Dewey nor Arendt sees the problem in the facts themselves, but rather in the 'truths' derived from these facts through the privileging of a particular method. In his book *The public and its problems*, published in 1927, Dewey makes his position very clear:

The power of facts to coerce belief does not reside in the bare phenomena. It proceeds from method, from the technique of research and calculation. *No one is forced by just the particular facts to accept a particular theory of their meaning*, so long as one retains intact some other doctrine by which he can marshal them. Only when the facts are allowed free play for the suggestion of new points of view is any significant conversion of conviction as to meaning possible.

(Dewey, cited in Weiss, 2011, p. 200, emphasis added)

Dewey believed that while facts ought to be recognised in the public realm, no one must be bound to follow or accept the method by which they were obtained. Arendt's concern is precisely that methods (including, of course, scientific methods based on instrumental reasoning) become constraining and hegemonic, so that in the end only conclusions that stem from these methods are recognised as correct and in fact as 'rational', and everything that departs from these recognised methods is deemed irrational. Dewey has a more positive (and perhaps idealised) view of science itself. The scientific process, as he understands it, is based on hypotheses, and hypotheses require verification. So to arrive at scientific truth means to 'test . . . one's opinions against the actual and possible experiences of others' (Weiss, 2011, p. 202). Science, for Dewey, should be a constant return to the facts rather than accepting one theory as the only rational interpretation. Thus construed, Dewey's perspective is indeed not so different from Arendt's notion of judgement, which we will turn to later in this chapter.

In summary, we can say that although Arendt considers the emphasis on instrumental rationality as the key problem in modern society and ultimately the culprit for the shrinking of the public sphere, she would readily concur with Dewey on a number of points. Revisiting the four pillars of critical inquiry that Dewey highlighted (as noted earlier), Arendt would agree on the importance of (a) a willingness to submit claims to public examination, and (b) collaboration. Experimentation, point (c), she would likely replace with not seeking false security in rules and orthodoxies but thinking 'without pillars and props' (Arendt, 1968a, p. 10), and Dewey's last point, argumentation through fact and analysis, point (d), she would replace by her notion of 'representative thinking' (Arendt, 2003), which, we will see momentarily, is based on a practical (and one might argue also emancipatory) rationality. According to Weiss's (2011) analysis these distinctions are more a matter of semantics than actual divisions. What happens in representative thinking is that all facts and interpretations are considered. This is not to deny that there are, nonetheless, important differences between Arendt and Dewey (and Weiss's article identifies their points of departure as well), but it is to say that the differences are not as profound as one might first expect.

I shall now examine some of the core concepts behind Arendtian *action*, which remained fundamental to all of Arendt's work, including freedom and deliberation, plurality and natality, unpredictability and irreversibility, forgiving and promising and, crucially, representative thinking and judgement. I end the chapter with a brief discussion of whether Arendt is easily placed within any political, let alone educational, tradition. In the chapter that follows I consider how university-based professional education might be transformed to foster practitioners' capacity to act as civic agents.

Who was Hannah Arendt and how does her work matter to professional practice?

Born to Jewish parents in Hanover, Germany, in 1906, Hannah Arendt studied first theology and then later philosophy with Husserl, Heidegger and Jasper, earning her doctorate under Carl Jasper's supervision at the University of Heidelberg in 1929. While Jasper stayed a close friend throughout her life, Arendt distanced herself from Heidegger whose (brief) collaboration with the Nazi regime she found deeply disturbing. With the rise of National Socialism in 1933 she first escaped to Paris where she befriended Walter Benjamin and also worked for various Jewish refugee organisations. In 1940, shortly before the German troops invaded France, she divorced her first husband and married Heinrich Blücher, also a German refugee, who was a Marxist philosopher. A few months later she and Blücher were interned, separately, in southern France. In 1941 they managed to escape and secure a passage to the United States. Arendt taught at many North American universities, holding a full professorship at Princeton and teaching also at the University of Chicago, Wesleyan University, and the New School for Social Research in New York. Arendt died in 1975 (Young-Bruehl, 2006).

Arendt was one of the most influential political theorists and philosophers of the twentieth century; nonetheless, her work is not typically drawn upon in either the higher education literature or the literature on the professions, although she has received some limited attention in education more generally (e.g., Greene, 1995; Gordon, 2001). On one level the paucity of attention she has received in the above fields is not surprising given that she did not address the professions, let alone any other occupational group, directly in her writing, as did John Dewey. She also contributed only one article specifically on education, and that one concerned the education of children. On another level, though, the limited attention Arendt has received in the fields of higher education and the literature on the professions *is* surprising as the concepts she developed in her work are of critical importance to both fields. At a time when intercultural, political and economic conflicts abound, Arendt's message of the importance of learning to live together in a world characterised by complexity, uncertainty and different viewpoints is perhaps more important than ever.

She leaves an enormous legacy of books and articles although her two masterpieces are widely considered to be the *Origins of totalitarianism*, published in 1951, and her more philosophical treatise, *The human condition*, published seven years later. She received particular attention in 1961 working for the

New Yorker reporting on the Eichmann trial in Jerusalem. Her newspaper articles, including her later book *Eichmann in Jerusalem* (1963), stimulated enormous public debate concerning the Holocaust. Witnessing Eichmann's responses during the trial led her to coin the expression 'The banality of evil'. It was meant to convey that the magnitude of sheer horror had its origin in the evolution of a new kind of criminal: individuals who lack the ability to think, specifically, to think representatively in a shared world (Young-Bruehl, 2006).

Below, I will discuss this idea of representative thinking and other concepts central to Arendt's notion of action as I see these as particularly relevant for professionals at a time when professional practice and the distribution of public goods are increasingly subject to neoliberal policies that tend to narrow the opportunities for public deliberation and task sharing.

The meaning of action

Action is one of the three modalities of the active life (the 'vita activa') that Arendt (1958) discusses in her major treatise *The human condition*. The other two modalities, as we saw in Chapter 2, are *labour* and *work*. In contrast to labour and work, which take place in the private sphere and thus serve mainly private interests, *action* is, by its very nature, a public activity. Arendt (1958) was deeply critical of matters of legitimate public concern being pushed into the 'private' arena. As d'Entreves (2014) makes clear:

> For Arendt modernity is characterized by the *loss of the world*, by which she means the restriction or elimination of the public sphere of action and speech in favor of the private world of introspection and the private pursuit of economic interests. . . . Modernity is the age of bureaucratic administration and anonymous labor, rather than politics and action, of elite domination and the manipulation of public opinion.
>
> (electronic source)

What does Arendt mean by *action*? Action is political for Arendt and refers to a particular mode of human togetherness that can be witnessed when and wherever people participate in public deliberation. It refers to a public space where human beings interact through speech as well as deeds, where they aim to persuade each other of their arguments and try to find solutions to common concerns. A public space does not refer to a particular geographical location (like the town hall, or market square). The point is not *where* the space is but what *kind* of a space it is. Town halls or market squares may be, or become, public spaces, but the same is true for schools, museums, cafés, streets, malls . . . even bus stops, or balconies. Any particular locality can become a public space if it is indeed representative of or open to the public and their concerns. What was a public space yesterday may not be one today. Public spaces are spaces where ordinary citizens get together and interact. Whenever that happens something is put in motion (i.e., there is a beginning of something) although what this something is, and where it might lead, cannot be determined in advance.

Arendt sees in public deliberation a necessary requirement for freedom. People are free as long as there is space to *act*. Freedom disappears if there is no space or opportunity for action. Adami (2014) observes that 'Freedom . . . can only be experienced and achieved *together with others* in the spontaneity of political action' (p. 303, emphasis added). Arendtian action is directly associated with a participatory democracy. The bureaucracy associated with many professional services, and how policy decisions are made, one might say poses a threat to people's freedom.

Action is made possible by two conditions. The first condition is 'natality', the second is 'plurality'.

Natality and plurality

'Natality' refers to the possibility of each individual starting something new. Arendt (2007) argues that each person who is born into the world offers the potential of a new beginning, or the potential of 'renewing the common world' (p. 192). Yet, importantly, each time a person initiates something by participating in *action*, natality is re-experienced and new opportunities are generated for renewal and change. Arendt (1958) comments on natality in this way: 'The new beginning inherent in birth can make itself felt in the world only because the newcomer possesses the capacity of beginning something anew, that is, of acting' (p. 9), and later:

> The fact that man is capable of action means that the unexpected can be expected from him, that he is able to perform what is infinitely improbable. And this is possible only because each man is unique, so that with each birth something uniquely new comes into the world.
>
> (p. 178)

In the above quote Arendt already alludes to the importance of the second condition of action, which is 'plurality'.

'Plurality' reflects both the reality of and the importance of valuing diversity. We live in a community with others who are different from us; yet, we share the common world as equals, which involves respecting and engaging the multiple perspectives and values of others. *Action*, as public deliberation, is by definition a collective activity. I cannot deliberate publicly on my own, and public deliberation involves recognising the perspectives of others. Action is always relational. Moreover, how our actions are received or interpreted is not up to us, despite us being the initiators of action. Actions, through speech and deed, gain their significance by how they are interpreted by others, those with whom we share the world. When Arendt argues that *action* leads to individuals being free, the freedom she has in mind is not individual sovereignty where one person can rule over others. In fact, Arendt emphasises 'the impossibility of [individuals] remaining unique masters of what they do' (1958, p. 244). Biesta (2012) further explains that by linking the collective activity of action to freedom Arendt shows that 'our freedom is fundamentally interconnected with the freedom of others; it is contingent upon the freedom of others' (p. 688). This same idea of our social interdependence I discussed earlier in this book as the foundation of civic-mindedness (see Chapters 4 and 5). Our freedom, or our individual flourishing, and indeed the choices we make as individuals, requires the support of others in the community who recognise such flourishing and choices as important.

In a particularly interesting section of *The human condition*, Arendt argued that through action people disclose to the world their distinct personalities.

> In acting and speaking, men [sic] show who they are, reveal actively their unique identities and thus make their appearance in the human world . . . This disclosure of 'who' in contradistinction to 'what' somebody is . . . is implicit in everything somebody says and does. . . . Although nobody knows who he reveals when he discloses himself in deed or word, he must be willing to risk the disclosure . . .
>
> (Arendt, 1958, pp. 179–180)

The public space of appearance is extremely important for Arendt and the foundation of democracy and freedom. Its existence cannot be taken for granted. It is only a potential space dependent on the preparedness of people to come out and disclose themselves, that is, take agency and make their perspective known. This, she contends, takes courage. 'Courage and even boldness are (already) present in leaving one's hiding place and showing who one is, in disclosing and exposing one's self' (p. 186). I think what is important here is whenever people come together to deliberate issues of public concern, thereby making their respective views or opinions witnessed by others, they also take responsibility for their actions rather than hide behind others. Participation in *action* encourages their authenticity. Note in this context also Nussbaum's (2006) review of research literature on the conditions under which people behave badly (for example, causing another person physical or psychological harm), leading her to conclude:

> First, people behave badly when they are not held personally accountable. People act much worse under shelter of anonymity, as parts of a faceless mass, than when they are watched and made accountable as individuals. . . . Second, people behave badly when nobody raises a critical voice . . . Third, people behave badly when the human beings over whom they have power are dehumanized and de-individualised.
>
> (pp. 43–44)

By recognising both 'plurality' and 'natality' through spaces or opportunities in which *action* can occur, we can build in some safeguards against such injustices and cruelty, often underpinned by ignorance, lack of empathy and spinelessness.

How are the two notions of 'plurality' and 'natality' relevant to professional practice? Recognising plurality would mean that professionals recognise their social interconnectedness with other members of the community, the importance of integrating their individual goals and those of their professional group with those of their larger community (Sullivan, 2005), and the existence of multiple perspectives on the same issue. Recognising natality would mean that professionals have a sense of personal agency, that is, an understanding that they can take advantage of the potential to act on the future differently. Perhaps even more importantly, they would recognise the potential of something new to emerge through the natality of each individual citizen, thereby seeing value in becoming enablers of democracy in their communities. D'Entreves (2014) concludes that, for Arendt, 'Political activity is valued . . . because it enables each citizen to exercise his or her powers of agency, to develop the capacity for judgment and to attain by concerted action some measure of political efficiency' (online source). This idea of citizens becoming involved in political activity, activity around important matters of public concern, resonates strongly with the notion of democratic professionalism discussed in the previous chapter.

While plurality and natality are conditions of action, two important characteristics of action are its *unpredictability* and *irreversibility*.

Unpredictability and irreversibility

Acting means to participate in an already existing web of (human) relations, in a context defined by plurality. When everyone has the same capacity to act in a community of equals, the consequences of an act are impossible to predict. 'No actor has the power to control the consequences of his or her deeds' (d'Entreves, 2014, online source). The power to influence, Arendt (1958) argues, is therefore never a guarantee; indeed it is no more than a 'potentiality in being together . . .' not an unchangeable, measurable, and reliable entity' (p. 200). In our professional practice we may aim to reach a good decision on a particular issue of public concern by providing complete information and creating spaces for open debate, but how our own actions will be interpreted, or how this information will influence others' decision, remains uncertain. This is what Arendt means by the *unpredictability* of action.

But not only can the outcomes of an action not be guaranteed the same way that IKEA guarantees that if we put the hundred screws and bolts together exactly the way they tell us in their instructions, the table we ordered will look like the one we saw in the catalogue; it is also the case that once a deed is done it cannot be undone the same way that we can simply take apart our IKEA table and return it if we do not like it. The consequences of actions are real and inevitable. This is the *irreversibility* of action. A poor decision cannot be undone. Consequences are real and they affect members of the community.

To cope with the *unpredictability* and *irreversibility* of action, Arendt suggests, we can find some limited comfort in two human faculties or potentialities: the acts of *forgiving* and *promising*. Forgiving can interrupt the otherwise endless chain of consequences of mistakes (or unrealised promises), while mutual promises provide a potential resource against an uncertain future and offer 'islands of certainty in an ocean of uncertainty' (Arendt, 1958, p. 244). By agreeing to and then becoming bound by certain courses of action we try to put some limits on unpredictability.

Readers might have realised already that these two potentialities, forgiving and promising, are highly relevant to professional practice, and are so in two ways. First, as already intimated, the judgements professionals make on how best to solve a problem do not always have the consequences that were intended. The potentiality of the public to forgive professionals what in the end turned out to be a poor decision perhaps with dreadful and long-lasting outcomes seems crucial for professionals to maintain, and perhaps, regain, public trust. At the same time, and reconnecting with the democratic ideal of professionalism discussed in the previous chapter, the promises professionals make about how issues are best solved are more likely to meet with acceptance by the public when these issues have been deliberated *with* them and not simply been decided *for* them. Thus construed, 'promising' is not unilateral. In a situation of task sharing, involving the flow of information in both ways and joint decision-making, the entire community, that is professionals and other citizens, make promises to each other. To the extent that the final decision on actual policy is made by (democratic) professionals, it is made not for the public but on behalf of, that is in representation of, the public.

I should add that whenever we speak of *representation of* the interests of others we are, strictly speaking, moving away from Arendt. The key point of Arendt's theory of action is that she contributed great significance to the active civic engagement of citizens, not their representation by others. In other words, rather than espousing the liberal value of a representative democracy she supported the classical republican tradition of a participatory democracy. As I hope to have pointed out, though, it is precisely active citizen engagement that I am driving at in this chapter. At the same time I feel it cannot be ignored that often, in the reality of our modern society and existing organisational structures, policy decisions themselves are made in settings where citizens themselves cannot vote. Given the complexity and busyness of modern life there simply is not the opportunity to hold a referendum every time a particular social or educational policy changes, for example. The Scots recently had a referendum on whether Scotland should become an independent country, a process that serves as a prime example of what is possible in a deliberative democracy and also of how opportunity for gatherings of the public to exchange divergent perspectives can actually bring a nation together rather than draw it apart. Yet, they did not organise a referendum a few years earlier before they decided on their new 'Curriculum for Excellence', a framework that substantially altered what was to be taught in Scottish schools and how (although surely, they consulted widely). It is for this reason that I emphasise that professionals, if they have the privilege to influence policy decisions, should do so in representation of the public, thereby becoming their spokesperson.

To some extent we can connect here also with Rawls's liberal position as discussed in Chapter 2. Rawls (1971) argued that social goods, such as liberty (or we might say now the freedom to vote), should be extended to everybody equally 'unless an unequal distribution of any or all of these primary goods is to the advantage of the least favoured' (p. 303). With Rawls we could argue that the concentration of the liberty to influence policy directly in a select minority of professionals can be justified only if the least advantaged of society (usually people with fewer capabilities to influence public debate) will be better off than would be the case if these privileges were not extended to professionals. While Arendt would maintain that this privilege should be extended to everyone, my point that in modern times a referendum in which everyone's voice is equally represented is simply not realistic each and every time should be persuasive. It is for this reason that I argue that what professionals should do is recognise that the privilege associated with having a vote carries the responsibility to represent the diverse views and positions of community members.

Second, we observe also that when professionals do make efforts to facilitate Arendtian action, and engage community members in public deliberation on the issues affecting their lives, they initiate a process that is irreversible with no guarantees of where this might lead. As I argued in Chapter 8, the outcome of debate cannot be foreseen. What follows from this observation is that professionals and other members of the community need to not only trust each other, but they must trust the democratic process itself. They need to believe in the value of public deliberation in their communities. To repeat an earlier point, although the process and outcome of the decision-making are perhaps less efficient, and perhaps even less just, than had been the case had the professional group made the decision, the value of shared decision-making lies in the strengthening of democracy itself.

Of central importance to Arendt's theory of action is her understanding of what it means to think critically, that is the relationship between the faculties of thinking and judging (Arendt, 2003).

Thinking and judgement

'Inability to think is . . .', for Arendt, 'the ever-present possibility for everybody' (2003, p. 187). Her interest in the moral implications of the capacity to think arose in response to her witnessing the trial of Adolf Eichmann in Jerusalem in 1961, leading her to pose the question: 'could the activity of thinking . . . be of such a nature that it "conditions" men [sic] against evildoing?' (Arendt, 2003, p. 160).

Arendt distinguished between three forms of thinking. The limitations and, by extension, dangers of the first form of thinking, 'abstract theorising', she recognised in Martin Heidegger's brief collaboration with the Nazi regime when he was Rector of the University of Freiburg from 1933 to 1934. As pure abstract thought is disconnected from *action*, it is, no matter how otherwise brilliant, disconnected from the world and in this sense both all too vulnerable to unrealistic romanticism and apolitical. The limitations and, by extension, dangers of the second form of thinking, 'technical reasoning', she recognised in Adolf Eichmann's horrific 'organization' of the Holocaust (see Arendt, 2003; Villa, 1996). The key problem with both pure abstract theorising and technical reasoning, Arendt realised, is that each lacks the capacity for morally astute judgements. Arendt argued that wise judgements were contingent on the capacity for a third form of reasoning, which she called 'representative thinking' (Arendt, 2003).

We witness representative thinking when we try to imagine what a situation looks like from the points of view of others with whom we share our world. Arendt comments on representative thinking this way:

> Political thought is representative. I form an opinion by considering a given issue from different viewpoints, by making present to my mind the standpoints of those who are absent; that is, I represent them . . . The more people's standpoints I have present in my mind while I am pondering a given issue, and the better I can imagine how I would feel and think if I were in their place, the stronger will be my capacity for representative thinking and the more valid my final conclusion, my opinion.
>
> (Arendt, 1968b, p. 241)

Importantly, astute judgement, in Arendt's view, depends on real encounters and confrontations with the opinions of others, thereby examining a particular issue from every possible angle. Such exchanges have achieved their goal when the issue 'is flooded and made transparent by the full light of human comprehension' (Arendt, as cited in D'Entreves, 2014, electronic source).

As we saw in Chapter 7, for Nussbaum (1998) greater understanding among people including those that are very different from ourselves can be nurtured by promoting among citizens what she calls the 'narrative imagination'. Narrative imagination refers to the empathy we feel for the situation of others or 'the ability to imagine what it is like to be in that person's place' (Nussbaum, 1998, p. 90). While it could be argued that there are some similarities between narrative imagination and representative thinking, Adami (2014), and also Benhabib (1988, 1990), emphasise that there is an important difference between evoking emotions, such as empathy and compassion through narrative imagination, and representative thinking as understood by Arendt (see also Silvane Busani, 2016). While thinking representatively means to bring to one's awareness the standpoint of the other, this representation of the other's perspective is not based on empathy (that is, we do not have to agree with it to represent it to ourselves in our minds).

And yet, something like the emotion of empathy is clearly important in public deliberation. Benhabib (1988) argues in reference to Arendt's notion of representative thinking that 'The cultivation of one's moral imagination flourishes in such a culture in which the self-centered perspective of the individual is constantly challenged by the multiplicity and diversity of perspectives that con-stitute public life' (p. 48). The feeling of friendship and solidarity, which are an extension of the sympathy and affection we naturally feel towards those we are close to, she claims,

> results precisely through the extension of our moral and political imagination . . . through the actual confrontation in public life with the point of view of those who are otherwise strangers to us, but who become known to us through their public presence as voices and perspectives we have to take into account.
>
> (p. 47)

Nussbaum (1998) sees the path to global citizenship, which is grounded in respect for diversity and a sense of social interdependence, in the furthering of emotions such as empathy and compassion through reading particular literature that allows us to learn *about others*. By contrast, both Adami (2014) and Benhabib (1988) would argue that respect for diversity is promoted through individual life narratives created in the course of participation in action, that is as people react to one another. According to this interpretation action *is* narrative expressed in deed and speech. It is through participation in the public sphere that we learn not *about the other* but learn *in relations* through narrative (Adami, 2014).

Arendt (1982) comments that in representative thinking we 'think with an enlarged mentality' and train our 'imagination to go visiting' (p. 43). Professionals and other citizens engage in representative thinking when they make efforts to imagine what a given situation looks like from the points of view of others with whom they share a common world. It both underpins and enables public deliberation, and thus *action*. Albert Dzur, I suggest, has representative thinking in mind, without calling it such, when he writes:

> [Democratic professionals] listen carefully to those outside their walls . . . in order to . . . encourage co-ownership of problems previously seen as beyond the laypeople's ability or realm of responsibility, and seek out opportunities for collaborative work.
>
> (Dzur, 2013, electronic source)

Elsewhere he argues that in order to inform public debate, professionals need to understand the kind of moral reasoning the public engages in when confronting ethical questions related to social or environmental issues that concern them (Dzur, 2008). In other words, we need to know how issues appear and are processed from the public's perspective.

Arendt emphasised that action includes both 'representative thinking' and 'judging'. Judging is, of course, not altogether independent of (representative) thinking, but is seen to follow from it. As Nixon (2012) explains: 'To judge is to engage in rational public dialogue, deliberating with others with whom I must finally come to an agreement and decision' (p. 58). What does all this mean for practitioners working in professional contexts?

When professional practice takes on the form of facilitating and participating in Arendtian *action*, practitioners evidently do not just apply their knowledge and skills in a technical sense (although they of course contribute their expertise), let alone publicise material based on abstract theories which bear little connection to the real situations people in the community find themselves in. Think of the typical scientists or scholars in the university who write articles mainly for their own professional group within the academy rather than to help the public explore and understand issues in depth and from a variety of perspectives. Instead, professionals engaged in Arendtian action facilitate and become engaged in public deliberation, thereby inviting, indeed encouraging, members of their community to make their respective perspectives known and to understand themselves likewise as civic agents capable of influencing the debate. As professionals seek solutions collaboratively with other members of the community, and provide a space for different voices to be heard, they engage in both representative thinking and judging. The facilitation of public deliberation serves to ensure not only that different perspectives are being considered but also that the community gains insight into the reasons why certain (policy or other) decisions are made. The potentialities of forgiving and promising, so crucial for helping us deal with the unpredictability and irreversibility of *action*, are vital for sustaining the necessary level of trust to engage in public deliberation.

In summary, when professional practice takes on the form of *action*, practitioners recognise the conditions of 'natality' and 'plurality' of our communities and participate with other community members in democratic discussions around how best to frame and address concerns affecting society's welfare. As facilitators of action, they become initiators and facilitators of community education and enablers of democracy.

Having argued earlier in this chapter that there is a certain affinity between Dewey and Arendt, I would like to, in the final section, address the question of whether Hannah Arendt's political theory of 'action' locates her firmly into any one political, let alone educational, tradition.

Categorising Arendt?

Arendt scholars tend to agree that she is not easily placed into any one existing tradition. Arendt's uniqueness lies in her sharing some of the assumptions underpinning certain traditions (such as liberalism, republicanism, communitarianism, progressivism, or Marxism) but departing from other assumptions that are also fundamental to the tradition in question but in her view problematic. So for example, as already mentioned, while Arendt was not anti-liberal, she was not a supporter of the liberal ideal of a representative democracy. Yet, while her values seem (classical) republican she certainly did not approve of the exclusion of many groups of society (e.g., women, slaves, etc.) from public deliberation in the ancient Greek assembly or agora. As well, while she strongly believed in civic participation she did not aim for people to hold a shared conception of the good, indicating both her appreciation for, yet also digression from, communitarianism. We already noted some of her similarities to and differences from Dewey, although I refer the interested reader to Weiss (2011) for a more in-depth discussion.

The notion of renewing the world that is at the centre of Arendt's theory of action offers the potential for social transformation. Yet, to what extent is it justified to consider Arendt a Marxist? As became evident in the biographical note on Arendt, she clearly had Marxist tendencies, and in an article written two years after Arendt's death, Habermas (1977) acknowledges that her 'concept of praxis is more Marxist than Aristotelian' (p. 13). However, Habermas's article is not simply an analysis but also a critique of Arendt's notion of *action* and it offers some clues as to why she cannot be located firmly within the Marxist tradition.

In defending his own comprehensive theory of rationality (later culminating in his theory of communicative action (Habermas, 1984)) over Arendt's views, Habermas argues that despite Arendt's interest in emancipation, and even the beginnings of a new political order through collective freedom by which power 'springs up between men [sic] when they act together and vanishes the moment they disperse' (Arendt, 1958, p. 200), her problem was that she remained stuck in an antiquated Aristotelian conceptualisation of knowledge separating praxis from both purpose-rational knowledge and abstract theory. Earlier in the discussion we saw that Arendt believed that through public deliberation based on representative thinking and the idea of *promising*, power is generated in the form of a social contract among equal partners placing them under mutual obligations. Habermas (1977) considers this contract view to be unsatisfactory as a basis for power, arguing instead that praxis itself needs to be infused with a comprehensive rationality, manifested in critical rational discourse, whereby validity claims underlying convictions or assertions can be subjected to critical scrutiny. It is through this process of critical discourse, assuming a set of ideal speech conditions, that structural violence (see Chapter 6) could be revealed.

According to this analysis of Arendt through the lens of Habermas's theory of communicative action, it would indeed appear that Arendt's concept of action and power does not neatly fit within critical theory. I add that a further reason why one would not put Arendt in the critical tradition is that Arendt's notion of freedom does not include a class analysis and thus Arendtian *action* is ultimately not about revolutionary class struggle.

Final comments

Given the above observations it should be obvious that Arendt is also not easily located within a particular educational tradition (e.g., liberal education, progressive education or Marxist/critical education, the latter aimed at social reform). She seems to tick all three boxes, while surely there are strong Marxist undertones in her work. Importantly, though, we do not need to assign a label to

Arendt to recognise that her emphasis on civic engagement resonates with approaches to higher education that encourage students to reflect on who they are, who they want to become and how they can make the world a better and fairer place. It also resonates with approaches that bring students in dialogue, not only with each other in the security of their classrooms but also with other members of their wider communities, about how to solve important issues of public concern. Participation of professionals, and other citizens, in Arendtian action encourages (and requires) *authenticity*. It encourages and requires a capacity to take risks, in a world characterised by 'uncertainty', 'unpredictability', 'challengeability' and 'contestability'; it encourages and requires an identity constructed around purposes of personal and public value; and it encourages and requires the opportunity to enact this identity in practice.

In the next chapter I shall consider the implications of Arendt's theory of action for higher education pedagogies.

Chapter 10

Imagining action-oriented pedagogies

Introduction

Arendt's concept of '*action*' emphasises free and spontaneous deliberation among citizens on issues of common concern whereby they try to persuade one another of their views with the purpose of coming to a shared understanding and decision. It is this particular notion of '*action*' that is at the centre of this chapter. If professionals are to become facilitators of action, that is of public spaces where citizens can gather to engage in public deliberation on important matters affecting their communities, and thus become enablers of democracy, what might this look like in concrete terms? And importantly, what are the implications for a university pedagogy that would prepare students on professional programmes to become facilitators of such community engagement? I shall suggest here that this pedagogy likewise would be guided by Arendtian action, involving students in precisely those processes they are meant to facilitate as practising democratic professionals upon graduation.

Such pedagogical practices are presently not widespread within the academy. Dzur (2008) comments that: 'those trained for professions currently have minimal instruction in the democratic consequences of their professional domain' (p. 132). He adds that while there are ethics courses offered as part of professional education programmes, discussions with students about the value of lay participation in decision-making and task sharing are rarely observed. This is not surprising given that most programme directors, and their colleagues teaching on the programme, view the principal contribution their profession makes to society as providing an efficient and useful service (that is doing things *for* the public), rather than as facilitating public understanding and practical abilities by stimulating open debate around decisions important to the public, but typically made by professionals on their behalf (doing things *with* the public). This is to say that professionals, including those teaching on professional programmes within the academy, often do not recognise or think much about the political potential of their profession. However, there are two further issues that work against fostering among academics and students a professional identity that is vested in democratic interests. The first is the challenge that a higher education pedagogy guided by

Arendtian action presents to the dominant perspective that sees the purpose of professional education in meeting employers' needs (Lucas, Spencer & Claxton, 2012). The second can be found in the assessment procedures that both faculty and students within the academy are subject to. In addressing the first point, I shall now first provide a few brief observations on what we typically mean by preparing people for work and contrast this prevailing conception of professional education with the one that guided workers' education in the early twentieth century. I then explore how these two different conceptions compare to the idea of democratic professionalism and/or Arendtian action discussed in the previous chapters. In addressing the second point, my emphasis will be on the priorities of government and how these can clash with the intent of academics to infuse their practice with a truly democratic spirit. Finally I discuss what a pedagogy oriented towards Arendtian action might look like.

Professional education

Professional education is rarely discussed in reference to early workers' education; however, such a comparative approach is quite enlightening in that it points to two radically different stances taken towards what it means to educate people for 'work'.

Early workers' education, at the beginning of the twentieth century, was characterised by strong linkages between educating for work, democracy, and social activism. Of course, what was meant by 'social activism' varied greatly. While the radical socialist initiatives were aimed at infusing worker education at the point of production with a Marxist agenda so as to equip them with the intellectual tools necessary to lead the anticipated political revolution (e.g., Crowther & Martin, 2010), the liberal movements occurring at the same time, such as those organised by the Workers' Educational Association in England, were aimed at promoting higher education of working people, and educating workers to contribute to democracy (e.g., Alfred, 2001; Elsey, 2001) and perhaps become social leaders. While Albert Mansbridge (1876–1952), an English pioneer of adult education, believed workers' participation in democracy could be achieved through personal cultivation facilitated through taught courses that would enlighten the mind (Alfred, 2001), his contemporary and colleague Richard Henry Tawney (1880–1962) added that the way to working-class power lay also in political education as provided through courses in political theory and economic history (Elsey, 2001).

Vocational education's concern with democracy and social activism, of either liberal or Marxist inclinations, weakened over time and actually, as some readers quite rightly will want to point out, was never very strong in university-based professional education. With the rise of the 'knowledge economy' (UNESCO, 2005), in particular, professional education (broadly conceived here as comprising the preparation for occupations ranging from those often referred to as 'vocations' to so-called 'professions') has come to mean increasingly the acquisition of knowledge and skills leading to employability, an ideology that is very different from either the liberal or the radical traditions that once characterised early workers' education initiatives.

Professional education in universities is often grounded in an instrumental rationality focused on ensuring that programme participants acquire the knowledge and skills necessary to perform well on the job, and by extension, on meeting the needs of their future employers. To an extent, one might like to point out, this is also how it should be; after all professions offer services that are fundamental to society's well-being by contributing to important public goods such as education, health, justice, safety, housing, access to information, the beauty and life-sustaining forces of the ecological environment, and so forth. University-based professional programmes then need to prepare individuals to perform services that contribute to these important public goods and ensure they are performed well. However, performing well, or doing good work, is not just a matter of performing at a certain level of technical proficiency but has ethical and social dimensions. And yet, professional education often seems little concerned with the public and political value of the work professionals do, let alone the personal meaning professionals themselves find in their work.

Harry Boyte (2004) argues that one significant challenge to democratic professionalism is rooted in how professionals are prepared for practice, specifically in how the relationships between professionals and society are portrayed. He observes:

> . . . in their normal training, professionals learn to see ordinary citizens in a particular fashion that greatly limits such interactions – as needy, victimized, and requiring rescue by educated elites . . . But changing professional practices and cultures is difficult, because the process entails changing identities and practices to make them more public.
>
> (p. 113)

Boyte suggests that the academy needs to pay greater attention to the professional identities it promotes in graduates and how they conceive of their role in society. Early workers' education was based on the assumption that workers would not just see themselves as applying a skill that they acquired to a set task but that their education would enable them to reflect on life and society more broadly and become active participants in their community, thereby contributing, perhaps even fostering, democracy. Civic professionalism, as conceptualised by Boyte (2004), and democratic professionalism as described by Dzur (2008), reconnect to some extent with this early twentieth-century ideal.

In Chapter 8 we saw that Boyte and Fretz (2012) encourage academics and students to engage with the community as equals, to infuse their practice with a more robust democratic orientation, and to make their work public in multiple ways. On one level then, recent government calls emphasising the need for academics to become more strongly engaged in knowledge exchange activities should be welcomed. However, steps undertaken by academics towards enacting a more democratic professional practice are associated with considerable challenges they confront from within the academy; challenges, as we shall see momentarily, that are linked to academic practices and cultures, which in turn are not unaffected by the wider policy context in which higher education institutions operate.

Challenges for academics and students

At first sight the call for greater knowledge exchange chimes well with the democratic orientation proposed by Boyte and Fretz (2010, 2012). However, the term knowledge exchange is open to more than one interpretation. The Higher Education Funding Council for England (HEFCE), for instance, chooses to define knowledge exchange this way:

> HEIs' engagement with businesses, public and third sector services, the community and wider public. It includes the transferring or exchanging of knowledge *with the aim of delivering external impact, such as improving products, services and profitability.*
>
> (www.hefce.ac.uk/glossary/, emphasis added)

Research Councils UK defines research impact consequently as 'the demonstrable contribution that excellent research makes to society and the economy'. It is seen to: 'embrace all the diverse ways that research-related skills benefit individuals, organisations and nations'. These include:

- fostering global economic performance, and specifically the economic competitiveness of the United Kingdom;
- increasing the effectiveness of public services and policy;
- enhancing quality of life, health and creative output.

> (www.esrc.ac.uk/funding-and-guidance/impact-toolkit/
> what-how-and-why/what-is-research-impact.aspx)

Although these statements leave no doubt that research is to benefit society, a strong emphasis on 'improving products, services and profitability' (HEFCE, see above) conveys a particular understanding of what is deemed beneficial. One gets little sense from the above statements that the impact government is after is a strengthening of critical debate in the public sphere. Indeed, in light of the larger policy context discussed in Chapters 1 and 2, we might argue that in a neoliberal environment the public sphere where critical engagement could happen is of no concern; if anything it is seen as a threat to the established order (Giroux, 2014). Projects that seek impact on a more political level in our communities are thus presently little valued by government, leading the Funding and Research councils to value *particular kinds* of impact.

The actual criteria against which faculty are assessed within the academy, which typically include level of external research income, number of articles published in top-tier journals, and more recently evidence of international partnerships, also are not conducive to having a strong impact on our local communities through genuine community engagement work. Woodrow Presley (2012) argued that the culture of the academy at present 'Will not notice or value community-based research until and unless it is published in a first-tier, peer reviewed journal' (p. 133).

At one institution in the UK that I'm especially familiar with, it was precisely those colleagues who were the most concerned with civic democratic engagement in their communities, and whose work had the greatest impact by involving citizens in participatory decision-making, who were the least recognised in the Research Assessment Exercise. For readers unfamiliar with the UK system I should briefly explain that the Research Assessment Exercise (RAE) is a highly competitive process of assessment of departmental research 'quality' led by the UK government. What is determined through the RAE (recently renamed the REF), on the basis of submissions of research output (by department) that are then assessed by nation-wide panels of experts, is direct institutional (departmental) operating funding for several years. Given that the stakes are this high, the REF is widely considered to be the most influential initiative in UK higher education policy. The REF takes place every six years, but institutions start preparing for the next REF cycle as soon as their scores from the latest one have been made public. Nothing, therefore, drives higher education research in the UK as strongly as the REF, and it does so incessantly. Might Arendt (1958) have considered this a prime example of the triumph of *labour* over *action*?

My colleagues' community-engaged scholarship was not valued since their associated publications were not considered to qualify as 'research' which, for the purposes of the REF, is defined as:

> a process of investigation leading to new insights, effectively shared . . . work of direct relevance to the needs of commerce, industry, and to the public and voluntary sectors . . . that is published, disseminated or made publicly available *in the form of assessable research outputs*, and confidential reports.
>
> (UK Government, 2011, p. 48, emphasis added)

Thus community-engaged work tends to be valued only if the associated scholarship is published in traditional academic journals, not through blog posts, films, websites, or articles in practitioner-oriented magazines. The Carnegie Foundation for the Advancement of Teaching in the United States recognised this dilemma many years ago when it introduced a four-faceted model of scholarship, including next to the scholarship of discovery also the scholarship of teaching, the scholarship of integration and the scholarship of application (Boyer, 1990), the latter eventually renamed the scholarship of engagement (Boyer, 1996). Boyer explained what he meant by the scholarship of engagement:

The scholarship of engagement means connecting the rich resources of the university to our most pressing social, civic and ethical problems, to our children, to our schools, to our teachers and to our cities . . . But at a deeper level it also means creating a special climate in which the academic and civic cultures communicate more continuously and more creatively with each other . . . enriching the quality of life for all of us.

(Boyer, 1996, pp. 19–20)

However, twenty years on, rewarding the scholarship of engagement remains a challenge also in the US (Saltmarsh, Wooding & McLellan, 2014; Woodrow Presley, 2012). What counts at present is still publications in the '*The Sacred Journal of REFable Research*' (or '*The Sacred Journal of the Scholarship of Discovery*'). The resulting problem is twofold. First, the impact of community-engaged work is not getting any more profound as a result of publishing the work in high-profile journals (the reason why many colleagues who are close to retirement decide to 'not play the game' (as they put it) and consider leaving early). Second, early and mid-career faculty are socialised into (or feel forced to adopt) a conception of scholarship that, while increasingly emphasising external impact and knowledge exchange, is not actually geared towards impact on wider public debate and the public's own critical inquiry into social issues.

Having identified how the university's policy context and, by extension, institutional assessment criteria (for tenure and promotion) present challenges for academics wishing to practise their profession as democratic professionals or 'public intellectuals', we now also should ask whether we can observe a parallel challenge with regards to students. Community-based learning opportunities are becoming more and more common on our campuses (e.g., Jacoby, 1996; Eyler & Giles, 1999; Peters, 2004; Taylor, 2014). However, on most programmes they tend to be voluntary and there is no expectation that all students will have had a community-based learning experience by the time they graduate. Perhaps more importantly, students graduating from our universities are typically examined not on how well they engaged with their communities but on how well they know the academic content of their field, and how well they can apply this knowledge to solve problems. Thus in the students' eyes, what actually counts, or what is perceived to be involved in doing well on the programme, and by extension being 'a good professional', is knowing your content and being able to solve problems. To be clear, knowing your content and being able to solve problems is important, but surely it is not all that we hope students will gain from community-based learning activities.

Professional programmes, typically, have an applied component, either incorporated into their regular (academic) study period at university and/or immediately following it. Student teachers usually complete fairly extensive field experiences in schools as part of their higher education, doctors complete a practicum in a hospital or private practice, and, at least on some journalism programmes, students go on placements with a newspaper or broadcasting station; and we usually find similar requirements in the curricula of social work, nursing, law, engineering, etc. The issue of concern is how these field experiences (or practical/applied components of the curriculum) are conceptualised. In most cases field experiences are conceived of as an opportunity for students to apply their academic knowledge in a concrete practical setting (one directly related to their future profession). Such concrete experiences are essential as a lot of professional knowledge is experiential and tacit in nature, and can only be acquired over time in real practical settings (e.g., Eraut, 1994). Taken on their own, though, in the context of an otherwise conservative professional education curriculum based on the philosophy of providing a useful service for others, such professional field experiences contribute little by way of enhancing students' democratic spirit, let alone the democratic spirit of the members of the communities their work is directed at. Compare such typical field experiences to the suggestions Haas (2000) made in the context of journalism education that were featured in Chapter 8. My point is that few of these experiences encourage students to view their clients as equals and to promote task sharing, public understanding and participatory democratic decision-making.

The purpose of this discussion was to show that the way both faculty and students are assessed within the university is counterproductive to promoting professional identities that are civic-minded and democratic. These contextual realities of higher education also have implications for the curricula and pedagogies we see employed on professional programmes, and thus the culture into which students become socialised.

In Chapter 8, I argued that when professionals become enablers of democracy by facilitating opportunities for the public to become engaged in decision-making around important issues in their community, this could be conceived of as them enabling a type of informal community education. Perhaps it requires clarifying that not all activities we see included today under the general umbrella of 'community education' are characterised by a democratic spirit or purpose, a reality that some commentators have highlighted as a crisis in community education brought about by the neoliberal policy context (e.g., Martin, 2006, 2008; Shaw, 2008). Given this crisis, it may be more accurate to say that all professionals, including those who are more oriented towards doing things *for* others than doing things *with* others, are involved in facilitating some type of 'community education'. Of note, though, is that the 'education' many thus support is likely to have a disabling effect, in the sense discussed by Illich and colleagues. In his own essay in his edited book Illich (1977) argued that we need to consider:

> the role that a new kind of professional elite plays in validating the worldwide religion that promotes impoverishing greed. It is therefore necessary that we clearly understand: 1) the nature of professional dominance, 2) the effects of professional establishment, 3) the characteristics of imputed needs and 4) the illusions that have enslaved us to professional management.
>
> (p. 15)

What the community learns from 'disabling professionals' (i.e., what they take away from their 'education') is that decisions on important matters are best left to professionals. My point about *democratic* professionals is that they are motivated to promote social activism and public deliberation among citizens; hence the type of community education *democratic professionals* facilitate is aimed at strengthening the public sphere and democracy.

Biesta (2012) recently proposed that community education can be conceived of in terms of three types of 'public pedagogy', which he chooses to call a pedagogy *for* the public, a pedagogy *of* the public, and a pedagogy that generates '*space through which freedom can appear*' (p. 683). The third type of community education, or 'public pedagogy', he argues, is defined by 'the enactment of a concern for the public quality of human togetherness' (Biesta, 2012, p. 683). In formulating the third type of public pedagogy, Biesta draws directly on Hannah Arendt's theory of action. When people gather publicly, we saw in the previous chapter, the potential of deliberation presents itself, and thus the potential for something new to begin is given.

Before I go any further in discussing Biesta's typology I should be clear about three points. First, in his article Biesta does not relate the three pedagogies to professional practice and he is also not concerned at all with higher education pedagogies. Second, when using the term 'pedagogy' he does not employ it in the narrow sense of teaching, learning and assessment strategies. The pedagogies he recognises in particular forms of community education are philosophies, or we might say broad approaches to practice supported by certain assumptions about the purposes of education. In the section that follows, I shall extrapolate from Biesta's own discussion and show how the 'pedagogies' of community education he identifies could play out in the lives of professionals, and how they might be modelled in higher education programmes that prepare future professionals for practice, thereby giving students first-hand experience of it. Third, I will deviate a little from Biesta's own conclusions as well as an interpretation of Biesta's typology I proposed in a recent article (Kreber, 2015). I now introduce the three public pedagogies in turn.

Public pedagogies

A pedagogy for the public

This type might be the most common. It is informed by the service ethic of doing things *for* others. When adapted to the higher education context, such a pedagogy might be modelled by universities opening their doors to the public and becoming places where students and educators on professional programmes meet together with members of their community and share their expertise with the public. In concrete terms this can be observed when students are engaged in (a type of) service learning whereby they offer their help or advice to the community. Often (but not always) in this scenario it is the community (or some community-based organisation) that identified the issue to be addressed. Once identified, this issue is handed over to the university unit responsible for organising the service learning experience of students, which, in turn, sends students out into the field. A definition of service learning emphasising seeking to achieve real objectives *for the community* (e.g., Eyler & Giles, 1999) might overlap with this first type of community education. Eyler and Giles (1999) make excellent suggestions for how a sense of citizenship can be promoted among students through engagement in service learning, but note that it is the *students'* sense of being or becoming active citizens that is the focus here, and how the *students'* new understanding of themselves and their activities can serve the community.

A pedagogy of the public

This pedagogy is in line with Boyte and Fretz's (2010, 2012) and Dzur's (2004, 2008) philosophy of doing things *with* rather than only *for* the public and thus is aimed at strengthening the public's agency. In this second type of public pedagogy, or second type of community education, professionals will share their expertise, but at the same time recognise the expertise of citizens and be careful not to deny community members the opportunity to act as civic agents. As part of the community education they facilitate, professionals might also assist in organising events that will bring people together in truly collaborative work and public deliberation on issues identified as common concerns. Applied to higher education, it might mean that universities invite members of the public to organised events where they can participate in open discussions of important issues of interest to the community. Events such as these may evolve into genuine debates where the voices of the community count as much as the voices of academics (often this is not the case), indeed where faculty teaching on professional programmes and future professionals (students) understand themselves as citizens and thus members of their broader community, and where decisions on how to address a particular issue of public concern are arrived at collaboratively with other members of that community. Through this public pedagogy real opportunities arise for community members to enact their freedom. Over the past several years some universities have begun to do some of this; however, such forms of engagement with the public are presently not core elements of professional curricula.

We can also observe this type 2 pedagogy when university service learning takes on the form of a strongly collaborative community project, facilitated by the university but organised or developed by the community itself. Perhaps Jacoby's (1996) notion of service learning overlaps with this second type. The author writes:

> Service learning is a form of experiential learning in which students engage in activities that address human and community needs . . . the human and community needs that service learning addresses are those needs that are *defined by the community.*
>
> (Jacoby, 1996, p. 5, emphasis in original)

Eyler and Giles (1999) also agree with this, commenting that engagement in service learning initiatives led to students feeling a stronger connection to their community and that this was enhanced when 'the community had a voice in shaping the service activities' (p. 158). Earlier I made the point that when communities identify their own issues but these ultimately are resolved by others ('experts' or students that are called in), the activity qualifies as the first type of public pedagogy (a pedagogy *for* the public). Important to Biesta's second type of public pedagogy (a pedagogy *of* the public) is that community education would meet the criteria of task sharing which features prominently also in Dzur's (2004, 2008) notion of democratic professionalism. This means that the community would not only define its needs but would have an equal say in how these might be addressed and what might qualify as the best solution.

The extent to which the projects discussed in Jacoby (1996) and Eyler and Giles (1999) fit into either one of these two types of public pedagogy is a little unclear. Both books highlight that meaningful service learning addresses the needs identified by the community. Yet I hope to have demonstrated also the significant difference between communities identifying their needs but having the solution provided by someone else and communities deciding for themselves how best to address their needs with some university support. Strand et al. (2003) proposed several principles of successful campus–community research partnerships, including agreeing on goals and strategies together as well as sharing power with the community. Unama'ki College (2016) at Cape Breton University recently released a strategy document highlighting research into issues relevant to aboriginal communities led by the aboriginal communities themselves as a key pillar of its activities. This idea of genuinely community-*led* research goes beyond doing research *for* the community enabling greater agency on the part of the community itself.

It is of interest as well that Eyler and Giles (1999, p. 103) make reference to Arendt's notion of action, suggesting that political (or Arendtian) action is promoted through service learning. However, the focus of their discussion is on the political action of *students* during service learning; there is no explicit mention that through service learning not only the students but ordinary citizens (members of the larger community) become involved in political action. The view that one of the important benefits of service learning is to promote the civic engagement of students is shared by a wide range of academics writing on service learning, as illustrated by the following quotation:

> One of the key elements that distinguishes service-learning from other types of experiential learning (e.g., conducting research) and community-based learning (e.g., internships, practica) is that service-learning intentionally identifies *the civic growth of students* fostered through structured reflection and meaningful experiences within community organizations (Ash & Clayton, 2009; Battistoni, 2002; Bringle & Hatcher, 1995, 2002, 2009).
>
> (Steinberg, Hatcher & Bringle, 2011, p. 19, emphasis added)

While I agree with the authors that service learning is valuable because it has been shown to have positive effects on students, and the students' work often addresses an issue identified as a need in the community, I am arguing that university-based service learning can go beyond this as it becomes oriented towards assisting the community to organise itself and find solutions to its own problems. It is this type of service learning that can help strengthen the public sphere and ultimately democracy. Put differently, university-based service learning can facilitate political action in citizens themselves.

In the previous chapter I connected Arendtian action with Dzur's notion of democratic professionalism. I should be clear though that Dzur (2004, 2008) means more by democratic professionalism than the facilitation of public debate. A community-based practice of type 2, where community members and professionals actually work together, would also be an example of task sharing (the idea Dzur takes from Alexis de Tocqueville); and, given that the community-based practice would involve mutual information sharing and exchange of opinions on all issues relevant to the project (e.g., what the project is meant to achieve, how it is to be achieved, etc.), it would also be a matter of facilitating public understanding (the idea Dzur takes from Dewey). This latter idea, as I demonstrated in the previous chapter, chimes well with Arendt's notion of action as freedom through public deliberation. Thus, when Biesta's typology of three public pedagogies is applied to university-based professional education, it is his type 2 ('a pedagogy *of* the public') that allows members of the community to participate in Arendtian action. It is for this reason that, in the context of university-based professional education, Biesta's type 2 and 3 public pedagogies actually merge into one. Having said this, I now nonetheless want to consider how a more intense form of engagement in Arendtian action might be achieved through professional education, building specifically on Biesta's type 3 pedagogy.

A pedagogy that generates 'space through which freedom can appear'

Biesta (2012) considers the third type of public pedagogy as separate from type 2. He argues that we can witness the third type of public pedagogy being enacted when true opportunities are created for public deliberation. It is a public pedagogy that offers the space for something new to be initiated through the interactions it encourages with people who quite naturally will hold different perspectives on issues. It thereby recognises both 'plurality' *and* 'natality'. The argument he is making is that this third type of pedagogy cannot be planned in the same way that pedagogies *for* the public (type 1) or pedagogies *of* the public (type 2) might be planned in advance. It either happens or it doesn't, but importantly the space or opportunity for something to happen is provided. The key issue here is that action for Arendt is spontaneous. It is up to the actors or citizens themselves, given the opportunity, to seize the moment and do something, or simply put, 'to act'.

Biesta's distinction between 'the community organising itself', for example, for the purpose of building a new school (type 2), and 'the community gathering to deliberate or debate particular issues which are of importance to them' (type 3) makes sense. Yet, as already argued, the distinction between the two blurs in situations where we are concerned with preparing students for democratic professionalism, because deliberations are already part of type 2 pedagogy.

Nonetheless, we can still identify a subtle difference between types 2 and 3 in the context of professional practice and education. Professionals practising the third type of public pedagogy go beyond collaborating with the community; they, additionally, offer opportunities for the public to make their views known, be heard and genuinely engaged with *when it was not known in advance that it would happen*. Biesta's type 3 public pedagogy is the most difficult to envisage for the context of higher education.

Imagine occasionally keeping classrooms open for members of the public to simply drop in for individual classes taught on professional programmes and contribute at any time (perhaps supported by new technologies). Or imagine sporadically holding regular classes in public places such as museums, schools, parks, community halls, thereby inviting members of the public to spontaneously participate if they wish. It is the unplanned nature of the interactions that might ensue from such opportunities (the class may just run as usual with no one joining in, but members of the public *might* become involved and share their particular views on the topic) which allows for something new to be created. I am not suggesting that classes themselves should be unplanned. To the contrary, outlines of courses should be made available publicly, perhaps through local newspapers and radio channels, to inform the public about which issues are likely to be addressed in a given class on a certain day; what is unplanned, and cannot be foreseen with certainty, is what might happen as a result of such opportunities for public engagement (what concerns might be raised, what perspectives might be shared, what insights might be gained, etc.). Imagine groups of students studying a particular issue of public concern, instead of presenting it to their classmates, writing a short article about it in the local paper (or telling their story over the course of a full month) thereby inviting the public to respond. Imagine a class being broadcast on local radio with twenty-minute breaks during which the public can call in to raise questions or offer opinions that are then discussed. Imagine students and teaching staff organising a conference that is open to the public where the students present their work. It would be critical that teachers lead on this as it requires considerable courage to put one's opinions forward in this way and engage in public discussion with members of one's community. Importantly, though, democratic professionalism, and Arendtian action, is about the community itself becoming involved. It is about the community being granted a voice. Further examples of how a type 3 pedagogy might be modelled and practised in higher education can be identified by letting our ideas flow freely regardless of how wild and unrealistic they might initially appear. While type 3 pedagogies are clearly valuable, at present community-based learning activities that qualify as type

2 pedagogy stand a greater chance to become more widely practised in higher education. Type 2 pedagogy might involve community groups, university teachers and students on professional programmes working together on timely issues, setting up a public discussion forum, publishing their joint report in a newspaper, organising a joint conference, making a joint film, etc. These are all real possibilities and it is in this spirit that I interpret the work of Strand et al. (2003) who emphasise in their discussion of community-based research partnerships in higher education the importance of working with and supporting community organisations and a 'commitment to social action and social change in the interest of advancing social justice' (p. 13).

The proposal outlined in this chapter is unorthodox as well as risky. Yet, it is through such participatory practices that educators can model the virtues of courage and imagination so crucial for Arendtian *action* and professional practice. By participating in public pedagogies, especially those of types 2 and 3, students learn what it takes to be open to community concerns and develop the disposition to become facilitators of action in their own professional practice.

Final comments

I proposed that professional practice, appropriately conceived, is not limited to rendering important services to a standard of technical proficiency. While doing good work in terms of technical proficiency is important, I argued that professional practice, ideally, also involves the professional's facilitation of, and engagement in, Arendtian *action*. Bridges were identified between community education and professional education in two ways. The argument, on the first level, has been that in so far as professional practice involves Arendtian *action*, professionals are enablers of democracy, and hence facilitators of informal democratic community education (and I further argued that this constitutes a form of social activism). On the second level I argued that such an understanding of professional practice has important implications for the formal professional education taking place in our universities. Specifically, I proposed that the public pedagogies of community education, especially of types 2 and 3 (Biesta, 2012), should be modelled on university programmes preparing future professionals for practice.

The proposition that all professional practices should include a civic or political element may not be accepted by everybody. Some will straightaway dismiss the idea as absurd, others will comment that it is neither what students want nor what employers expect of professional education, and again others might argue that while they agree that a civic or democratic spirit should inform professional practices there is simply not enough space in the syllabus to teach students all the technical expertise they need and also encourage them to develop an identity as civic agents, let alone facilitate such agency in others. My proposal to conceptualise professional practice as the facilitation of Arendtian *action*, and model this during professional education, therefore, will be met with a good degree of scepticism and, in some corners, outright opposition.

Nonetheless, I believe it is both possible and necessary to transform university professional education to play its role in promoting a civic spirit and the enactment of a truly democratic professionalism, and thereby contribute to a flourishing deliberative democracy. Fortunately positive examples in the right direction already exist especially for the higher education sector (e.g., Haas, 2000; Sullivan & Rosin, 2008). Yet, as English and Mayo (2012) concluded, 'different needs and interests have to be reconciled for a more effective critical engagement with the world of work' (p. 93).

The final chapter now takes a broader view, connecting with the other themes addressed in this book to develop a vision of university-based professional education that is transformative of graduates/professionals, pedagogies, professional practices and the world we share with others.

Chapter 11

Nurturing authentic professional identities

Introduction

It is the people graduating with good degrees from our best colleges and universities 'that are leading us down the current unhealthy, inequitable, and unsustainable path', Cortese (2003, p. 17) wrote more than a decade ago. To counter this disturbing trend it is vital that higher education institutions put opportunities in place that allow students to develop 'the awareness, knowledge, skills and values needed to create a just and sustainable future' (Cortese, 2003, p. 17). Universities then are more than knowledge factories (Aronowitz, 2000) whose ultimate purpose it is to produce skilled workers to fulfil predetermined roles in society. While playing an important role in preparing students for the world of work, universities are still places where students can become educated in a broader sense, where they can grow intellectually and personally, recognise their place in their communities and where some even identify a new purpose in life. No matter what school or faculty we are based in, we are preparing students to fulfil adult roles as citizens and 'workers'. The fundamental disposition and two qualities (or values) that were identified in Chapter 3 as core, and 'ideal', educational outcomes, therefore, are proposed as core outcomes for any graduate. *Openness to experience*, risk and uncertainty (linked to the existential dimension of authenticity), a *moral commitment* to stand up for and help create a fairer world, based on an awareness of who is and who is not served by the status quo, and by what mechanisms of power (linked to the critical dimension of authenticity), and *responsible engagement* with our local and global communities (linked to the communitarian dimension of authenticity), are attributes that are desirable in every graduate. They are desirable as they bolster the overarching professional capability of civic-mindedness, which comes about through the interplay of self-cultivation of the practitioner and his or her responsiveness to the needs of others, and they are developed, as was argued in Chapters 6 and 7, through relevant types of knowledge and reasoning as well as appropriate political emotions. Professional education, then, too, is more than the provision of training in a certain body of domain-specific knowledge and technical skills. Indeed, more and more educators believe that what is important given the challenges of our times is that universities graduate people who appreciate the public value of their work, have learned to distinguish between practices that are fair and sustainable and those that are not, and have developed the disposition to work towards a fairer and more sustainable world (e.g., Colby et al., 2003).

Promoting civic democratic professionalism through education

What then does it mean to be civic-minded? It means being oriented towards the needs of the community, but it goes beyond that. It involves recognising that the best service to be rendered is often tied to creating genuine opportunities for community empowerment. For professionals this implies not simply making informed decisions *for* others, but to serve a larger purpose that includes working *with* others thereby strengthening democracy and social justice. It was further argued in this book that to be civic-minded is not just a matter of commitment to serving the needs of others but hinges on practitioners also being self-cultivating. Self-cultivation is associated with recognising and furthering one's fundamental need for growth or self-actualisation (see Chapter 5). While self-cultivation is made possible by being open to experience (as well as critical reflection and recognition of social interdependence) I argued that it can be fostered also through engagement in the professional practice itself. As practitioners are afforded opportunities to develop the virtue of civic-mindedness, or the professional capabilities they need to make the world a better place (such as practical reasoning; integrity; emotional awareness; informed vision; confidence to act for change; resilience; affiliation; public reasoning; relationship and rapport across special groups and status hierarchies; etc. (see Figure 8.1)), they are involved in a process of self-cultivation. To be clear, self-cultivation occurs not exclusively through engagement in professional practices, but professional practices that are self-cultivating stand a higher chance of being sustainable and civic-minded.

How can we foster this orientation towards civic and democratic professionalism through higher education, or to put it differently, *how might we cultivate authentic professional identities through transformative higher education?* As outlined in Chapter 1, and discussed in greater detail in subsequent chapters, professional identities are authentic in that they are grounded in authentic desires, meaning desires that have not been shaped by hegemonic forces. Professional identities are authentic in that they are rooted in both self-regard and regard for other individuals (including other species) and communities; they are attentive to their environment and thus are oriented toward a common good. As Sullivan (1995) suggests: 'The goal of self-actualization itself must be transcended, or perhaps, reoriented by integrating individual goals with those of the larger community' (p. 237). Professional identities are authentic in that they are informed by the ideals of civic and democratic purpose and social justice. Professional identities are authentic in yet another way: they are actually enacted. This can be achieved by supporting the ideals of a decent profession and society, which we arrived at through reason and deliberation, by means of appropriate political emotions. These emotions include a love or care for the ideals themselves, and empathy and compassion towards those in need.

Pedagogies of contemplation (Kahane, 2009) and pedagogies of compassion (Nussbaum, 2006, 2010) recognise our mutual interrelatedness and make us reflect on our values (Chapter 7). Public symbols can generate emotions that serve to remind us of our ideals and can create spaces where we can come together despite our differences to interact openly, peacefully and joyfully with one another. One powerful example of a symbol is the idea of the 'living campus' that reminds students and faculty, through the life- and environment-sustaining practices put in place across different levels of the institution, of the ideal of finding solutions to our most pressing problems that are socially and environmentally sustainable (O'Brien & Adam, in press; O'Brien & Howard, 2016). Community-engaged pedagogies, as discussed in Chapters 9 and 10, that offer opportunity for professionals and other community members to participate in Arendtian action, foster reflection on self and other, including our ideals. Types of community-based research and service learning that are *led* by the community and thus involve the community in identifying both its own needs *and* how these might best be addressed also resonate well with the idea of educating for civic-mindedness.

How ready are we to embrace these notions? In Chapter 8, I noted some of the challenges to more democratic forms of professional engagement. These include, first, the wider community being reluctant to share responsibility as a function of having been socialised into wanting others to take care of their needs (the power of 'disabling' professions), and, second, practitioners not necessarily being prepared to enact the role of social activists, or enablers of democracy, given a learned professional identity as providers of technical services. In addition, as I argued in Chapter 10, the academy itself is often a hindrance rather than a facilitator of community-engaged scholarship (e.g., Woodrow Presley, 2012).

Yet, what purpose should higher education serve? As noted in Chapter 1, the key questions we need to confront urgently in higher education include:

- Do we have a shared vision of what we consider a 'decent profession', and, by extension, a 'good graduate', to be?
- How might professions contribute most effectively to their broader communities, and how might higher education support future professionals in making this contribution?
- What ideals can we identify and agree on, and how can we work towards stabilising them?
- How can higher education play its role in nurturing authentic professional identities?

Nussbaum's suggestions, already discussed in Chapter 7, seem profoundly relevant if we want to ensure that the education our students are receiving is more than training in solving technical problems. At the core of Nussbaum's argument is the importance of helping students to think critically, recognise the perspective of others, and be motivated to work towards a world that is more just and fair than the one they inhabit at present. Critical of a higher education that is principally oriented towards economic profit and employability of graduates, she offers these challenging remarks:

> . . . democracies are prone to some serious flaws in reasoning, to parochialism, haste, sloppiness, selfishness, narrowness of the spirit. Education based mainly on profitability in the global market magnifies these deficiencies, producing a greedy obtuseness and a technically trained docility that threaten the very life of democracy itself, and that certainly impede the creation of a decent world culture.
>
> (Nussbaum, 2010, p. 142)

In a strong plea for the importance of the humanities in the higher education curriculum, Nussbaum further comments that, while they do not make money,

> They do what is much more precious than that, make a world that is worth living in, people who are able to see other human beings as full people, with thoughts and feelings of their own that deserve respect and empathy, and nations that are able to overcome fear and suspicion in favour of sympathetic and reasoned debate.
>
> (p. 145)

In a book published already twelve years earlier she urges us to recognise that: 'we must produce citizens who have the Socratic capacity to reason about their beliefs' (Nussbaum, 1998, p. 19), and 'can operate as world citizens with sensitivity and understanding' (p. 52). While reason is important to help develop a vision of a just or decent society, it is the emotions that can support us in upholding these good principles or ideals (Nussbaum, 2013).

What are the qualities of a higher education that is transformative?

The British philosopher of higher education Ron Barnett argued that a distinguishing feature of higher education is precisely that it is meant to be transformative; it is not meant to be a comfortable, cosy experience that re-inforces pre-existing assumptions in students. It is only when education brings the students in direct contact with the uncertain and complex, when it leads them to critically interrogate dominant arguments and question the status quo, that it exceeds technical training and prepares them for life in our contemporary world, characterised by multiple and often conflicting perspectives and multi-faceted social, economic, political and environmental problems. 'A genuine higher education', Barnett (1990) writes,

is subversive in the sense of subverting the student's taken-for-granted world
. . . A genuine higher education is unsettling; it is not meant to be a cosy
experience. It is disturbing because, ultimately, the student comes to see that
things could always be other than they are.

(p. 155)

Students may experience transformative learning (i.e., a significant reorientation
in assumptions, beliefs or values), as they develop relevant professional capabilities
(see Chapter 4), especially the overarching professional capability of civic-
mindedness, which is grounded in 'authenticity', and supported by certain
dispositions and qualities, types of knowledge and reasoning processes and
emotions (see Figure 8.1). As students strive towards authenticity in their
professional identity they become aware of socially constructed, often hegemonic,
assumptions, beliefs or values that led them to hold a limited, indiscriminate
and incomplete perspective (Mezirow, 1991) on the actual possibilities of
their professional practice. Students experience transformation as they come to
reject professional practices that are oriented either towards personal profit or
towards being 'disabling' of the community. They experience transformation as
they become aware of the many blatant injustices and unsustainable practices
in the world and decide to act upon this awareness.

Our learning communities become transformed, and have the potential to be
transformative, as they employ pedagogies and curricula that encourage the development of civic-mindedness and thus professional identities that are authentic.
Whereas the *curriculum* concerns the alignment of courses within a programme
and wider university learning experience with the broad goals and purposes we
identify, *pedagogies* refer to the actual approaches taken by teachers to guide
students through these learning experiences. So while questions over whether or
not students should participate in community-based service learning, or should
have an opportunity to exercise their practical reasoning (Sullivan & Rosin, 2008),
are essentially *curriculum* decisions, questions over how to support students'
learning in particular courses are decisions regarding university *pedagogy*.
Pedagogies themselves are not neutral teaching approaches but the outcome of
certain worldviews or ideologies; think, for instance, of critical (Kincheloe, 2008),
feminist (Crabtree, Sapp & Licona, 2009), postcolonial (Turcotte, 2004), or
radical pedagogies (Brookfield & Holst, 2010). Unlike the general notion of
'learner-centred pedagogy', critical, feminist, postcolonial and radical pedagogies
go further than that by being explicit about their social justice agenda and concern
with recognising and addressing relations of power. These latter pedagogies might
ask, for example, what, in a given context, counts as relevant knowledge, where
does knowledge reside and how is knowledge (de)legitimised. Such pedagogies
are especially well suited to help students reflect on the various power relations
inherent in professional practices and promote identities that are authentic.

Finally, the world in which we live and share with others becomes transformed as fewer graduates put up with unhealthy, inequitable, and unsustainable

practices as a consequence of universities teaching students 'the awareness, knowledge, skills and values needed to create a just and sustainable future' (Cortese, 2003, p. 17).

Similar to Nussbaum (2010), Sullivan and Rosin (2008) criticise the dominance of technical reasoning encouraged in many professional subjects and suggest infusing the professions with the spirit of the humanities. However, Sullivan and Rosin's (2008) argument, as we saw in Chapter 3, is to recognise that professional education ought to be informed by practical reasoning, connecting the ability and disposition to think critically, typically fostered through the study of the humanities, with real-world application. Rather than preparing students on professional programmes for a narrowly defined domain of work by helping them acquire instrumental knowledge and technical skill, an emphasis on practical and critical reasoning ensures that students are prepared for analysing complex issues and for a life as active citizens. Ideally, all courses taught within a professional programme are infused by all three forms of knowledge (instrumental, communicative and emancipatory), rather than dealing with communicative and emancipatory knowledge by adding a couple of electives in humanities subjects. Indeed there are two problems with this 'add-on' approach.

First, the courses students choose may not be the most appropriate ones or may simply happen to be available at a convenient time ('"Introduction to moral philosophy" got cancelled on Thursday afternoons but I was able to take Spanish instead'). Yet, even when students choose a challenging humanities course emphasising communicative and emancipatory knowledge, it often remains unclear to students how their humanities electives help them achieve learning outcomes important to their professional practice. The connections between the learning outcomes to be achieved in these courses and the broader programme learning outcomes, therefore, ought to be made explicit to students as early as they begin their programme. Students need to understand how humanities courses are relevant to them as nurses, as teachers, as engineers, etc. Yet, in addition, and just as importantly, practical reasoning aimed at promoting communicative and emancipatory knowledge should not only be taught through humanities courses but ought to be a central element of all courses offered as part of the professional programme. This is to say that even if very relevant humanities courses (think of the study of different cultures, epistemologies and theories of justice) were added to the professional curriculum, making up a certain percentage of required programme credits, this would still not be good enough; *all courses* offered as part of the professional curriculum ought to be infused with the exercise of practical reasoning.

Is this an unreasonable expectation? Most certainly, individual courses necessarily differ in the emphasis they need to place on instrumental reasoning (or knowledge) versus communicative and emancipatory knowledge. Moreover, professional fields such as health sciences or engineering will have a greater instrumental knowledge base than the fields of social work, theology, and even nursing. And yet, is the practice professionals in engineering or public health are engaged in best conceptualised as requiring exclusively theoretical and productive knowledge based on a technical rationality and skill, or does it also call for communicative/interpretive knowledge and values? Dall'Alba (2009) argued that 'A key task for professional programmes is to promote integration of knowing, acting and being in our world as they relate to particular professional practices, including opening up new possibilities for being the professionals in question' (p. 33). Achieving this task depends on all three kinds of knowledge.

It is also necessary to acknowledge that most professional programmes include at least one or two ethics courses. While some of these courses advocate an 'ethics of principles' (e.g., Beauchamp & Childress, 2001) based either on Kant's duty-ethics or Mill's utilitarian principle of universal benevolence, others emphasise an 'ethics of character', often in reference to Aristotle's notion of practical wisdom or 'phronesis' (e.g., Bondi et al., 2011; Kinsella & Pitman, 2012). The need for teaching practical wisdom is often rationalised by pointing to the fact that next to technical 'know-how' professionals also need to know how to make good judgements in particular situations (e.g., Schön, 1983). This notion of practical wisdom is closely linked to *practical reasoning* discussed earlier.

It seems important at this point to make two additional observations concerning Aristotelian practical wisdom (or as we said earlier, practical reasoning) that seem particularly relevant to the present discussion.

First, while according to Aristotle practical wisdom is indeed critical for making good judgements, there is a tendency in some of the practical wisdom literature to portray it as a form of positive knowledge that one can come to hold and then deploy to solve a problem in an instrumental way, rather than as a developed disposition of the professional to make good judgements based on moral virtue (as indeed an 'ethics of character' would imply). This disposition of practical wisdom, importantly, would include mustering the courage to make a decision (i.e., act) when the circumstances are complex, the aims open to debate, and positive (intended) outcomes cannot be guaranteed by the person making the decision (Carr, 2000; Kemmis, 2012).

Second, such a conceptualisation of practical wisdom as a means to solve a problem ignores Aristotle's emphasis on citizenship and democracy, and thus conceals the close affinities between Arendt and Aristotle. Dana Villa comments in reference to this observation:

> Arendt and Aristotle are one in their emphasis on the primacy of *participation*. Politics is action for Arendt: her debt to Aristotle's conception of citizenship, which makes participation in 'judgement and authority' the criterion that 'effectively distinguishes citizens from all others', is manifest. . . . Both theorists have an essentially deliberative conception of politics, in which debate and deliberation of diverse equals is granted an intrinsic value.
>
> (Villa, 1996, p. 35, emphasis in original)

The fact that many professional education programmes highlighting the importance of practical wisdom in professional life fail to acknowledge the political dimensions of Aristotle's work is perhaps an indication that professional practice often is construed as essentially 'apolitical'. Indeed, Dzur (2008) observes that ethics courses on professional programmes rarely engage with the democratic possibilities of professionalism. Both observations made here, that regarding character and that regarding the political dimension of deliberation, have implications for pedagogy. As Young-Bruehl (2006) in her book on Arendt also remarks: acting means to 'rise to an occasion' (p. 87) and thereby it requires 'courage in the face of the unknown' (p. 89). Developing practical reasoning and judgement in students, therefore, means to encourage them to engage in representative thinking but then to leap forward and make their appearance in the world through action. Practical reasoning as advocated by Sullivan and Rosin, I argued in Chapter 3, involves this challenge of authenticity.

Looking ahead

It might be worth asking faculty members responsible for professional programmes questions broadly similar to those Dzur (2013) asked of professionals across the United States about their democratic processes (note though that Dzur talked to self-identified 'democratic professionals' and he was not interested in their education, let alone the pedagogical implications of preparing professionals for practice). If the aim is to gain a deeper understanding of pedagogical practices employed by faculty teaching on professional programmes, an opening question could be:

> *Imagined at its best, how do you think your profession might contribute most effectively to its broader communities, and how in your view might higher education best support future professionals in your field in making this contribution?*

Answers to this question might vary greatly, ranging from (1) providing an efficient and competent technical service, to (2) serving the public, to (3) facilitating public engagement.

   If the response is associated with option (3), additional insight could be gained by asking some follow-up questions including:

(a) Have you created spaces of proximity and collaboration between the community and students studying on your programme, and if so, how? Have you, for example, brought citizens into reflective contact with each other, as well as with people teaching on the programme and the students?
(b) Have you managed to incorporate into your programme any opportunities for students to become involved as facilitators of shared decision-making, allowing clients or citizens to make their views on issues heard? If so, how did you ensure students learned what they needed to learn so as not to compromise on competence and accountability?

(c) More generally, how do you attempt to prepare students for a professional practice that tries to break down traditional barriers between clients and professionals?

(d) Is it your sense that you are preparing students as enablers of democracy? If not, why not, if yes, why would you say that?

An outline was provided in this book of what transformative higher education entails. Yet it is by developing thoughtful and concrete responses to the above types of questions that we move closer towards finding ways of nurturing authentic professional identities through transformative higher education. Many examples of innovative, democratic and community-engaged practices already exist in professional education in our colleges and universities, but they are not mainstream. Perhaps what needs doing now is gathering these isolated examples from across as many professional fields as possible, disseminating these more widely to demonstrate what is already happening on our campuses and thus start building a shared ideal of what professional education could, or should, be.

References

Adami, R. (2014). Re-thinking relations in human rights education: The politics of narratives. *Journal of Philosophy of Education*, 48(2), 293–307.

Alfred, D. (2001). Albert Mansbridge. In P. Jarvis (ed.), *Twentieth century thinkers in adult and continuing education* (pp. 15–31). London: Kogan Page.

Alverno College (2011). *The eight core abilities*. Milwaukee, WI. www.alverno.edu/academics/ourability-basedcurriculum/the8coreabilities/ (accessed 24 February 2015).

Arendt, H. (2007). The crises in education. In R. Curren (ed.), *Philosophy of education: An anthology* (pp. 188–192). Oxford: Blackwell Publishing. (Previously published in *Between past and future*. London: Faber & Faber, 1961.)

Arendt, H. (2003). *Responsibility and judgment*, ed. with an introduction by Jerome Kuhn. New York: Schocken Books.

Arendt, H. (1982). *Lectures on Kant's political philosophy*, ed. R. Beiner. Sussex: Harvester Press (originally published in 1970).

Arendt, H. (1968a). *Men in dark times*. New York: Harcourt Publishing.

Arendt, H. (1968b). *Between past and future* (rev. edn). New York: Viking Press.

Arendt, H. (1958). *The human condition*. Chicago, IL: University of Chicago Press.

Armstrong, D. (2006). Dreaming our future: Developing democratic professional practice? *The Australian Educational Researcher*, 33(1), 1–11.

Aronowitz, S. (2000). *The knowledge factory: Dismantling the corporate university and creating true higher education*. Boston, MA: Beacon Press.

Arthur, J. (with Richard Bailey) (2000). *Schools and community: The communitarian agenda in education*. London: Falmer Press.

Aspin, D. N., Chapman, J. D., Hatton, M. & Sawano, Y. (eds) (2001). *International handbook of lifelong learning*. Boston: Kluwer Academic Publishers.

Ball, S. (2003). The teacher's soul and the terrors of performativity. *Journal of Education Policy*, 18(2), 215–228.

Barnett, R. (2011). Towards an ecological professionalism. In S. Sugrue & T. D. Solbrekke (eds), *Professional responsibility: New horizons of praxis* (pp. 29–41). London: Routledge.

Barnett, R. (2008). Critical professionalism in an age of supercomplexity. In B. Cunningham (ed.), *Exploring professionalism* (pp. 190–207). London: Institute of Education, University of London.

Barnett, R. (2007). *A will to learn*. Buckingham: Society for Research into Higher Education/Open University Press.

Barnett, R. (2006). Graduate attributes in an age of uncertainty. In P. Hager & S. Holland (eds), *Graduate attributes, learning and employability* (pp. 49–65). Dordrecht: Springer Verlag.

Barnett, R. (2005). Recapturing the universal in the university. *Educational Philosophy and Theory*, 37(6), 785–796.

Barnett, R. (2004). Learning for an unknown future. *Higher Education Research and Development*, 23(3), 247–260.

Barnett, R. (2000). *Realising the university in an age of supercomplexity*. Buckingham, UK: Society for Research into Higher Education/Open University Press.

Barnett, R. (1990). *The idea of higher education*. Buckingham, UK: Society for Research into Higher Education/Open University Press.

Barrie, S. C. (2007). A conceptual framework for the teaching and learning of generic graduate attributes. *Studies in Higher Education*, 32(4), 439–458.

Baxter-Magolda, M. (1999). *Creating contexts for learning and self-authorship: Constructive-developmental pedagogy*. Nashville, TN: Vanderbilt University Press.

Bayne, S. (2008). Uncanny spaces for higher education: Teaching and learning in virtual worlds. *Alt-J, Research in Learning Technology*, 16(3), 197–205.

Beauchamp, T. L. & Childress, J. F. (2001). *Principles of biomedical ethics*. Oxford: Oxford University Press.

Beck, U. (2000). *The brave new world of work*. Cambridge, UK: Polity Press.

Benhabib, S. (1990). Hannah Arendt and the redemptive power of narrative. *Social Research*, 57(1), 167–196.

Benhabib, S. (1988). Judgment and the moral foundations of politics in Arendt's thought. *Political Theory*, 16(1), 29–51.

Biesta, G. J. (2012). Becoming public: Public pedagogy, citizenship and the public sphere. *Social and Cultural Geography*, 13(7), 683–697.

Biesta, G. J. (2007). Why 'what works' won't work: Evidence-based practice and the democratic deficit of educational research. *Educational Theory*, 57(1), 1–22.

Biesta, G. J. (2006). *Beyond learning: Democratic education for a human future*. Boulder, CO: Paradigm Publishers.

Bondi, L., Carr, D., Clark, C. & Clegg, C. (2011). *Towards professional wisdom: Practical deliberation in the people professions*. Farnham, UK: Ashgate.

Bonnett, M. (1978). Authenticity and education. *Journal of Philosophy of Education*, 12, 51–61.

Bonnett, M. & Cuypers, S. (2003). Autonomy and authenticity in education. In N. Blake, P. Smeyers, R. Smith & P. Standish (eds), *The Blackwell guide to the philosophy of education* (pp. 326–340). Blackwell Philosophy Guides. Oxford: Blackwell Publishing.

Boud, D. (2007). Reframing assessment as if learning were important. In D. Boud & N. Falchikov (eds), *Rethinking assessment in higher education* (pp. 14–26). London: Routledge.

Bourdieu, P. & Passeron, J. C. (1977). *Reproduction in education, society and culture*. Beverly Hills, CA: Sage.

Bowden, J., Hart, G., King, B., Trigwell, K. & Watts, O. (2000). *Generic capabilities of ATN university graduates*. Canberra: Australian Government Department of Education, Training and Youth Affairs.

Bowen, G. A. (2010). Exploring civic engagement in higher education: An international context. *Asian Journal of Educational Research and Synergy*, 2(2), 1–8.

Bowes, J. M., Chalmers, D. & Flanagan, C. (1996). Adolescents' ideas about social and civic responsibility. Paper presented at the 9th Australasian Human Development Conference, Perth, Australia, April.

Boyer, E. L. (1996). The scholarship of engagement. *Bulletin of the American Academy of Arts and Sciences*, 49(7), 18–33.

Boyer, E. L. (1990). *Scholarship reconsidered: Priorities of the professoriate*. The Carnegie Foundation for the Advancement of Teaching. Princeton, NJ: Princeton University Press.

Boys, C. J., Brennan, J., Henkel, M., Kirkland, J., Kogan, M. & Youll, P. (1988). *Higher education and the preparation for work*. London: Jessica Kingsley Publishers.

Boyte, H. (2008). A new civic politics. Review of L. Benson, I. Harkavy & J. Puckett (2007). *Dewey's dream: Universities and democracies in an age of education reform*. Temple University Press. *Journal of Higher Education Outreach and Engagement*, 12(1), 107–112.

Boyte, H. (2004). *Everyday politics: Reconnecting citizens and public life*. Philadelphia, PA: Pennsylvania University Press.

Boyte, H. C. & Fretz, E. (2012). Civic professionalism. In J. Saltmarsh & M. Hartley (eds), *To serve a larger purpose: Engagement for democracy and the transformation of higher education* (pp. 82–101). Philadelphia, PA: Temple University Press.

Boyte, H. C. & Fretz, E. (2010). Civic professionalism. *Journal of Higher Education, Outreach and Engagement*, 14(2), 67–90.

Breneman, D. W. (1990). Are we losing our liberal arts colleges? *AAHE Bulletin*, 43(2): 3–6.

Bringle, R. G. & Steinberg, K. S. (2010). Educating for informed community involvement. *American Journal of Community Psychology*, 46, 428–441.

Brint, S. (1994). *In an age of experts: The changing role of professionals in politics and public life*. Princeton, NJ: Princeton University Press.

Brint, S. & Levy, C. S. (1999). Profession and civic engagement: Trends in rhetoric and practice 1975–1995. In T. Skocpol & M. Firrina (eds), *Civic engagement in American democracy* (pp. 163–210). Washington, DC: Brookings Institution Press.

Brint, S., Riddle, M., Turk-Bicakci, L. & Levy, C. S. (2005). From the liberal to the practical arts in American colleges and universities: Organizational analysis and curricular change. *Journal of Higher Education*, 76(2): 151–180.

Brookfield, S. (2005). *The power of critical theory: Liberating adult learning and teaching*. San Francisco, CA: Jossey-Bass.

Brookfield, S. (1990). *The skilful teacher*. San Francisco, CA: Jossey-Bass.

Brookfield, S. D. (1987). *Developing critical thinkers: Challenging adults to explore alternative ways of thinking and acting*. San Francisco, CA: Jossey-Bass.

Brookfield, S. & Holst, J. D. (2010). *Radicalising learning: Adult education for a just world*. San Francisco, CA: Jossey-Bass.

Carr, D. (2000). *Professionalism and ethics in teaching*. London: Routledge.

Casey, K. (1995). *Work, self and identity after industrialism*. London: Routledge.

Chapman, S. (2017). Changing the discourse: Self-cultivation for a sustainable teaching profession. Unpublished doctoral thesis. University of Edinburgh, UK.

Coetzee, M., Botha, J., Eccles, N., Holtzhausen, N. & Nienaber, H. (eds) (2012). *Developing student graduateness and employability: Issues, provocations, theory and practical guidelines.* Randburg, South Africa: Knowres.

Colby, A., Ehrlich, T., Beaumont, E. & Stephens, J. (eds) (2003). *Educating citizens: Preparing America's undergraduates for lives of moral and civic responsibility.* San Francisco, CA: Jossey-Bass.

Collini, S. (2012). *What are universities for?* London: Penguin Books.

Cortese, A. (2003). The critical role of higher education in creating a sustainable future. *Planning for Higher Education,* 31(3), 15–22.

Crabtree, R. D., Sapp, D. A. & Licona, A. C. (eds) (2009). *Feminist pedagogy: Looking back to move forward.* Baltimore, MD: Johns Hopkins University Press.

Cranton, P. A. (1998). *No one way: Teaching and learning in higher education.* Toronto, ON: Wall & Emerson.

Crowther, J. & Martin, I. (2010). Adult education in Scotland: Past and present. *The Journal of Contemporary Community Education Practice Theory,* 1(3), electronic journal. http://concept.lib.ed.ac.uk/ (accessed 6 May 2015).

Croxford, L. & Raffe, D. (2012). Social class, ethnicity and access to higher education in the four countries of the UK: 1996–2010. *International Journal of Lifelong Education,* 33(1), 77–95 (CES Ref 1222).

Dall'Alba, G. (2009). *Learning to be professionals: Innovation and change in professional education.* Dordrecht, Netherlands: Springer.

Damrosch, D. (1995). *We scholars: Changing the culture of the university.* Cambridge, MA: Harvard University Press.

Deggs, D. M., Machtmes, K. L. & Johnson, E. (2008). The significance of teaching perspectives among academic disciplines. *College Teaching Methods and Styles Journal,* 4(8), 1–8.

Deem, R. & Brehony, K. J. (2005). Management as ideology: The case of 'new managerialism' in higher education. *Oxford Review of Education,* 31(2), 217–235.

d'Entreves, M. P. (2014) Hannah Arendt. In Edward N. Zalta (ed.), *The Stanford encyclopedia of philosophy* (Summer 2014 edition). http://plato.stanford.edu/archives/sum2014/entries/arendt/ (accessed 4 May 2015).

Department of Trade and Industry (1998). The Competitiveness White Paper: Our competitive future; building the knowledge driven economy. London: HMSO.

Dewey, J. (1927). *The public and its problems.* New York: H. Holt and Company.

Dewey, J. (1991). *How we think.* Buffalo, NY: Prometheus Books (originally published in 1910).

Dirkx, J. M. (2006). Authenticity and imagination. In P. A. Cranton (ed.), *Authenticity in teaching* (pp. 27–39). New Directions for Adult and Continuing Education, No. 111. San Francisco, CA: Jossey-Bass.

Donald, J. G. (2002). *Learning to think: Disciplinary perspectives.* San Francisco, CA: Jossey-Bass.

Dunne, J. (2005). An intricate fabric: Understanding the rationality of practice. *Pedagogy, Culture and Society,* 13(3), 367–389.

Dunne, J. (1993). *Back to the rough ground: 'Phronesis' and 'techne' in modern philosophy and in Aristotle.* Notre Dame, IN: University of Notre Dame Press.

Dunne, J. & Pendlebury, S. (2003). Practical reason. In N. Blake, P. Smeyers, R. Smith & P. Standish (eds), *The Blackwell guide to the philosophy of education* (pp. 194–211). Blackwell Philosophy Guides. Oxford: Blackwell Publishing.

Durkheim, E. (1957). *Professional ethics and civil morals.* New York: The Free Press.

Dzur, A. (2013). Trench democracy: Participatory innovation in unlikely places. *Boston Review,* 11 October. www.bostonreview.net/blog/dzur-trench-democracy-1.

Dzur, A. (2008). *Democratic professionalism: Citizen participation and the reconstruction of professional ethics, identity, and practice.* University Park, PA: Penn State University Press.

Dzur, A. W. (2004). Democratic professionalism: Sharing authority in civic life. *The Good Society,* 13(1), 6–14.

Eagleton, T. (2007). *The meaning of life: A very short introduction.* Oxford: Oxford University Press.

Elsey, B. (2001). R H Tawney – patron saint of adult education. In P. Jarvis (ed.), *Twentieth century thinkers in adult and continuing education* (pp. 49–61). London: Kogan Page.

English, L. & Mayo, P. (2012). *Learning with adults: A critical pedagogical introduction.* Rotterdam, Netherlands: Sense Publishers.

Ennis, R. H. (1996). Critical thinking dispositions: Their nature and assessability. *Informal Logic,* 18(2 & 3), 165–182

Entwistle, N. J., Tait, H. & McCune, V. (2000). Patterns of response to an approach to studying inventory across contrasting groups and contexts. *European Journal of the Psychology of Education,* 15(1), 33–48.

Eraut, M. (1994). *Developing professional knowledge and competence.* London: Falmer Press.

Erikson, E. H. (1965). *Childhood and society.* New York: Norton.

Evetts, J. (2012). Professionalism in turbulent times: Changes, challenges and opportunities. Paper presented at the Propel International Conference, Stirling, UK, 9–11 May.

Evetts, J. (2009). The management of professionalism: A contemporary paradox. In S. Gewirtz, P. Mahony, I. Hextall & A. Cribb (eds), *Changing teacher professionalism: International trends, challenges and ways forward* (pp. 19–30). Abingdon, UK: Routledge.

Exworthy, M. & Halford, S. (eds) (1999). *Professionals and the new managerialism in the public sector.* Buckingham, UK: Open University Press.

Eyler, J. & Giles, D. E. (1999). *Where's the learning in service-learning?* San Francisco, CA: Jossey-Bass.

Facione, P. A., Sanchez, C. A. & Facione, N. C. (1994). *Are college students disposed to think?* Millbrae, CA: California Academic Press.

Faure, E. (1972). *Learning to be: The world of education today and tomorrow.* Paris: UNESCO Publishing.

Felton, P., Gilchrist, L. Z. & Darby, A. (2006). Emotion and learning: Feeling our way toward a new theory of reflection in service-learning. *Michigan Journal of Community Service Learning,* 12(2), 38–46.

Fleming, P. (2009). *Authenticity and the cultural politics of work: New forms of informal control.* Oxford: Oxford University Press.

Flyvbjerg, B. (2001). *Making social science matter: Why social inquiry fails and how it can succeed again.* Cambridge, UK: Cambridge University Press.

Fournier, V. (2000). Boundary work and the (un)making of the professions. In N. Malin (ed.), *Professionalism, boundaries, and the workplace* (pp. 67–86). London: Routledge.

Fournier, V. (1999). The appeal of professionalism as a disciplinary mechanism. *The Sociological Review*, 47, 280–307.

Fox, D. (1983). Personal theories of teaching. *Studies in Higher Education*, 8(2), 151–164.

Frankfurt, H. G. (2004). *The reasons of love*. Princeton, NJ: Princeton University Press.

Fraser, G. (2005). Parents rebel in junk food ban row. *The Cumberland News & Star*, 20 October. www.newsandstar.co.uk/news/parents-rebel-in-junk-food-ban-row-1.434637 (accessed 30 April 2015).

Fraser, N. (1992). Rethinking the public sphere: A contribution to the critique of actually existing democracy. In C. Calhuon (ed.), *Habermas and the public sphere* (pp. 109–142). Cambridge, MA: MIT Press.

Freidson, E. (2001). *Professionalism: The third logic*. Chicago, IL: University of Chicago Press.

Freire, P. (1971). *Pedagogy of the oppressed*. New York: Continuum.

Gallagher, S. (1992). *Hermeneutics and education*. New York: SUNY Press.

Gardner, H. (2011). *Truth, beauty, and goodness reframed: Educating for the virtues in the twenty-first century*. New York: Basic Books.

Gibbons, M., Limoges, C., Nowotny, H., Schwartzman, S., Scott, P. & Trow, M. (1994). *The new production of knowledge: The dynamics of science and research in contemporary societies*. London: Sage.

Giddens, A. (1991). *Modernity and self-identity: Self and society in the late-modern age*. Cambridge, UK: Polity Press.

Giroux, H. (2014). Neoliberalism, democracy and the university as a public sphere. Interview with Victoria Harper, *Truthout*, 22 April. www.truth-out.org/opinion/item/23156-henry-a-giroux-neoliberalism-democracy-and-the-university-as-a-public-sphere (accessed 10 May 2015).

Giroux, H. (2011). Beyond the limits of neoliberal higher education: Global youth resistance and the American/British divide. Blog posted by Campaign for the Public University on 7 November. http://publicuniversity.org.uk/2011/11/07/beyond-the-limits-of-neoliberal-higher-education-global-youth-resistance-and-the-americanbritish-divide/ (accessed 7 March 2015).

Giroux, H. (2006). Higher education under siege: Implications for public intellectuals. *Thought & Action. The NEA Higher Education Journal*, Fall, 63–78. www.nea.org/assets/img/PubThoughtAndAction/TAA_06_08.pdf (accessed 17 February 2015).

Goode, W. J. (1957). Community within a community: The professions. *American Sociological Review*, 22, 194–200.

Gordon, M. (ed.) (2001). *Hannah Arendt and education: Renewing our common world*. Boulder, CO: Westview Press.

Gramsci, A. (1971). *Selection from the prison notebooks*. London: Lawrence and Wishart.

Greene, M. (1995). *Releasing the imagination: Essays on education, the arts and social change*. San Francisco, CA: Jossey-Bass.

Grimmet, P. & Neufeld, J. (ed.) (1994). *Teacher development and the struggle for authenticity: Professional growth and restructuring in the context of change*. New York: Teachers College Press.

Gutmann, A. (1987). *Democratic education*. Princeton, NJ: Princeton University Press.

Haas, T. (2000). Public journalism challenges to curriculum and instruction. *Journalism & Mass Communication Educator*, 55(3), 27–41.

Habermas, J. (1984). *The theory of communicative action*, vol. 1 (English translation by Thomas McCarthy). Boston, MA: Beacon Press.

Habermas, J. (1977). Hannah Arendt's communications concept of power. *Social Research*, 44(1), 3–24.

Habermas, J. (1971). *Knowledge and human interests*. Boston, MA: Beacon Press.

Hampton, J. (2007). *The intrinsic worth of persons: Contractarianism in moral and political philosophy*, ed. Daniel Farnham. New York: Cambridge University Press.

Hargreaves, D. (1997). In defence of research for evidence-based teaching: A rejoinder to Martyn Hammersley. *British Educational Research Journal*, 23, 141–161.

Hativa, N. & Marincovich, M. (eds) (1995). *Disciplinary differences in teaching and learning: Implications for practice*. San Francisco, CA: Jossey-Bass.

Heidegger, M. (1962). *Being and time*, trans. John Macquarrie and Edward Robinson. London: SCM Press (originally published in 1927).

Henderson, L. W. & Knight, T. (2012). Integrating the hedonic and eudaimonic perspectives to more comprehensively understand wellbeing and pathways to wellbeing. *International Journal of Wellbeing*, 2(3), 196–221.

Higgins, C. (2011). *The good life of teaching: An ethics of professional practice*. Chichester, UK: Wiley Blackwell.

Hoggan, C. & Cranton, P. A. (2014). Promoting transformative learning through reading fiction. *Journal of Transformative Education*, doi: 10.1177/1541344614 561864.

Hounsell, D. & Anderson, C. (2009). Ways of thinking and practising in biology and history: Disciplinary aspects of teaching and learning environments. In C. Kreber (ed.), *The university and its disciplines: Teaching and learning within and beyond disciplinary boundaries* (pp. 71–84). New York: Routledge.

Hoyle, E. & John, P. (1995). *Professional knowledge and professional practice*. London: Cassell.

Hughes, C. & Barrie, S. (2010). Influences on the assessment of graduate attributes in higher education. In Fourth Biennial EARLI/Northumbria Assessment Conference. Challenging Assessment, Berlin, Germany, 27–29 August 2008 (pp. 325–334).

Hutchings, P., Huber, M. Y. & Ciccone, A. (2011). *The scholarship of teaching and learning reconsidered: Institutional integration and impact*. The Carnegie Foundation for the Advancement of Teaching. San Francisco, CA: Jossey-Bass.

Illich, I. (1977). Disabling professions. In I. Illich, I. Zola, J. McKnight, J. Caplan & H. Sharken (eds), *Disabling professions*. London: Marion Boyars.

Jackson, D., Firtko, A. & Edenborough, M. (2007). Personal resilience as a strategy for surviving and thriving in the face of workplace adversity: A literature review. *Journal of Advanced Nursing*, 60(1), 1–9.

Jacoby, B. (2009). Civic engagement in today's higher education: An overview. In B. Jacoby (ed.), *Civic engagement in higher education: Concepts and practices* (pp. 5–30). San Francisco, CA: Jossey-Bass.

Jacoby, B. (1996). Service-learning in today's higher education. In B. Jacoby and Associates (eds), *Service-learning in higher education: Concepts and practices*. San Francisco, CA: Jossey-Bass.

Jarvis, P. (2007). *Globalization, lifelong learning and the learning society: Sociological perspectives*. New York: Routledge.

Johnson, T. (1972). *Professions and power.* London: Macmillan.

Jones, A. (2009). Re-disciplining generic attributes: The disciplinary context in focus. *Studies in Higher Education*, 34(1), 85–100.

Kahane, D. (2009). Learning about obligation, compassion and social justice. In C. Kreber (ed.), *Internationalizing the curriculum in higher education* (pp. 49–60). New Directions for Teaching and Learning, No. 118. San Francisco, CA: Jossey-Bass.

Keeley, B. (2007). *Human capital: How what you know shapes your life*. Paris: OECD Publishing.

Keen, S. & Todres, L. (2007). Strategies for disseminating qualitative research findings: Three exemplars. *Forum: Qualitative Social Research: Sozialforschung*, 8(3), Article 17. www.qualitative-research.net/index.php/fqs/article/view/285/625 (accessed 14 May 2015).

Kember, D. (1997). A reconceptualisation of the research into university academics' conceptions of teaching. *Learning and Instruction*, 7(3), 255–275.

Kemmis, S. (2012). Phronesis, experience, and the primacy of praxis. In E. A. Kinsella & A. Pitman (eds), *Phronesis as professional knowledge: Practical wisdom in the professions* (pp. 147–161). Dordrecht, Netherlands: Sense Publishers.

Kincheloe, J. (2008). *Critical pedagogy primer*. New York: Peter Lang.

Kinsella, E. A. & Pitman, A. (eds) (2012). *Phronesis as professional knowledge: Practical wisdom in the professions*. Dordrecht, Netherlands: Sense Publishers.

Kirkpatrick, I., Ackroyd, S. & Walker, R. (2005). *The new managerialism and public service professions: Developments in health, social services and housing*. New York: Palgrave Macmillan.

Kreber, C. (2015). Transforming employment-oriented adult education to foster Arendtian action: Rebuilding bridges between community and vocational education. *Adult Education Quarterly*, 65, 100–115.

Kreber, C. (2013a). *Authenticity in and through teaching in higher education: The transformative potential of the scholarship of teaching*. London: Routledge.

Kreber, C. (2013b). Rationalising the nature of 'graduateness' through philosophical accounts of authenticity. *Teaching in Higher Education*, 19(1), 90–100.

Kreber, C. (2012). Critical reflection and transformative learning. In E. Taylor and P. A. Cranton (eds), *Handbook of transformative learning: Theory, research and practice* (pp. 323–342). San Francisco, CA: Jossey-Bass.

Kreber, C. (ed.) (2009). *The university and its disciplines: Teaching and learning within and beyond disciplinary boundaries*. New York: Routledge.

Kreber, C. (ed.) (2001). Scholarship revisited: Perspectives on the scholarship of teaching. In *New directions for teaching and learning*. San Francisco, CA: Jossey-Bass.

Lagemann, E. C. & Lewis, H. (eds) (2012). *What is college for? The public purpose of higher education*. New York: Teachers College Press.

Langstraat, L. & Bowdon, M. (2011). Service-learning and critical emotion studies: On the perils of empathy and the politics of compassion. *Michigan Journal of Community Service Learning*, 17(2), 5–11.

Larson, M. S. (1977). *The rise of professionalism: A sociological analysis*. Berkeley, CA: University of California Press.

Leitch Report (2006). Prosperity for all in the global economy – world class skills. Norwich, UK: HMSO.

Lisbon European Council (2000). Presidency conclusion. www.consilium.europa.eu/en/uedocs/cms_data/docs/pressdata/en/ec/00100-r1.en0.htm (accessed 6 March 2015).

Lucas, B., Spencer, E. & Claxton, G. (2012). *How to teach vocational education: A theory of vocational pedagogy*. London: City and Guilds Centre for Skills Development.

MacIntyre, A. (2009). *Dependent rational animals: Why human beings need the virtues*. Illinois: Open Court Publishing.

MacIntyre, A. (2007). *After virtue: A study in moral theory* (3rd edn). London: Duckworth.

MacIntyre, A. (1987). The idea of an educated public. In G. Haydon (ed.), *Education and values* (pp. 15–37). London: Institute of Education.

Malpas, J. (2003). Martin Heidegger. In R. C. Salomon & D. L. Sherman (eds), *The Blackwell guide to continental philosophy* (pp. 143–162). Oxford: Blackwell.

Marshall, T. H. (1963). The recent history of professionalism in relation to social structure and social policy. Reprinted in *Sociology at the crossroads*. London: Heinemann (originally published in 1939).

Martin, I. (2008). Reclaiming social purpose: Framing the discussion. In M. Shaw and Associates (eds), *Reclaiming social purpose in community education*. The Edinburgh Papers (pp. 13–16). Edinburgh: Reclaiming Social Purpose Group. https://criticallychatting.files.wordpress.com/2008/11/theedinburghpapers-pdf.pdf (accessed 10 May 2015).

Martin, I. (2006). 'Principled positions' for adult learning: Where have all the flowers gone? Paper presented at the 36th Annual SCUTREA Conference, 4–6 July, Trinity and All Saints College, Leeds.

Marton, F. (1981). Phenomenography – describing conceptions of the world around us. *Instructional Science*, 10, 177–200.

Maslow, A. H. (1972). *Abraham Maslow: A memorial volume*. Monterey, CA: Brooks/Cole.

May, T. & Buck, M. (1998). Power, professionalism and organisational transformation. *Sociological Research Online*, 3(2). www.socresonline.org.uk/3/2/5.html (accessed 10 January 2015).

McIlrath, L., Lyons, A. & Munck, R. (eds) (2012). *Higher education and civic engagement: Comparative perspectives*. New York: Palgrave Macmillan.

McLean, M. & Walker, M. (2012). The possibilities for university-based public-good professional education: A case-study from South Africa based on the 'capability approach'. *Studies in Higher Education*, 37(5), 585–601.

McMillan, J. (2015). Developing civic-minded university graduates. *University World News. The global window on higher education*, 353, 6 February.

McPeck, J. E. (1981). *Critical thinking and education*. Oxford: Martin Robertson.

Mentkowski, M. & Associates (2000). *Learning that lasts: Integrating learning, development, and performance in college and beyond*. San Francisco, CA: Jossey-Bass.

Mezirow, J. (1991). *Transformative dimensions of adult learning*. San Francisco, CA: Jossey-Bass.

Miller, D. (1994). Virtues, practices and justice. In J. Horton & S. Mendus (eds), *After MacIntyre: Critical perspectives on the work of Alasdair MacIntyre* (pp. 245–264). Indiana: University of Notre Dame Press.

Mooney, G. & Scott, G. (2012). Devolution, social justice and social policy: The Scottish context. In G. Mooney & G. Scott (eds), *Social justice and social policy in Scotland* (pp. 1–25). Bristol, UK: The Policy Press.

Mount Royal University (2012). Inspiring learning. Academic Plan 2012–2017. www.mtroyal.ca/cs/groups/public/documents/pdf/academic_plan.pdf (accessed 25 February 2015).

Neumann, A. (2001). Disciplinary differences and university teaching. *Studies in Higher Education*, 26(2), 135–146.

Nixon, J. (2012). *Interpretive pedagogies for higher education: Arendt, Berger, Said, Nussbaum and their legacies.* London: Continuum International Publishing Group.

Nixon, J. (2007). Excellence and the good society. In A. Skelton (ed.), *International perspectives on teaching excellence in higher education* (pp. 23–53). New York: Routledge.

Nixon, J., Marks, A., Rowland, S. & Walker, M. (2001). Towards a new academic professionalism: A manifesto for hope. *British Journal of Sociology of Education*, 22(2), 227–244.

Noddings, N. (2003). Is teaching a practice? *Journal of Philosophy of Education*, 37(2), 241–251.

Norris, S. P. (ed.) (1992). *The generalizability of critical thinking: Multiple perspectives on an educational ideal.* New York: Teachers College.

Nussbaum, M. (2013). *Political emotions: Why love matters for justice.* Cambridge, MA: Harvard University Press.

Nussbaum, M. (2012). Recoiling from reason: Review of MacIntyre, Whose justice? Which rationality? In *Philosophical interventions: Reviews 1986–2011* (ch. 4, pp. 53–68). Oxford: Oxford University Press.

Nussbaum, M. (2011). *Creating capabilities.* Cambridge, MA: Harvard University Press.

Nussbaum, M. (2010). *Not for profit: Why democracy needs the humanities.* Princeton, NJ: Princeton University Press.

Nussbaum, M. C. (2006). Education and democratic citizenship: Capabilities and quality education. *Journal of Human Development*, 7(3), 385–395.

Nussbaum, M. (2005). Beyond compassion and humanity: Justice for non-human animals. In C. R. Sunstein & M. Nussbaum (eds), *Animal rights: Current debates and new directions* (pp. 299–314). Oxford: Oxford University Press.

Nussbaum, M. (2004a). *Hiding from humanity: Disgust, shame and the law.* Princeton, NJ: Princeton University Press.

Nussbaum, M. (2004b). *Upheavals of thought.* Cambridge, UK: Cambridge University Press.

Nussbaum, M. (2000). *Women and human development: The capabilities approach.* New York: Cambridge University Press.

Nussbaum, M. (1998). *Cultivating humanity: A classical defense of reform in liberal education.* Cambridge, MA: Harvard University Press.

Nussbaum, M. (1986). *The fragility of goodness: Luck and ethics in Greek tragedy and philosophy.* New York: Cambridge University Press.

Nussbaum, M. & Sen, A. (eds) (1993). *The quality of life*. Oxford: Clarendon Press.

O'Brien, C. & Adam, C. (in press). Sustainable happiness, living campus and well-being for all. *International Journal of Innovation, Creativity, and Change.*

O'Brien, C. & Howard, P. (2016). The living school: The emergence of a transformative sustainability education paradigm. *Journal of Education for Sustainable Development*, 10(1).

O'Neil, O. (2002). *A question of trust. The Reith lectures* (lectures 1 to 5). www.bbc.co.uk/radio4/reith2002/.

Pace, D. & Middendorf, J. (eds) (2004). *Decoding the disciplines: A model for helping students learn disciplinary ways of thinking*. New Directions for Teaching and Learning, No. 98. San Francisco, CA: Wiley.

Palmer, P. (1998). *The courage to teach*. San Francisco, CA: Jossey-Bass.

Parsons, T. (1954). Professions and social structure. In *Essays in sociological theory*. Glencoe, IL: The Free Press.

Paul, R. (1990). *Critical thinking: What every person needs to survive in a rapidly changing world*. Rohnert Park, CA: Center for Critical Thinking and Moral Critique.

Pederson, A., Durrant, I. & Bentley, B. (2014). Student teachers' perceptions of their role as civic educators: Evidence from a large higher education institution in England. *British Educational Research Journal*, 41(2), 343–364.

Perkins, D. N., Jay, E. & Tishman, S. (1993). Beyond abilities: A dispositional theory of thinking. *Merrill-Palmer Quarterly*, 39(1), 1–21.

Peters, S. J. (2004). Educating the civic professional: Reconfigurations and resistances. *Michigan Journal of Community Service-Learning*, 11, 47–58.

Potter, A. (2010). *The authenticity hoax*. New York: HarperCollins.

Pratt, D. D., Collins, J. B. & Jarvis Selinger, S. (2001). Development and use of the Teaching Perspectives Inventory (TPI). Paper presented at the American Educational Research Association. https://facultycommons.macewan.ca/wp-content/uploads/TPI-online-resource.pdf (accessed 8 March 2015).

Pratt, D. D. & Associates (1998). *Five perspectives on teaching in adult and higher education*. Malabar, FL: Krieger Publishing. Ch. 3: Alternative frames of understanding: An introduction to five perspectives on teaching. www.academia.edu/317235/Five_Perspectives_on_Teaching (accessed 13 March 2015).

Putnam, R. (2000). *Bowling alone: The collapse and revival of American community*. New York: Simon & Schuster.

Ranson, S. (2003). Public accountability in the age of neo-liberal governance. *Journal of Education Policy*, 19(5), 459–480.

Raphael, D. (2002). *Poverty, income inequality, and health in Canada*. York University, Toronto, Canada: The CSJ Foundation for Research and Education. www.socialjustice.org/uploads/pubs/PovertyIncomeInequalityandHealthinCanada.pdf (accessed 8 March 2015).

Rawls, J. (1971/1999). *A theory of justice*. Cambridge, MA: Harvard University Press.

Richardson, J. T. E. (2010). Widening participation without widening attainment: The case of ethnic minority students. *Psychology Teaching Review*, 16(1), 37–45.

Riddell, S., Tinklin, T. & Wilson, A. (2004). Disabled students in higher education: A reflection on research strategies and findings. In C. Barnes & G. Mercer (eds),

Disability policy and practice: Applying the social model (pp. 81–98). Leeds: The Disability Press.

Robinson, S. (2005). Enabling professions. In J. Strain & S. Robinson (eds), *The teaching and practice of professional ethics* (pp. 199–211). Leicester, UK: Troubador.

Rosenberg, C. (2000). Beyond empathy: Developing critical consciousness through service learning. In C. O'Grady (ed.), *Integrating service learning and multicultural education in colleges and universities* (pp. 23–44). Mahwah, NJ: Lawrence Erlbaum.

Rowland, S. (2006). *The enquiring university: Compliance and contestation in higher education*. Maidenhead, UK: Open University Press.

Ruitenberg, C. W. (2009). Educating political adversaries: Chantal Mouffe and radical democratic citizenship education. *Studies in Philosophy and Education*, 28, 269–281.

Ryle, G. (1949). *The concept of mind*. Chicago, IL: University of Chicago Press.

Saltmarsh, J. & Hartley, M. (2012). Democratic engagement. In J. Saltmarsh & M. Hartley (eds), *To serve a larger purpose: Engagement for democracy and the transformation of higher education* (pp. 14–26). Philadelphia, PA: Temple University Press.

Saltmarsh, J., Wooding, J. & McLellan, K. (2014). The challenges of rewarding new forms of scholarship: Creating academic cultures that support community-engaged scholarship. A report on a Bringing Theory to Practice seminar held 15 May 2014. Boston, MA: New England Resource Center for Higher Education.

Sandeen, C. (2013). Confronting the liberal arts conundrum. The blog. *Huffington Post*, 16 October. www.huffingtonpost.com/cathy-sandeen/confronting-the-liberal-a_b_4107404.html (accessed 20 February 2015).

Schön, D. (1983). *The reflective practitioner*. San Francisco, CA: Jossey-Bass.

Scott, S. M. (1997). The grieving soul in the transformation process. In P. Cranton (ed.), *Transformative learning in action: Insights from practice* (pp. 41–50). New Directions for Adult and Continuing Education, No. 74. San Francisco, CA: Jossey-Bass.

Sellman, D. (2000). Alasdair MacIntyre and the professional practice of nursing. *Nursing Philosophy*, 1, 26–33.

Sen, A. (2009). *The idea of justice*. London: Allen Lane.

Sennett, R. (1998). *The corrosion of character: The personal consequences of work in new capitalism*. New York: W.E Norton & Company.

Serrano del Pozo, I. & Kreber, C. (2014). The professionalization of the university and the profession as MacIntyrean practice. *Studies in Philosophy and Education*. DOI 10.1007/s11217-014-9453-0.

Shaw, M. (2008). Policy, politics and practice: Community development. In M. Shaw and Associates (eds), *Reclaiming social purpose in community education*. The Edinburgh Papers (pp. 13–16). Edinburgh: Reclaiming Social Purpose Group. https://criticallychatting.files.wordpress.com/2008/11/theedinburghpapers-pdf.pdf (accessed 10 May 2015).

Sherman, D. L. (2003). Jean-Paul Sartre. In R. C. Salomon & D. L. Sherman (eds), *The Blackwell guide to continental philosophy* (pp. 163–187). Oxford: Blackwell Publishing.

Shulman, L. (2000). From Minsk to Pinsk: Why a scholarship of teaching and learning? *Journal of Scholarship of Teaching and Learning (JoSoTL)*, 1(1), 48–53.

Shulman, L. (1987). Knowledge and teaching: Foundations of the new reform. *Harvard Educational Review*, 57(1), 1–22.

Siegel, H. (1988). *Educating reason: Rationality, critical thinking and education.* New York: Routledge.

Silvane Busani, C. (2016). A plural moral philosophical perspective on citizenship education. Unpublished doctoral thesis. University of Edinburgh, UK.

Small, H. (ed.) (2002). *The public intellectual.* Oxford: Blackwell Publishing.

Smart, D., Sanson, A., Da Silva, L. & Toumbourou, J. (2000). The development of civic mindedness. *Family Matters*, 57, 4–9.

Steinberg, K. S., Hatcher, J. A. & Bringle, R. G. (2011). Civic-minded graduate: A north star. *Michigan Journal of Community Service Learning*, Fall, 19–33. http://quod.lib.umich.edu/cgi/p/pod/dod-idx/civic-minded-graduate-a-north-star.pdf?c=mjcsl;idno=3239521.0018.102 (accessed 17 February 2016).

Strain, J. (2005). Professional ethics and higher education. In J. Strain & S. Robinson (eds), *The teaching and practice of professional ethics* (pp. 3–17). Leicester, UK: Troubador.

Strand, K., Marula, S., Cuttforth, N, Stoecker, R. & Donohue, P. (2003). *Community-based research and higher education: Principles and practices.* San Francisco, CA: Jossey-Bass.

Sugrue, S. & Solbrekke, T. D. (eds) (2011). *Professional responsibility: New horizons of praxis.* London: Routledge.

Sullivan, W. (2005). *Work and integrity: The crisis and promise of professionalism in America* (2nd edn). San Francisco, CA: Jossey-Bass.

Sullivan, W. (1995). *Work and integrity: The crisis and promise of professionalism in America.* San Francisco, CA: Jossey-Bass.

Sullivan, W. M. & Rosin, M. S. (2008). *A new agenda for higher education: Shaping a life of the mind for practice.* San Francisco, CA: Carnegie Foundation for the Advancement of Teaching and Jossey-Bass.

The Sutton Trust (2012). Social mobility and education gaps in the four major Anglophone countries. Social Mobility Summit. London.

Tackey, N. D., Barnes, H. & Khambhaita, P. (2011). *Poverty, ethnicity and education.* Institute for Employment Studies. York, UK: Joseph Rowntree Foundation. www.jrf.org.uk/publications/ (accessed 14 February 2015).

Tawney, R. (1920). *The acquisitive society.* New York: Harcourt, Brace and World.

Taylor, A. (2014, July). Community-university engagement: Exploring the tensions. European Group for Organizational Studies (EGOS) Colloquium. Erasmus University, Rotterdam, Netherlands.

Taylor, C. (2007). *A secular age.* Cambridge, MA: Harvard University Press.

Taylor, C. (1991). *The ethics of authenticity.* Cambridge, MA: Harvard University Press.

Taylor, C. (1989). *Sources of the self: The making of the modern identity.* Cambridge, MA: Harvard University Press.

Taylor, R., Barr, J. & Steele, T. (2002). *For a radical higher education: After postmodernism.* Buckingham, UK: SRHE and Open University Press.

Teichler, U. (1999). Research on the relationships between higher education and the world of work: Past achievements, problems and new challenges. *Higher Education*, 38, 168–190.

Thames, B. (2011). Authentically virtuous: Heidegger, Taylor, and MacIntyre. International Society for MacIntyrean Enquiry 5th Annual Conference, Providence College, Providence, RI, July 2011.

Thompson, J. L., Mallet-Boucher, M., McCloskey, C., Tamlyn, K. & Wilson, K. (2013). Educating nurses for the twenty-first century: Abilities-based outcomes and assessing student learning in the context of democratic professionalism. *International Journal of Nursing Education Scholarship*, 10(1), 219–226.

Thomson, J. A. K. (1976). *The ethics of Aristotle. The Nicomachean ethics.* Middlesex, UK: Penguin Books.

Trigwell, K. & Prosser, M. (1996). Changing approaches to teaching: A relational perspective. *Studies in Higher Education*, 21(3), 275–284.

Turcotte, G. (2004). Compr(om)ising postcolonialisms: Postcolonial pedagogy and the uncanny space of possibility. In C. Sugars (ed.), *Home-work: Postcolonialism, pedagogy and Canadian literature* (pp. 151–166). Ottawa, ON: University of Ottawa Press.

UK Government (2014). *Elitist Britain*. London: Child Poverty and Social Mobility Commission. www.gov.uk/government/uploads/system/uploads/attachment_data/file/347915/Elitist_Britain_-_Final.pdf (accessed 28 August 2014).

UK Government (2011). REF 2014. Assessment framework and guidance on submissions. REF 02.2011 Northavon House, Bristol. Department for Employment and Learning. www.ref.ac.uk/media/ref/content/pub/assessmentframeworkand guidanceonsubmissions/GOS%20including%20addendum.pdf.

Unama'ki College (2016). Restructuring plan. Cape Breton University, Sydney, NS, Canada.

UNESCO (2005). Toward knowledge societies. *UNESCO World Report*. Conde-sur-Noireau, France: Imprimerie Corlet. http://unesdoc.unesco.org/images/0014/001418/141843e.pdf (accessed 18 February 2015).

UNESCO Institute for Statistics (2010). *Global education digest. Comparing education statistics across the world. Special focus on gender.* Montreal, Canada. www.uis.unesco.org/Library/Documents/GED_2010_EN.pdf (accessed 15 February 2015).

University of Edinburgh (2011). Graduate attributes framework. www.employability.ed.ac.uk/GraduateAttributesFramework.htm (accessed 25 February 2015).

Villa, D. R. (1996). *Arendt and Heidegger: The fate of the political.* Princeton, NJ: Princeton University Press.

Vu, T. & Dall'Alba, G. (2011). Becoming authentic professionals: Learning for authenticity. In L. Scanlion (ed.), *'Becoming' a professional: An interdisciplinary analysis of professional learning* (pp. 95–108). Lifelong Learning Book series. Dordrecht, Netherlands: Springer.

Walker, M. (2012). A capital or capabilities education narrative in a world of staggering inequalities. *International Journal of Educational Development*, 32, 384–393.

Walker, M. & McLean, M. (2013). *Professional education, capabilities and contributions to the public good: The role of universities in promoting human development.* London: Routledge.

Walker, M. & McLean, M. (2011). Making lives go better: University education and professional capabilities. *South African Journal of Higher Education*, 24(5), 847–869.

Walker, M. & McLean, M. (2009). A public good professional capability index for university-based professional education in South Africa. Paper presented at the

Annual Meeting of the Society for Research into Higher Education, Newport, Wales, 8 December.

Walker, I. & Zhu, Y. (2013). The impact of university degrees on the lifecycle of earnings: Some further analyses. BIS Research Paper No. 112. Department for Business, Innovation and Skills, UK Government. www.gov.uk/government/uploads/system/uploads/attachment_data/file/229498/bis-13-899-the-impact-of-university-degrees-on-the-lifecycle-of-earnings-further-analysis.pdf (accessed 17 February 2016).

Watson, G. & Glaser, E. M. (1984). *The Watson-Glaser Critical Thinking Appraisal*. San Antonio, TX: The Psychological Corporation.

Watson, D., Hollister, R. M., Stroud, S. E. & Babcock, E. (2011). *The engaged university: International perspectives on civic engagement*. New York: Routledge.

Weiss, R. (2011). Arendt and the American pragmatists: Her debate with Dewey and some American strains in her thought. *Philosophical Topics*, 39(2), 183–205.

Wenger, E. (1998). *Communities of practice: Learning, meaning and identity*. Cambridge, UK: Cambridge University Press.

Williams, B. (1985). *Ethics and the limits of philosophy*. Cambridge, MA: Harvard University Press.

Wilson, A., Akerlind, G., Walsh, B., Stevens, B., Turner, B. & Shield, A. (2013). Making professionalism meaningful to students in higher education. *Studies in Higher Education*, 38(8), 1222–1238.

Wolf, A. (2011). *The Wolf report – Review of vocational education*. UK Department for Education. Ref: DFE-00031–2011.

Wolf, A. (2002). *Does education matter? Myths about education and economic growth*. London: Penguin Books.

Woodrow Presley, J. (2012). Chief academic officers and community-engaged faculty work. In J. Saltmarsh & M. Hartley (eds), *To serve a larger purpose: Engagement for democracy and the transformation of higher education* (pp. 130–154). Philadelphia, PA: Temple University Press.

World Bank (2002). Building knowledge economies: Opportunities and challenges for EU accession countries. Final Report of the Knowledge Economy Forum 'Using Knowledge for Development in EU Accession Countries', Paris, 19–22 February 2002. http://siteresources.worldbank.org/EXTECAREGTOPKNOECO/Resources/Building_Knowledge_Economies_final_final.pdf (accessed 6 March 2015).

Wright, K. (2008). Authentic and eudaimonic. *Psychology Today*. www.psychologytoday.com/articles/200805/authentic-and-eudaimonic (accessed 6 May 2015).

Young, M. D. (2008) *Bringing the knowledge back in*. Abingdon, UK: Routledge.

Young, M. D. & J. Muller (2014). *Knowledge, expertise and the professions*. Abingdon, UK: Routledge.

Young-Bruehl, E. (2006). *Why Arendt matters*. New Haven, CT: Yale University Press.

Index

Note: Page numbers followed by 'f' refer to figures and followed by 't' refer to tables.